Electronic Voting Machines

Unconstitutional and Tamperable

Editors

Subramanian Swamy
S. Kalyanaraman

www.visionbooksindia.com

ISBN 10: 81-7094-798-7
ISBN 13: 978-81-7094-798-1

First Published in 2010
by
Vision Books Pvt. Ltd.
(Incorporating Orient Paperbacks & CARING imprints)
24 Feroze Gandhi Road, Lajpat Nagar 3
New Delhi 110024, India.
Phone: (+91-11) 2983 6470 and 2983 6480
E-mail: visionbk@vsnl.com

Printed at
Ravindra Printing Press
1590, Madarsa Road, Kashmere Gate
Delhi 110006, India.

Contents

Preface

The electronic voting machines (EVMs) used in Indian elections are known as Direct Recording Electronic (DRE) voting machines which record votes directly in the electronic memory. Such voting machines have, however, been banned in many countries such as Germany, the Netherlands, Ireland and Italy — and the list is growing. DRE machines are permitted in the States of the US but only with a paper backup or receipt. While there are voices raised in the US about the dangers of "vote fraud", more importantly, it is the lack of transparency and verifiability associated with these machines that has prompted some countries to ban or impose restrictions on their use. Thus there is a growing lack of confidence in EVMs the world over. This is because the EVM system of recording and counting votes is shrouded in secrecy, thereby violating the basic and fundamental right of transparency in voting.

The German Supreme Court has recently handed down a landmark judgement (text included in Chapter 5) which should be applicable to all democratic republics.

The two fundamental arguments that led the German Supreme Court to declare EVMs unconstitutional are:

1. The principle of the public nature of elections emerging from the German Basic Law requires that all essential steps in the elections are subject to public "examinability" unless other constitutional interest is proved to justify an exception.
2. When electronic voting machines are deployed, it must be possible for the citizen to check the essential steps in the election and to ascertain the results reliably *and without special expert knowledge.*

List of Countries Which Have Banned EVMs

1. Netherlands (cited lack of transparency and risk of eavesdropping and securing cannot be guaranteed)
2. Ireland (after spending 51 million pounds for three years due to lack of transparency and trust)
3. Germany considered e-voting unconstitutional due to lack of transparency to a common voter.
4. Italy (because EVMs are easy to falsify)
5. US (California and other states banned EVMs without paper trail).
6. CIA security expert Mr. Stigall, monitoring use of Electronic Voting Systems in developing nations such as Venezuela, Macedonia and Ukraine reported abuse using Electronic Voting Machines.
7. When Chavez won in Venzuela, mathematicians challenged and found a "very subtle algorithm" that appeared to adjust vote in Chavez's favour. Summarised at: http:// saveindiandemocracy.wordpress.com
8. The Supreme Court of Finland declared the result of pilot electronic voting machines invalid in the municipal corporation elections of 2009.
9. Election of the Pope takes place by paper ballot and not through the use of EVMs.

List of Countries Which Continue to Use Paper Ballot

1. United Kingdom.
2. France.
3. Japan.

The corresponding principle of the German Basic Law is defined in Article 324 of the Indian Constitution read with the Objects of the Symbols Order (1968), which makes it an imperative that public nature of elections should be ensured without Election Commission (EC) making secret arrangement or transactions. The EC must ensure total transparency to the satisfaction of a voter of ordinary prudence, i.e. a voter without special expert knowledge, *that the result of an election is arrived at reliably and correctly*. It is not enough that the EC is satisfied, but that the voter is satisfied that his or her vote will be accurately recorded and counted.

Thus, the most transparent system of voting is voters assembling in a room and voting by a show of hands and these being counted there and then. But in country of half-a-billion voters, and the power of the vote becoming known, this most transparent system is not practical. Thus, the next most transparent system is the paper ballot where the voter sees his vote physically being registered by him on the paper which he himself or she herself puts into a ballot box. These sealed boxes are then transported to a counting centre and openly counted one by one ballot paper and totalled. If a fraud occurs, then it will be localized or at the "retail" level and not wholesale fraud unless it is a dictatorship like Saddam Hussein's.

The EVMs have no such transparency. Many knowledgeable experts, computer science professors and Information Technology professors have repeatedly pointed out that EVMs are tamperable and no such electronic computing system can be rendered secure. Any such man-made system can be tampered with; India's EVMs are no exception. Remember that stakes are high in winning elections. And just by managing at the chip embedding stage, for example, an election can be wholesale rigged. This risk, however small; cannot be accepted in a democracy. Hence, we need to pool our intellectual resources to ensure greater transparency in the electronic voting system or revert back to the paper ballot.

For this purpose, the Centre for National Renaissance, New Delhi convened an international conference in Chennai on 13 February 2010 and called for papers to be read from international and national experts (Chapters 1 to 9). This volume, based on the conference papers and proceedings on the illegal and unreliable features of India's EVMs will be a revelation for those who care and want to listen.

Italy, Ireland, Germany, United Kingdom, Japan and many other tech-savvy countries have reverted back to or stayed with the paper ballots, which can be traced to our ancient system of Parantakachola model. Why should India persist with a failed electronic system that has been abandoned worldwide when even the Pope's election is now conducted only through secret paper ballot and Italy is the latest to revert to paper ballot? The present CEC Mr. Chawla, therefore, should have no objection to going back to paper ballots till a genuine transparent electronic system is invented.

A vote of "no confidence" against the EVMs also emanates from the personal experiences of parties and leaders as well as the nature of results thrown up by the EVMs. Parties are looking at EVMs with great suspicion and dread the prospect of EVMs "defeating" them. This mistrust in EVMs is not confined to any single party and is all pervasive.

Almost all mainstream Indian political parties, including the BJP, Congress, Left parties, Janata Party, regional parties, such as the Telegu Desam Party (TDP), AIADMK, Samajwadi Party, Rashtriya Lok Dal (RLD), Janata Dal (United), etc. have all expressed reservation about EVMs in the aftermath of 2009 Lok Sabha polls. Even the Congress party, which surprisingly won the 2004 and the 2009 general elections, seems shy to defend the EVMs.

The Election Commission has adopted the EVM technology about which it has practically no knowledge. As a result, it has little control over many aspects of the election process.

The only source of technical understanding for the Election Commission is a committee of experts led by its Chairman, Prof. P. V. Indiresan who is a completely out-dated electrical engineer. He has little knowledge of electronics.

Even the Expert Committee seems very weak in its capacities and understanding. Alex Halderman, Professor of Computer Science at the University of Michigan and an expert on the security of voting systems who was present in the Conference in Chennai, commented, "When I read the 2006 technical report prepared by the Expert Committee of the Election Commission, I scribbled on it that there was a cause for alarm and quickly decided to agree to come here."

The most deadly way to hack Indian EVMs is by inserting a chip with Trojan inside the display section of the Control unit. This requires access to the EVM for just two minutes and these replacement units can be made for a few hundred rupees. Bypassing completely all inbuilt securities, this chip would manipulate the results and give out "fixed" results on the EVM screen. The Election

Commission is completely oblivious to such possibilities. A demonstration of these vulnerabilities was made by Dr. Hari Prasad and Mr. V. V. Rao whom I accompanied to the Election Commission on 3 September 2009. Half-way through our demonstration, the EC abruptly aborted the demonstration. The EC which videoed the proceedings is refusing to part with a copy of the same.

Unlike in the traditional ballot system where only the election officials were the "insiders", electronic voting machine regime has spawned a long chain of insiders, all of whom are outside the ambit and control of the Election Commission of India.

There is every possibility that some of these "insiders" are involved in murky activities in fixing elections. The whole world — except us in India — is alive to the dangers of insider fraud in elections.

The "insiders" include the public sector manufacturers of India's electronic voting machines namely, the Bharat Electronics Limited (BEL) and Electronics Corporation of India (ECIL), the foreign companies supplying micro controllers, private players (some of which are allegedly owned by some political leaders) for carrying out checking and maintenance of electronic voting machines during elections. These organizers have bluffed us that they have intellectual property to protect in EVMs. In fact, they had to withdraw their applications for Patent to the World Intellectual Property Organization when they could not prove the uniqueness of the Indian EVMs.

The EVMs are stored at the district headquarters or in a decentralized manner in different locations. Election Commission's concern for EVM safety becomes apparent only during elections, whereas security experts say that voting machines must remain in a secure environment throughout their life cycle.

There could be many malpractices associated with electronic counting. "Everybody watches polling closely. No body watches counting as closely," says Bev Harris, an American activist.

Our Election Commission takes three months to conduct parliamentary elections but wants counting to be over in just three hours! In the rush to declare results and the winners, several serious lapses go unnoticed in the counting process. As a result, parties cannot give it the kind of attention that this activity deserves. Massive discrepancies between votes polled and counted in a large number of polling stations across the country raise serious concerns in this regard. Efficient counting cannot be a constitutional justification for violating the basic feature of public nature of elections in a democracy. In this context, it is pertinent to recall that the German Supreme Court held that efficiency of elections is not a constitutional interest. What is of constitutional interest is the imperative of public nature of the entire election process in a democratic republic. "The voter himself or herself must be able to verify — also without a more detailed knowledge of computers — whether his or her vote as cast is recorded truthfully as a basis for counting or — if the votes are initially counted with technical support — at least as a basis for a subsequent re-count. It is not sufficient if he or she must rely on the functionality of the system without the possibility of personal inspection. For this reason, a comprehensive bundle of other technical and organisational security measures (e.g., monitoring and safe-keeping of the voting machines, comparability of the devices used with an officially checked sample at any time, criminal liability in respect of election falsifications and local organisation of the elections) is also not suited by itself to compensate for a lack of controllability of the essential steps in the election procedure by the citizen."

Cutting across all sides of the divide, there is just one verdict on everyone lips: "We don't trust either OTP-ROM or masked chips".

The danger for EVM manipulations is not just from its software. Even the hardware isn't safe. Dr. Alex Halderman says, "EVMs used in the West require software attacks as they are sophisticated voting machines and their hardware cannot be replaced cheaply. In contrast, the Indian EVMs can easily be replaced either in part or as wholesale units."

One crucial part that can be faked is micro controllers used in the EVMs in which the software is copied. EVM manufacturers have greatly facilitated fraud by using generic micro controllers rather than more secure ASIC or FPGA.

Not just only micro controllers, mother boards (card which contains micro controllers) and entire EVMs can be replaced. Neither the Election Commission nor the manufacturers have undertaken any hardware or software audit till date. As a result, such manipulation attempts would go undetected.

To detect such fraud, the upgraded EVMs have a provision to interface with an Authentication Unit that would allow the manufacturers to verify whether the EVM being used in the election is the same that they have supplied to the Election Commission. The EVM manufacturers developed an "Authentication Unit" engaging the services of SecureSpin, a Bangalore based software services firm. The Unit was developed and tested in 2006 but when the project was ready for implementation, the project was mysteriously shelved at the instance of the Election Commission. Several questions posted to the Election Commission for taking this decision went unanswered.

The Indian EVMs can be hacked both before and after elections to alter election results. Apart from manipulating the EVM software and replacing many hardware parts discussed above, discussions with knowledgeable sources revealed that Indian EVMs can be hacked in many ways. I mention just two of them below.

Each EVM contains two EEPROMs inside the Control Unit in which the voting data is stored. They are completely unsecured and the data inside EEPROMs can be manipulated from an external source. It is very easy to read (data from) the EEPROMs and manipulate them.

India is an exception to this international trend and we continue to use these voting machines long discarded by the world due to lack of awareness and appreciation of the lay public of the concerns.

Indian EVMs may also be held unconstitutional because they infringe upon the fundamental rights of the voters. In India, right to vote is a legal right but how that vote should be exercised by a voter is his / her individual expression covered by Article 19(1)(a) of the Constitution, which guarantees fundamental rights to the citizens. In the 2002 case pertaining to disclosure of assets and criminal background of candidates, the Supreme Court ruled that voters have a right to know the antecedents of the contesting candidates and this is fundamental and basic for survival of democracy.

Accordingly, a voter has the right to know that his vote which he exercised as a part of freedom of expression has really gone in favour of the candidate whom he / she has chosen. This right, fundamental in nature, is absent in the electronic voting system. In the traditional paper ballot system, that fundamental right was preserved because a voter knew exactly how his / her vote was recorded and counted.

Universal use of EVMs in Indian elections is illegal too! In 1984, the Supreme Court of India held that the use of electronic voting machines in elections was "illegal" as the Representation of the People (RP) Act, 1951 did not permit use of voting machines in elections. Later, the RP Act was amended in 1989 incorporating Section 61A. However, the amendment says voting machines "may be adopted in such constituency or constituencies as the Election Commission may, having regard to the circumstances of each case, specify".

Violating the provisions of the RP Act, the Election Commission has conducted 2004 and 2009 nationwide general elections only using electronic voting machines. Going by the 1984 judgement of the Supreme Court, parliamentary elections of 2004 and 2009 may be held illegal.

The electronic voting machines are safe and secure only if the source code used in the EVMs is genuine. Shockingly, the EVM manufacturers, the BEL and ECII, have shared the "top secret" EVM software programme with two foreign companies, Microchip (USA) and Renesas (Japan) to copy it onto micro controllers used in EVMs. This process should have been done securely in-house by the Indian manufacturers.

Worse, when the foreign companies deliver micro controllers fused with software code to the EVM manufacturers, the EVM manufacturers cannot "read back" their contents as they are locked. That is why the ECIL and BEL had to suffer the humiliation of withdrawing their application for patents for their EVMs from the

World Intellectual Property Organisation after three years of correspondence with the WIPO.

We hope, therefore, through this volume we can create the necessary public opinion to make the EC withdraw the EVMs if they cannot be safeguarded to public satisfaction, and thus return to the paper ballot system.

Chennai, SUBRAMANIAN SWAMY
September 2010 S. KALYANARAMAN

1

Use of Electronic Voting Machines in Indian Elections

Transparency and Audit

Dr. Roxna Swamy*

The Problem of EVMs in India

> "Voting by electronic machines (hereinafter for convenience referred to as EVMs) was supposed to be the cure for ballot fiascos during elections, but in its present system / form it has only worsened the problem and these EVMs also do not meet the legal requirements set out by the relevant laws and rules there under. It also creates worries about the future of our democratic system."

The duties of the Election Commission of India as set out in Article 324 of the Constitution of India, include an obligation to ensure that such elections conducted by it, are free and fair, and reflect the will of the voters.

(a) For several thousand years, voting has been practised in many parts of the world, as a means of determining who will govern. But it is only since the seventeenth century that the paper ballot emerged for this purpose. Thereafter, there have been many modifications thereon, for the purpose of ensuring that elections conducted with it are free and fair, untainted by force or fraud and that the individual voter's choice is secret.

* B.A. (Hons), M.A., M.S. (Harvard), Ph.D (IIT / D), LL.B, Advocate, Supreme Court.

(b) However, the process of sorting and hand counting such paper ballots can be laborious and time consuming; and it requires all concerned to be vigilant over a period which may extend to some days. In India, for example, where a parliamentary constituency today usually has over a million eligible voters of whom several lakhs cast their votes, merely physically counting them can take two or three days — even longer if the result is close and more than usual vigilance is required. Hence in the last few decades, many countries have experimented with using EVMs which tabulate electronically and so can announce the result in a few hours. But, convenience cannot take precedence over reliability.

(c) International standards an election has to meet, to be considered free and fair, comprehend:

   (i) Individuals have to be accurately identified as eligible voters who have not already voted;

   (ii) Voters are allowed only one anonymous ballot each, which they can mark in privacy;

   (iii) The ballot box is secure, observed and, during the election, only able to have votes added to it by voters: votes cannot be removed;

   (iv) When the election ends, the ballot box is opened and counted in the presence of observers from all competing parties. The counting process cannot reveal how individual voters cast their ballots;

   (v) If the results are in doubt, the ballots can be checked and counted again by different people;

   (vi) As far as the individual voter is concerned, he must be assured that the candidate he casts his vote for, actually gets that vote.

(d) Over the last few centuries, the system of paper ballots has been developed which can meet all six requirements. But, it is submitted, the present system of EVMs as utilized in the last few general elections in India, (though admittedly it gives results very fast and dispenses with the labour of hand counting) do not meet requirements (v) and (vi) set out in subpara (c) above.

(e) It became necessary to file a Writ Petition in the Delhi High Court, because of the refusal of the Election Commission of India to incorporate in its EVMs, a certain obvious safeguard, called the "paper backup" or "paper trail" — presently in use in the USA and various European countries — which would easily and cheaply meet the requirements of (v) and (vi).

(f) When such an obvious safeguard — the paper trail — used all over the USA and some European countries, is easily and relatively cheaply available, it is submitted that the Election Commission's refusal to even consider its induction, is unreasonable and smacks of malafide.

As suggested and developed by many experts, this "paper trail" procedure is to supplement the procedure of voting, as follows:

> "Once approved, the voter views the ballot and makes the desired selections . . . If the voter confirms that the choices displayed are correct, the machine records the vote on some storage medium such as a CD-ROM or flash memory and overwrites the smart card with random numbers to prevent its reuse . . . The voting machine then prints out a human readable ballot, which is confirmed by the voter, who then deposits it in the ballot box, which poll workers are monitoring. If the election is later disputed, officials can optically scan these paper ballots or hand-count them."(See May 2009 issue of the IEEE Computer Society, pages 23 to 29, Article by Nathanael Paul and Andrew S. Tannenbaum: "Trustworthy Voting: From Machine to System").

A further safeguard to the above procedure, has also been developed, viz. that at the time of issuing the stamped paper ballot, the EVM also issues to the voter to take home, a print out receipt indicating exactly whom he voted for. The reason why this receipt is a good precaution, is as follows: presently, if an election is challenged on the ground that some particular identified voter's vote or the vote of a group of voters has been suppressed / not been correctly assigned, the accepted procedure is for such voter / voters to submit an affidavit stating as to how he / they had voted; and then it is for the Court to decide the credibility of such depositions. Under the new procedure, no affidavit is necessary: all that the voter has to do, is to submit the printout receipt the EVM had issued to him.

(g) To summarise, when a voter votes, the modified EVM with a paper trail, does three things:

1. It records the vote electronically;
2. It prints a paper vote that the voter can read, and verify before depositing in a separate ballot box; or
3. It prints a receipt for the voter that he can take home as proof whom he voted for, or deposit it in a box in the booth which is sealed and kept safely after the voting is over.

Thus in the event that any group of voters look at their receipts and detect an anomaly with the electronic result, they have due cause to require an election audit, and the ballot box provides the audit trail that can actually be counted.

With the above set-up in place, in order to rig this election, the intending fraudster would need to identically rig:

(a) The electronic counter;
(b) The paper ballot boxes; and
(c) The distributed receipts;

Which is virtually impossible.

(If further, the EVM is linked with the UID (Unique Identity) system being developed throughout India, and the EVM can check the voters' fingerprints — biometric details —, before allowing them to vote, this will eliminate bogus voters as well).

The Law on the Use of EVMs in Elections in India

The Law on the Use of EVMs in elections in India has been developed as under:

(a) The Constitution of India Part XV, Articles 324 to 329 deals with Elections. To summarise, Article 324 requires that the superintendence, direction and control of elections be vested in the Election Commission of India; Article 326, that the elections to the House of People and to the Legislative Assemblies shall be on the basis of adult suffrage; and under Article 327, Parliament has the power to make provisions with respect to elections to the Legislatures.

(b) In particular Parliament has enacted the Representation of the People Act 1951 to provide *inter alia* for the conduct of elections; and this includes specifically the manner of polling: Section 59 lays down that where a poll is taken, votes shall be given by ballot in such manner as may be prescribed. Section 61A, enacted w.e.f. 15.3.1989, states:

> "Section 61A — Voting machines at Elections — Notwithstanding anything contained in this Act or the rules made there under, the giving and recording of votes by voting machines in such manner as may be prescribed, may be adopted in such constituency or constituencies as the Election Commission may, having regard to the circumstances of each case, specify.
>
> Explanation — For the purpose of this section, "voting machine" means any machine or apparatus whether operated electronically or otherwise used for giving or recording of votes and any reference to a ballot box or ballot paper in this Act or the rules made there under shall, save as otherwise provided, be construed as including a reference to such voting machine wherever such voting machine is used at any election."

(c) There has also been promulgated the Conduct of Election Rules 1961.Part IV Chapter I, thereof deals in detail with Voting By Ballot. Part IV Chapter II, incorporated in these Rules as from 24.3.1992 deals in detail with Voting By Electronic Voting Machines. Part V deals in detail with the Counting of Votes in Parliamentary and Assembly Constituencies.

(d) Thus, it is evident that the Election Commission is empowered to utilize EVMs of its choice in any of the elections carried out by it. The procedure for such utilization has also been laid out. Naturally this must only be done in a manner which ensures free and fair elections: thus the Respondent must not utilize any procedure which cannot ensure that the voter's choice is in any way altered by fraudulent practices. In the case of EVMs, in particular, doubts have been raised whether justified or not, that their software is liable to be misutilized by "Trojan Horses", i.e. whether before or after polling the machine is programmed to alter the voter's indicated choice, in order to favour some other candidate.

Worldwide Acceptance of the Need for a Paper Trail in Conjunction with EVMs

Particularly in the last two decades, electronic voting was introduced in many countries worldwide; but after utilizing them for a short while serious doubts were raised about the security, accuracy, reliability and verifiability of electronic elections. In October 2006 the Netherlands banned all EVMs. In 2009, the Republic of Ireland declared a moratorium on their use. As did Italy. In March 2009, after hearings that stretched over almost two years, the Supreme Court of the Federal Republic of Germany ruled that voting through EVMs was unconstitutional. In 2007, after conducting a top-to-bottom review of many of the voting systems certified for use in California, its Secretary of State strengthened the security requirements and use conditions, requiring all EVMs to have paper backups. Thereafter, till today a further 27 states of the US have followed suit.

Position and Proceedings in India

The question then arises why, despite the recent enormous demand for EVMs that incorporate such a paper trail, the Election Commission of India has not introduced the use of such a paper trail. So far, the official attitude of the Election Commission is that its EVMs are hundred percent reliable and tamper proof: that the functioning chips have their instructions indelibly burnt into them at the time of manufacture and that these chips are then "mother sealed" into the

EVM; and this sealing can never be altered. The above claim is presented as an immaculate premise of the Election Commission, or a mantra requiring no proof thereof.

It is submitted that this claim (which incidentally has never been submitted before any body of world scholars, or published in the known and respected journals dealing with the subject, where it would have to undergo the scrutiny of world experts) is not correct, to the knowledge of the Election Commission.

(a) Around 1970, the Election Commission, with the idea of introducing EVMs in the election process, induced two government companies —Electronics Corporation of India Ltd, Hyderabad (ECI) and Bharat Electronics Corporation Ltd., Bangalore (BEL) — to design and develop suitable machines. They were first used in 1982 when EVMs were introduced in 11 constituencies; they were reported to work satisfactorily.

Despite persistent questioning, however the Election Commission has always refused to reveal the internal programming of its EVMs.

(b) In 1990, at the instance of the Electoral Reforms Committee, which desired the evaluation of the functioning of these EVMs, with special reference to the possibility that they could be tampered with, the Department of Electronics constituted an Expert Committee. This Expert Committee recommended accepting the EVMs while requiring certain precautions. With these precautions, the EVMs were used in a limited number of constituencies, for the 1994, the 1997 and the 1998 general elections to the Lok Sabha. In December 2005, as the EVMs had been in operation for 15 years — their lifetime — and were due for replacement, a further Technical Expert Committee, headed by Professor Indiresan a former Director of the I.I.T., Chennai, to evaluate the working of the machines, and to suggest improvements based on the experience of the first period of 15 years. Its Report came out in September 2006, and its recommendations were carried out so that the improvements could be used in elections due in 2009

(c) In particular, it has been publicized widely that in terms of the Indiresan Committee Recommendations, the EVMs in current use now, have all been modified so that each vote cast is date-time stamped INSIDE the machine.

(d) The significance of this admitted alteration is as follows. There are three ways to implement an electronics system:

   (i) A fixed electronic is called an ASIC i.e. an Application Specific Integrated Circuit. Once manufactured, the functionality of this ASIC is fixed and cannot be changed with new software;

   (ii) An EEPROM (i.e. an Electrically Erasable and Programmable Re Only Memory), a FPGA (i.e. a Field Programmable Gate Array) or other such chip that is programmable by complex means such as a field or electric charge;

   (iii) A generalized processor circuit that is freely programmable and re-programmable using software (like the ordinary computers in use today).

   For a system to be post-manufacture tamper proof, it must belong to type (i). One can still tamper with the election count by just replacing the whole machine (as is alleged to have been done in the recent Sivaganga Lok Sabha election) or swapping out the EEPROM with a reprogrammable one or even just re-programming *in situ* in certain cases. (For example, the EVM displayed to the Petitioner's team in 1999, was an EEPROM, which was admittedly reprogrammable, but it took some effort).

   However, the disclosure of the post manufacture introduction of the time-date stamp device using software (like clocks, etc.) indicates that the EVM system must now be of the third category (iii).

(e) This is a most hazardous condition: not only does it mean that the functionality is not set in stone, but there was actually an authorized event (the introduction into the machine of the new date-time stamp procedure) that provided a golden opportunity to introduce a "Trojan" (i.e., a malicious programme that is sneaked in under the guise of another programme . . . the Trojan then executes its malicious code after which quite often it will self destroy.)

(f) After the Lok Sabha General Elections of April-May 2004, Professor Satinath Choudhary approached first the Kerala High Court; and later the Supreme Court of India, explaining how very possible it is to rig EVMs. Both courts directed the Election Commission to consider his suggestions seeking changes in the EVMs. But till today, the Election Commission, continuing to reiterate the "100% impossibility" of tampering with its machines, has not done so.

(g) In April 2009, there was filed W.P. No. 2506 / 2009, a PIL in the High Court of Madhya Pradesh, pointing out that in the Madhya Pradesh Vidhan Sabha General Election of 2008, in the election to 152 Bhopal South West Constituency, (from where the first Petitioner was a candidate) in Booth No. 32, the EVM recorded that the Petitioner candidate had got only three votes, nevertheless at least 12 voters in this Booth, have sworn on affidavit that they had voted for him. The Election Commission has opposed the same. Although in April 2009 itself, the Madhya Pradesh High Court issued notice in the above matter to the Election Commission of India, till today the Election Commission has failed to explain the indubitable mal-recording / mal-counting aforesaid.

(h) The latest General Elections to the Lok Sabha, held in April-May 2009, were conducted wholly with the use of EVMs. Around 13,60,000 such machines were used in 8,28,000 polling booths. Thereafter, Writ Petitions voicing concern over the credibility of EVM results have been filed in various High Courts. An Andhra Pradesh based NGO, Election Watch, filed in the Supreme Court of India W.P.(C) No.292 / 2009, a P.I.L. which itemized in detail the manner in which such EVMs can be manipulated. Its prayers were:

> "The petitioners, therefore, pray that in the facts and circumstances of the present case this Hon'ble Court may be pleased to issue a writ of Mandamus / certiorari or a writ / direction of like nature to:

(i) Direct the Respondents to provide such mechanism which is free from any manipulation / tampering so that free and fair elections in the parliamentary democracy are ensured and that the votes cast by the citizens as their right of free expression under Article 19(1)(a) of the Constitution are reflected correctly in such mechanism, whether EVM or ballots or any other device.

(ii) Direct appointment of an Independent Expert Committee to study in details all the aspects / objections concerning the present EVMs and submission of the said report before this Hon'ble Court for passing appropriate orders.

(iii) Pass such other order / orders as this Hon'ble Court may deem fit and proper in the circumstance of the case."

On 27.7.2009, the Hon'ble Supreme Court disposed of W.P.(C) No.292 of 2009, with a direction to the Petitioners to approach the Election Commission with its information. This the Election Watch has done, with what result is set out herein below.

(i) Thus, after studying all the data in regard to the results of the 2009 Lok Sabha General Elections, Dr. Subramanian Swamy sent a legal notice, dated 29.5.2009, to the Election Commission demanding that a paper trail, as indicated be put in place.

(j) In the Election Commission's reply dated 27.7.2009, to his aforesaid letter of demand the Election Commission reiterated its stand that its EVMs were tamper proof and it had taken all precautions to ensure that they never fall into the hands of any unauthorized persons. As to the Petitioner's specific demand that it set up a paper trail, the Election Commission simply declined to do so, stating:

> "As regards your suggestion for introduction of the paper trail in the ECI-EVMs, it is stated that when vote is recorded, light glows against the name and symbol of the candidate, which is electronic equivalent of a paper output. The Commission, therefore, does not consider that a parallel maintenance of paper trail is necessary since the person who is bent

on doubting would ever doubt the paper output by the machines."

(k) By then, the Hon'ble Supreme Court's Order disposing of Election Watch's Writ Petition was issued; and the Election Commission had invited Election Watch to demonstrate before it how its EVMs could be tampered with. Election Watch invited Dr. Subramanian Swamy to accompany them and obtained the Election Commission's leave to be present at their demonstration.

(l) Two hearings of the Election Watch have been held before the Election Commission. At the first hearing, on 17.8.2009, the Election Commission failed to present its EVMs and the manufacturers' engineers who serviced them, so the matter had to be adjourned.

(m) Before the next hearing, on or around 1.9.2009, Election Watch was served with a legal notice from ECIL, threatening them with a suit for defamation, for stating that their EVMs could be tampered with, and demanding an apology in writing.

(n) Accordingly at the second hearing, Election Watch requested the Election Commission's representative there to assure them that they would be ensured / indemnified against such suit for defamation, by the manufacturers of the Election Commission's EVMs. This assurance, the Election Commission's representative stated that he was not authorised to give, but the Commission requested the ECIL to "consider" withdrawing the said Notice. The ECIL, however, remained adamant. Despite this attempt at intimidation, the Election Watch decided to go ahead with the demonstration after consultations with Dr. Subramanian Swamy. It was agreed that as a first stage, only ECIL's employees would open the actual machines and then Election Watch experts would handle the parts and make notes thereon.

(o) However, when the Election Watch experts began to make notes about the parts, the manufacturers' engineers objected and demanded that the notes be confiscated. The Election Commission representative stated that he was not authorized to let the inspection go on under these circumstances. The demonstration was therefore adjourned by the Election Commission so that orders thereon from the Election Commissioners could be obtained. So far Election Watch has not been informed of the Election Commissions order on this vexed question; so no demonstration can proceed.

(p) Meanwhile ECIL's legal notice has not been withdrawn. Accordingly it is apprehended that further tests on the EVMs maybe delayed indefinitely until the legal liability issues are decided and that election after election will be scheduled and carried out without any safeguard in place.

(q) Meanwhile on the same date, 3.9.2009, Dr Subramanian Swam (who had merely asked for videos of the demonstrations), was e-mailed a letter from the Election Commission challenging him to prove that the EVMs could be tampered with. Since at no stage had Dr. Subramanian Swamy averred that these EVMs were tampered with (at this stage, he is only demanding a paper trail to be put in place as per international consensus for building voter confidence) at the hearing, Dr. Subramanian Swamy demanded that the letter be withdrawn.

(r) The demonstration has still not been carried out, simply because the Election Commission is now demanding that Election Watch come before it to demonstrate the tamperability of its EVMs; but at the same time, the Election Commission is refusing to deal with Election Watch's demand that first the ground rules for such a demonstration should be clearly laid down, and that Election Watch be indemnified from the legal action threats of the EVM manufacturers.

(s) In the above circumstances, on 14.9.2009 Dr. Subramanian Swamy has filed in the Delhi High Court Writ Petition (C) No.11879 of 2009, praying that the Court direct the incorporation of a paper trail. Notice was issued thereon; and in November 2009, the Election Commission filed its counter-affidavit, based on only one immaculate premise: that its EVMs were untamperable: a claim they have never substantiated before anybody of world scholars, or published in the known and respected journals dealing with the subject, when it would have to undergo the scrutiny of world experts.

The High Court is expected to take the matter on 28 August 2010.

Election Commission is Evading the Main Issue

Throughout, the Election Commission is evading the main issue:

(a) Its whole counter-affidavit is based on just one immaculate premise: viz. that the present system of EVMs is tamperproof, because the vote is recorded on a chip which is:

1. Specially designed;
2. Only one-time programmable;
3. Firmly embedded by robotic soldering in the Control unit, at the time of manufacture of the EVM in the factory itself; and
4. The programme once written on the chip at the time of its production cannot be altered or overwritten.

The above is stated repeatedly as an immaculate premise, or a mantra, requiring no proof thereof. It is in fact the self serving statement of the Election Commission's suppliers. The Technical Report appended to support this claim is that of an interested party, the contractor to whom the job of supplying the EVMs has been given. But there is nothing in this Report that can indubitably prove that the EVMs are tamper proof.

All that the Technical Report is actually claiming is that once the voter in the polling booth presses the key in the Ballot Unit (to record his vote), the Ballot Unit gets locked, and thereafter (until the Election Official unlocks it so that some other voter can cast his vote), the Ballot Unit will not record any other vote even if the voter himself wants to alter his vote.

(b) It is submitted that this is not how ballot units are manipulated: to take one instance (tried out successfully elsewhere), the chip in the EVM can be injected with a Trojan which will be activated / triggered after some predesignated event or sequence occurs. For example, the programmed Trojan will activate only if one voter votes for Candidate A, the next voter votes for Candidate B, and the next voter votes for Candidate C, in a sequence. Thus the EVM will function as required properly recording votes until the three designated conspirators cast their vote in sequence; and thereafter, as per the Trojan's design, the EVM will record that all further votes (or perhaps a predetermined high percentage of votes) will be cast for the candidate of the conspirator's choice.

(c) The Manufacturers Technical Report is concerned with Quality Control, and a "Company Profile" which points out *inter alia* that this is a "Navratna PSU"— all of which apparently do not equip it to understand how Trojans work. Interestingly, the Navratna PSU has never submitted its fancy claim before any body of world scholars, or published it in the known and respected journals dealing with the subject, when it would have to undergo the scrutiny of world experts.

(d) A considerable body of the Technical Report, is concerned with "Additional Features of Upgraded EVMs", "Improved data encryption", "Date-time stamp features", etc. all of which beg the question: if the chip (despite being "specially designed one-time programmable" and "firmly embedded by robot soldering in the control unit") can accept a date-time stamp programme, why can it not accept some other Trojan?

(e) Unfortunately, claiming that this is all that the Hon'ble Court needs to know, the counter-affidavit has not dealt at all with the Petitioner's averments in respect to the short-comings of the present system of EVMs but only with the difficulties and expenditure which would be incurred in improving the system with the addition of a paper trail.

(f) In the same fashion, the Respondent has failed to deal at all in its counter-affidavit, with the Petitioner's main contention:

   (1) In para 5 (c) of his Writ Petition, the Petitioner had laid down six internationally accepted standards which have to be comprehended, for elections to be credibly considered free and fair. The Petitioner had pointed out that the present system of EVMs as utilized in the last few general elections, did not meet two of these criteria, viz,

"(v) If the results are in doubt, the ballots can be checked and counted again by different people; (vi) As far as the individual voter is concerned, he must be assured that the candidate he casts his vote for, actually gets that vote."

(2) The Election Commission's counter-affidavit has failed to deal with these:

(i) The meat of the criticism is that when the voter presses the button of his choice, a light certainly shines on the symbol of the candidate of his choice, but there is nothing to assure this voter that the vote recorded inside the EVM is according to his indicated choice (Requirement (vi) above); and

(ii) The EVM can certainly recount the totals; but if anyone doubts the election result and demands a recount, all that can be done is that the EVM can go through its stored electronic data (which may not, right from the recording, have reflected the voter's actual choice) once more: it cannot check whether someone's vote has been properly recorded and stored because it has just the one record . . . . So all that happens is that the EVM goes through the same record and gets exactly the same result, i.e. a recount is not a fresh operation, but merely the same operation carried out again on the same (perhaps flawed) data. Also, the recount is not carried out by a different set of persons.

Thus, the requirement of (v) and (vi) are not met. Yet the counter affidavit has not even commented on the essentiality of the above two requirements.

(g) Much has been made of the fact that if the voter is allowed to take out, or even to handle the paper ballot, this can be misused by parties intent on terrorizing or buying up the voter's vote. For this, there are certain modifications of procedure available, which have been tried abroad. For example, in one suggested procedure, the voter does not actually handle the printed ballot paper, but he sees it behind a glass cover, and he confirms it correctly reflects his choice and then he actually sees this ballot paper peeled off and mechanically deposited in the designated ballot box. That would confirm his confidence that his vote has actually been recorded in favour of the candidate of his choice.

(h) The key question before the Hon'ble Delhi High Court, is the question of transparency and voter confidence. The most transparent system practised yet is the ballot paper system. Today, the most opaque is the EVM. There is no corroboration of the Election Commission's claim that it is unriggable. The two contractors, ECIL and BEL have made no presentation in any international conference that this is so; so its claim has not stood the test of scrutiny by acknowledged world experts. On the other hand, the Petitioner has sought advice from and received it from two of the foremost contemporary and up-to-date scholars in this field, Professor David L. Dill of Stanford University, and Dr. Ulrich Wiesner of Germany, (who spearheaded the case which led to the use of EVMs being struck down by the German Federal Supreme Court). It must be remembered that the field of hacking is a continually developing field and, with due respect, ECIL and BEL's expert advisors, who worked in the field of electrical engineering (not electronic engineering) in the 1960s to 1980's period, (the so-called "diode and triode era"), have long since retired and ceased to keep current with new developments in the field. They have published nothing for the last twenty years: the period of greatest strides in this field. Thus, they are hardly in a position to counter the averment of Professor Dill and Dr. Weisner: that no electronic machine has been devised that cannot be rigged or hacked, and that only safeguards can minimize the hacking, or more accurately, its detection.

(i) Furthermore, in paras 14, 16 and 17 of the counter-affidavit, the Election Commission claims that EVMs in India are not networked while those outside India are networked and claims that because of non-networking of Indian EVMs they are not riggable. On this the foremost German expert, Dr. Ulrich Weisner, who had spearheaded the case leading to the ban by the German

Federal Supreme Court, and who has been consulted by the Petitioner, states:

> "The Nedap voting computers now banned in the Netherlands, Ireland and Germany are not networked either. Similar to the Indian EVMs, they need to be connected to a configuration device before the election, but work stand alone with no connection to internet or other networks during the election and counting phase. The lack of the missing network connection was one of the (invalid) reasons given by the vendor and by authorities in the three countries why the machines could not be hacked. The vendor also claimed that his devices were no real computers but special purpose devices which were designed to only count votes and could not be used for any other purpose. Rop and his team have proven that someone with access to the machines can replace the implemented software with any software, including vote stealing software and a chess programme. When the Indian Election Commission claims the machines are not riggable, this can only refer to "by user operation via keys". It is common sense that someone who has sufficient access to open the machines and replace soft- or hardware can implement virtually any functionality, including vote stealing functionality that is only activated under certain circumstances and would not be spotted in tests. In neither of the three countries security concerns have been the main driver for banning e-voting. In all three countries the main reason for the removal of the EVMs was their negative impact on the transparency of the election process, and the fact that any malfunction of the devices due to malfunction or manipulation would remain undetected." (emphasis supplied)

It is submitted that the fact of the matter is not-networking will only prevent those vulnerabilities related to networking but it still is as vulnerable as any EVMs outside India on the aspects of malicious code, Trojans, malfunctioning, etc.

(j) The Petitioner has also approached Professor David L. Dill of Stanford University in regard to the Election Commission's claim that its EVMs are tamper proof. Thereon Professor Dill had to state as under:

> "At this time, there is no reliable way to detect the presence of malicious changes to software or hardware in a computer system, even a simple computer system. Although many discussions of "hacking" electronic voting systems focus on corruption of the machines by third parties, the greatest threat comes from changes made by someone with legitimate access to the hardware or software design or manufacturing process. Malicious changes to computer systems create a greater threat of undetected election fraud than conventional paper ballot systems because a relatively small team of individuals, perhaps just one, could change systems that could affect thousands or millions of votes.
>
> Since the legitimacy of elections depends on whether the populace can trust the results, I believe that the burden of proof should be on the advocates of an election system to show that it is difficult to commit undetected election fraud. It is difficult to find any significant number of computer scientists who to say there are effective ways to find malicious changes to computer systems. No such claims should be accepted unless the methods are disclosed and debated openly with experts on the other side." (emphasis supplied)

(k) As to the administrative precautions, set out in para 15 of the counter-affidavit, it is accepted that these are all salutary precautions; but they also highlight how very many officers have legitimate access to the EVMs: and therefore the number of points at which a very few officers, if suborned or part of a conspiracy, can mal-inject material in the EVMs.

(l) As to the Election Commission's main contention in its counter-affidavit, regarding cost (set out in para 9), and practical difficulties (set out in paras 8,10,11, and 25), it is submitted that these considerations can never be paramount when the very fate of the country could be at stake, with a bogus result obtained from mal-fixed EVMs. If, in fact, there are insurmountable practical difficulties, then it is better to return to the paper ballot system: but on the grounds of expense and technical difficulties, the EVMs cannot be imposed on democracy's most sacred arena.

(m) It may, however, be pointed out that in its letter dated 27.2.2009 to Dr. Subramanian Swamy the Election Commission had stated that already the "ECI-EVMs have the facility of a paper trail"; so perhaps the cost and practical difficulties would not be as high as is now being made out.

Requirements of the Information Technology Act 2000

It should be pointed out that a receipt safeguard is also mandatory in terms of Section 12 and 13 of the Information Technology Act 2000: there under, the Election Commission has a duty to provide a receipt. The space having been occupied by this legislation, the plenary power of the Election Commission under Article 324 of the Constitution, must yield to the requirement of Sections 12 and 13 of the Information Technology Act. Yet the Election Commission is vigorously opposing the Petitioner's demand for providing a paper receipt.

Conclusion

It is once again emphasized that at no stage, have we made the averment that there has actually been any fraud through the EVMs of the Election Commission of India: only that any electronic machine can be hacked or rigged and hence adequate safeguards are essential to meet the constitutional obligation for conducting free and fair elections.

Postscript

When ECI prevented the process of review to prove tamperability of India's EVMs, infringement of intellectual property rights was claimed. The ECIL has not mentioned clearly as to what IP will be violated. the entire box CANNOT be an IP since they have built it with

3rd party components. Almost all of the components used are 3rd party and not developed by ECIL / BEL and hence the IP of the chips etc. are not owned by ECIL / BEL. Moreover, an IP can be protected only if one such application has been filed either in the WIPO or even Indian IPO. The best part is that both ECIL & BEL have been granted patent for the exact same thing under 2 different patent numbers. This is a miracle which has happened only in India. How can this be legally possible, that the same invention is claimed by two parties? How can 2 companies be given the patent on 2 different patent numbers but have filed the SAME FILING papers? Is this valid?

Here's the link to the IPO search (http://124.124.193.243/ patentgrantedsearch/%28S%282ueasd45zv1kdx45cvzmokuq%29%29/quicksearchnew.aspx) and

The patent numbers are:

ECIL — 199087;
BEL — 196285.

Type "Voting" in the text box and select Title and click search

2

EVMs are Not Tamper-Proof

Falsity of the Election Commissioner's Claim

Dr Subramanian Swamy*

Jayalalitha, Chandrababu Naidu want to return to ballot papers. In Orissa, parties are approaching EC with dozens of complaints. Nowhere in Europe or US are EVMs used.

Numerous electronic voting inconsistencies in developing countries, where governments are often all too eager to manipulate votes, have only added to the controversy. After Hugo Chavez won the 2004 election in Venezuela, it came out that the government owned 28 per cent of Bizta, the company that manufactured the voting machines.

There is much talk today about the possibility of rigging of the electoral outcome in the recent general elections to the Lok Sabha. These doubts have arisen from the unexpected number of seats won by the Congress nation-wide, and these doubts are accentuated by the recent spate of articles published in reputed computer engineering journals as also in the popular international press which raises doubts about the EVMs.

For example, the respected *International Electrical & Electronics Engineering Journal* (*The IEEE*, May 2009, p.23) has published an article by two eminent professors of computer science, titled: "Trustworthy Voting" in which they conclude that while electronic voting machines offer a myriad of benefits, these cannot be reaped unless suggested safeguards are put in place for protecting the integrity of

* Former Union Law Minister.

the outcome. None of the safeguards are in place in Indian EVMs. Electronic voting machines in India today do not meet the standard of national integrity and safeguard the sanctity of democracy.

Newsweek magazine issue (dated 1 June 2009) has published an article by Evgeny Morozov, who points out that when Ireland embarked on an ambitious e-voting scheme in 2006, such as fancy touch-screen voting machines, it was widely welcomed: Three years and expense of Euro 51 million later, in April, the government scrapped the entire initiative. What doomed the effort was a lack of trust: The electorate just didn't like that the machines would record their votes as mere electronic blips, with no tangible record.

Morozov points out that one doesn't have to be a conspiracy theorist to suspect the fallibility of electronic voting machines. As most PC-users know by now, computers can be hacked. We are not unwilling to accept this security risk in banking, shopping and e-mailing since the fraud is at the micro-level, and of individual consequence which in most cases is rectifiable. But the ballot box needs to be perfectly safeguarded because of the monumental consequence of a rigged or faulty vote recording. It is of macro-significance much like an "e-coup d'etat". At least that's what voters across Europe seem to have said loud and clear.

Thus, a backlash against e-voting is brewing all over the European continent. After almost two years of deliberations, Germany's Supreme Court ruled last March that e-voting was unconstitutional because the average citizen could not be expected to understand the exact steps involved in the recording and tallying of votes. Political scientist Ulrich Wiesner, a physicist who filed the initial lawsuit, said in an interview with the German magazine *Der Spiegel* that the Dutch Nedap machines used in Germany are even less secure than mobile phones! The Dutch public-interest group Wij Vertrouwen Stemcomputers Niet (We Do Not Trust Voting Machines) produced a video showing how quickly the Nedap machines could be hacked without voters or election officials being aware (the answer: in five minutes!). After the clip was broadcast on national television in October 2006, the Netherlands banned all electronic voting machines.

Numerous electronic voting inconsistencies in developing countries, where governments are often all too eager to manipulate votes, have only added to the controversy. After Hugo Chavez won the 2004 election in Venezuela, it came out that the government owned 28 per cent of Bizta, the company that manufactured the voting machines. On the eve of the 2009 general elections in India, I had in a press conference in Chennai raised the issue and pointed out that those who had been convicted in the US for hacking of bank accounts on the internet and credit cards had been recruited just before the elections. In the US, the Secretary of State of California has now set up a full-fledged inquiry into EVMs, after staying all further use.

Why are the EVMs so vulnerable? Each step in the life cycle of a voting machine — from the time it is developed and installed to when the votes are recorded and the data transferred to a central repository for tallying — involves different people gaining access to the machines, often installing a new software. It wouldn't be hard for, say, an election official to paint a parallel programme under another password, on one or many voting machines that would ensure one outcome or another pre-determined even before voters arrived at the poll stations.

These dangers have been known to the Election Commission since 2000, when Dr M. S. Gill, the then CEC, had arranged at my initiative for Professor Sanjay Sarma of Massachusetts Institute of Technology (MIT) and Dr Gitanjali Swamy of Harvard to demonstrate how unsafe guarded the chips in EVMs were. Some changes in procedures were made subsequently by the EC, but not on the fundamental flaws that make it compliant to hacking. In 2004, the Supreme Court First Bench of Chief Justice V. N. Khare, Justices Babu and Kapadia had directed the Election Commission to consider the technical flaws in EVMs put forward by Prof. Satinath Choudhary, a US-based software engineer, in a PIL. But the EC has failed to consider his representation.

There are many ways to prevent EVM fraud. One way to reduce the risk of fraud is to have machines print a paper record of each vote, which voters could then deposit into a conventional ballot box. While this procedure would ensure that each vote can be verified, using paper ballots defeats the purpose of electronic voting in the first place. Using two machines produced by different manufacturers would decrease the risk of a security compromise, but wouldn't eliminate it.

A better way, it is argued in the above-cited IEEE article, is to expose the software behind electronic voting machines to public scrutiny. The root problem of popular electronic machines is that the computer programmes that run them are usually closely held trade secrets (it doesn't help that the software often runs on the Microsoft Windows operating system, which is not the world's most secure). Having the software closely examined and tested by experts not affiliated with the company would make it easier to close technical loopholes that hackers can exploit. Experience with web servers has shown that opening software to public scrutiny can uncover potential security breaches.

However, as the *Newsweek* article points out, the electronic voting machine industry argues that openness would hurt the competitive position of the current market leaders. A report released by the Election Technology Council, a US trade association, in April this year says that disclosing information on known vulnerabilities might help would-be attackers more than those who would defend against such attacks. Some computer scientists have proposed that computer code be disclosed only to a limited group of certified experts. Making such disclosure mandatory for all electronic voting machines would be a good first step for preventing vote fraud, and also be consistent with openness in the electoral process.

Now Madras High Court is hearing soon a PIL on the EVMs. This is a good news. I believe time has arrived for taking a long, hard look at these riggable machines that favour the ruling party which has ensured a pliant Election Commission. Otherwise, elections would soon become ridiculed and lose their credibility. The demise of democracy would then be near. Hence, evidence must now be collected by all political parties to determine how many constituencies they suspect rigging. The number would not exceed 75 in my opinion. We can identify them as follows:

> "In the 2009 general elections, any result in which the main losing candidate of a recognised party finds that more than 10 per cent of the polling booths showed less than five votes per booth,

should be taken *prima facie* a constituency in which rigging has taken place. This is because the main recognised parties usually have more than five party workers per booth, and hence with their families would poll a minimum of 25 votes per booth for their party candidate. Hence if these 25 voters can give affidavits affirming who they had voted for, then the High Court can treat it as evidence and order a full inquiry."

(*Source:* http://www.organiser.org/dynamic/modules.php?name=Content&pa=showpage&pid=294&page=2_)

Annexure 2.1

Dr. Subramanian Swamy's Statement* Regarding Falsity of the Chief Election Commissioner's Claim

1. The German Supreme Court has recently banned the use of EVMs in German elections based on these reports. The Delhi High Court has been hearing my PIL on the use of EVMs in Indian elections. The next date of hearing is scheduled for February 17th. In that petition, I have given two examples of two constituencies, Madurai (2004), Madhya Pradesh (2006) where *prima facie* rigging has taken place.
2. The Chief Election Commissioner, Mr. Navin Chawla has been telling a blatant lie to the media that no one has yet been able to demonstrate the tamperability of Indian EVMs. In fact on 3 September 2009, I was accompanied by two IT software engineers, Dr. Hariprasad and Dr. V. V. Rao (both of whom will attend this conference) to the Election Commission for a demonstration. Half way through our demonstration, the EC officials abruptly aborted the meeting stating that they cannot allow us to continue the demonstration since it involved the patent rights of the ECIL, and needed special permission of the CEC! Since then no meeting has been held for us. However, ECI continues to "inform" us that Indian EVMs are special and somehow different from International EVMs and that concerns about Indian EVMs are misplaced. But activists, technologists contest that position. These conferences will throw light how Indian EVMs lack the many safeguards that international EVMs have and they can be easily hacked (perhaps much more easily) than many internationally used EVMs and if corrective actions are

---

* Statement of 4 February 2010.

not taken, it will have serious implications to the democracy of the country.

3. *What is at core is the issue of transparency*, as German Supreme Court has enumerated, the ability of a common voter understand the process form the time vote is cast to the counting of that vote to the candidate specified by the voter. When that transparency is lost, the elections are greatly beholden to experts and election officials and leaves field open for fraud, potentially in a very large scale.
4. The challenge in India is also that the public is under the impression that EVM solved many issues related to paper ballots such as booth capturing, booth stuffing, etc. and is viewed as using technology to improve efficiency. However, crimes of booth capturing, etc. at the local level by physical means have now been replaced by the dangerous possibility of national level rigging by electronic means. The planned sessions in this conference are geared to bring an open discussion on these issues with international and national experts and help protect Indian Democracy.

3

EVM Hacking — EC Accountable Under Cyberlaws

Dr. S. Kalyanaraman

(I have collated and summarised arguments demonstrating EVM hacking and the imperative of subjecting EC to a forensic audit by an independent agency under the directions of the Supreme Court. The splendid contributions made by Prof. J. Krishnayya, Dr. Anupam Saraph, Prof. M. D. Nalapat, Rajeev Srinivasan, Prof. Sohan Prabhakar Modak, Senthi Raja are gratefully acknowledged.)

The freedom we have earned has to be defended resolutely. Eternal vigilance is the price of liberty.

EC like Caesar's wife should be above suspicion. Now, EC is tainted as it has entered the complex cyber world, has to justify its constitutional status before the peoples' court and explain fully the measures taken to guard against cyber frauds in the wireless technology age exemplified by a chip the size of a pencil head can transmit and receive messages when buttoned on to a device like the EVM.

Our ancestors of the 10th century (919 CE) seem to have conducted elections — with secret ballots using pots — much more efficiently as recorded in the Uttaramerur (near Kanchipuram) inscription of King Parantaka Chola (*See* Appendix 2 at the end of the book). This was mentioned during the Constituent Assembly debates by T. Prakasam (who was Chief Minister of Madras Presidency) while referring to the democratic traditions of our nation.* This inscription which refers to adult suffrage and secret ballot, was cited during Constituent Assembly deliberations for drafting the Constitution of independent Bharat. "Shri T. Prakasam (Madras: General): The Honourable Mr. Madhava Rau said that the ballot box and ballot paper were not known to our ancestors. I would like to point out to him, that the ballot box and the ballet papers were described in an inscription on the walls of a temple in the villages of Uttaramerur, twenty miles from Conjeevaram (Kanchipuram). Every detail is given there. The ballot box was a pot with the mouth tied and placed on the ground with a hole made at the bottom and the ballot paper was the kadjan leaf and adult franchise was exercised. The election took place not only for that village but for the whole of India. This was just a thousand years ago. It is not known to my honourable friend and that is why he made such a wrong statement — a grievously wrong statement and I want to correct it."**

EC Accountable under Cyber Law: Information Technology Act, 2000

How Can an Accused Become a Judge?

All parties have expressed concerns about functioning of EVMs (Ghulam Nabi Azad about Orissa polls, Advani about Lok Sabha polls, PMK/MDMK in Tamil Nadu, etc.). EC is going through a make-believe, non-transparent exercise. How can the accused become a judge?

---

* http:// parliamentofindia.nic.in/ls/debates/debates.htm (Constituent Assembly Debates).

** http://parliamentofindia.nic.in/lsdebates/vol7p5b.htm (Constituent Assembly debate on 9th November, 1948) (http://parliamentofindia.nic.in/ls/debates/vol4p8.htm Constitution 1000 years ago).

EC has Not Explained Who Manufactures the Chips in the EVMs

The manufactures of the Chips are still not revealed by the EC, and most probably the manufacturer of the chip would be a foreign company. Again, this is another national security issue, where we mortgage our credibility of our election process to a foreign company. Ultimately we never inspect the foreign company premises too.

There are also reports that ECIL / BEL have outsourced the making of the EVMs to private parties thus introducing another trojan horse. EC has to confirm the situation.

Introduction of Timer Device in EVMs Violates Secrecy of Ballot

The latest EVMs record the time of each vote. This violates the fundamental principle of secret voting. When the polling booth agent, notes down the time a particular voter had voted, he will be able to find which party he voted for, if he has access to EVM vote logs. This is a violation of constitutional rights, which can invalidate the last Lok Sabha election itself, since about 16% of EVMs had time details.

Use of two types of machines — one with timer (introduced in January 2009 first in Delhi Assembly polls) and another without timer device. EVMs with timer devices are said to be about two lakh in number (out of a total of about 13 lakh EVMs). Thus, in 16% of the constituencies or about 80 Lok Sabha constituencies the timer device EVMs were used rendering them to internet frauds because timer device makes the device non-local and directly amenable to internet crime. There is a good possibility that the 80 constituencies selected for manipulation were in Tamil Nadu, Orissa, Punjab, Rajasthan, UP and Delhi. EC is accountable to provide information on how the timer-device EVMs were distributed and how they were certified by manufacturers, audited by EC, before being deployed. Party polling agents should be allowed access to such regular system audits to ensure transparency and accountability of EC.

Just as ATMs are subject to cyber laws audited by RBI, EVMs also should be subject to cyber laws and a controller should be appointed under the Information Technology Act 2000

Section 61A of Representation of the People Act, 1951 was introduced Effective 15 March 1989

It is clear that EVM = ballot paper + ballot box. It is usable as evidentiary document under the Indian Evidence Act, 1872. Under Information Technology Act 2000 (the cyber law of the country) "electronic record" means date, record or date generated, image or sound stored, received or sent in an electronic form. (Definition in Section 2 of the IT Act 2000).

Thus, it constitutes a document / evidence under the IT Act 2000 and hence should be subject to the cyber law of the land.

EVM employs a chip and counting involves a computer network. Hence, it should be adjudicated under IT Act 2000.

The requirement of a paper printout receipt as in an ATM is VERY SOUND and is consistent with the mandatory principle of AUDIT TRAIL when computer systems are used.

The Representation of the People Act, 1951

2[61A. Voting machines at elections — Notwithstanding anything contained in this Act or the rules made there under, the giving and recording of votes by voting machines in such manner as may be prescribed, may be adopted in such constituency or constituencies as the Election Commission may, having regard to the circumstances of each case, specify.

Explanation — For the purpose of this section, "voting machine" means any machine or apparatus whether operated electronically or otherwise used for giving or recording of votes and any reference to a ballot box or ballot paper in this Act or the rules made there under shall, save as otherwise provided, be construed as including a reference to such voting machine wherever such voting machine is used at any election.]

Ins. by Act 1 of 1989, s. 11 (w.e.f. 15-3-1989)

The IT act defines itself as "An Act to provide legal recognition for transactions carried out by means of electronic data interchange and other means of electronic communication, commonly referred to as 'electronic commerce', which involve the use of alternatives to paper-based methods of communication and storage of information, to facilitate electronic filing of documents with the Government agencies and further to amend the Indian Penal Code, the Indian Evidence Act, 1872, the Bankers' Books Evidence Act, 1891 and the Reserve Bank of India Act, 1934 and for matters connected therewith or incidental thereto."

Comments

The IT Act was brought into effect in the year 2000. This act should be seen as an elaboration of the Representation of Peoples Act 1951 which refers to the optional use of any machine operated electronically.

Since the EVM is clearly a computer, a computer network under the IT Act, the electronic record (mentioned in the Representation of Peoples Act 1951) should be seen to be consistent with the electronic document mentioned in the IT Act 2000.

The IT Act also mandates the appointment of a Controller. Government of India should, by a notification, appoint such a Controller without any further delay.

The plea for a paper printout during the voting process is to ensure the public nature of the election process as clearly enunciated by the German Supreme Court in defining the basic structure of a democratic republic. This should be done immediately; if the Government Election Commission fails to act within a reasonable period, the Court should declare the process of polling and counting using a network of machines (polling unit, control unit, counting machine and EC electronic spreadsheet compilation) unconstitutional since they violate the principle of transparency and public nature of the election process which is the very foundation of our sovereign democratic republic as mentioned in the Preamble of the Constitution of India.

"India Needs a Separate Cyber Police Force" *

India urgently needs a well-trained special police force to deal with cyber crimes and it must be equipped and trained to deal with all kinds of internet bugs, holds India's incumbent Law Minister Veerappa Moily. "India does not have a specific police force to deal with cyber crimes and implementation of laws against crimes in the virtual world. India needs it urgently following the footsteps of US and South Korea," Moily said at an interactive seminar for judges, heads of police forces and prosecuting agencies here.

He said there were many impediments that needed to be overcome soon. While a vast majority of the police force or prosecutors in the country had no experience of tackling cyber crime, judges too lacked experience in appreciating evidence in such cases. As cyber crime knows no geographical boundary, the absence of international cooperation between police forces adds to the woes of victims and lets the culprit go scot free, he said.

It was attorney general G. E. Vahanvati who pointed out the danger potential of cyber crime as was shown by "trojan horse" and " love you" bug and said cyber crime was not limited to the web world but had been extended to mobile phones, which could be used to bombard a victim with messages and send illicit MMSes.

Chief Justice of India K. G. Balakrishnan said cyber crimes caused irreparable damage to the victims though it may not involve inflicting of physical pain. "Someone's bank account can be wiped off depriving him of life-long savings and others can face huge loss of reputation when his face is morphed and put in an obscene video on the net," he said while emphasising on sensitisation of the police, prosecutors and judiciary about the consequences of the crime.

Supreme Court judge and Cyber Law Enforcement Committee chairman, Justice Altamas Kabir, said the attending DGPs and judges should make efforts to understand the nitty-gritty of the anti-cyber crime law enacted by the country in the shape of IT Act, 2000. However, he said going by the growing ingenuity of cyber criminals, there was a need for expanding the definitions of various crimes listed in the law.**

---

* Moily, TNN, 1 February 2010, 2.32 a.m., New Delhi

** http://timesofindia.indiatimes.com/india/India-needs-a-separate-cyber-police-force-Moily/articleshow/5521142.cms

Tampering with EVMs should be declared a crime under the Information Technology Act of 2000 and the full force of law should apply to EVMs which are part of the cyber space of India.

Election Commission cannot dodge the issue that EVMs are not computers or computer networks.

Does the Election Commission of India have the competence and does it have cyber specialist teams knowledgeable about controlling computer network devices? Can it deal with cyber crime related to EVMs?

IT Act of 2000 introduces salutary measures to control cyber crime related to ATMs for instance, by making the RBI responsible to institute control measures.

Getting BHEL, ECI to certify the EVMs supplied is a good first step. Not enough. More needs to be done. A microchip of the size of a pencil head is enough to pry into any EVM and network used by EC to consolidate vote count. The revelation of spreadsheets used by EC well before the declaration of results is a shocker. Most of the "so-called dummy numbers" used turned out to be valid final results for over 100 constituencies in the last Lok Sabha election. (http://government.wikia.com/wiki/Case_to_ban_EVM).

EVM is Not a Super Calculator but a Computer Network under Information Technology Act, 2000

Chief Election Commissioner Navin Chawla misled the public by calling the electronic voting machine a super calculator. (*See* Annexure 3.3 News Report of 2 January 2010 and also Annexure 3.4 "A Remote Wireless Manipulation of EVM"). Chawla was wrong. EVM is a computer network as defined under the Information Technology Act 2000. From EC's own website, it is clear that EVM is:

(1) An electronic system composed of a Control Unit and a Balloting Unit and hence is a computer network;
(2) Has a memory to store the results for 10 years; and
(3) Is based on an "imported" electronic chip. (*See* excerpts from the CEC website appended, Annexure 3.1).

Are EVMs Unconstitutional in India?

EVMs should be declared unconstitutional because:

- The basic feature of Constitution of India is that India is a democracy and India is a republic.
- Republican nature demands that all citizens have a say in the formation of the State.
- Democratic form of governance demands that all citizens should publicly participate in the process of government formation.
- Public nature of the election process is inherent in these fundamental features of the Constitution.
- EVMs are held in secrecy by the Election Commission of India. Even ECI does NOT know what programmes have been burnt into the control unit microprocessors of the EVMs.
- Hence, EVMs which are outside public scrutiny for casting of ballots and counting of votes is unconstitutional.

Secrecy of the ballot cannot mean that ECI holds complete control over and secretly manages the EVMs outside of anyone's continuous testing, verification and validation. Such a testing, verification and validation process should be openly done in the presence of the public and by systems audit agencies outside the control of ECI. This is to ensure checks and balances which is ANOTHER basic feature of the Constitution.

Indian Constitution has created a democratic republic and not an autocracy run by ECI, beyond the control of and accountability to the people of India.

Public Nature of Election Process: Parakesarivarma Chola's Thousand-Year Old Intellectual Property Right of Secret Ballot.
Source: https://sites.google. com/site/hindunew/electronic-voting-machines http:// tinyurl.com/ylb57tr (Stone inscription, slab 1).

The EVM is a computer network used for the most important function under the Constitution of India: the recording of public will to elect public officials to perform under the democratic system of the Constitution. Since the introduction of the EVMs in 1989-90, the Parliament has enacted an Information Technology Act, 2000 to regulate and control the use of computers, computer systems and networks. (*See* excerpts from the Act appended in Annexure 3.2). Under the provisions of this Act, EVMs clearly fall within the ambit of this Act. Government of India should appoint appropriate controlling authorities to monitor the use of EVMs as computer systems and networks, similar to the authority given to RBI to control and monitor the use of ATMs for banking transactions. This will ensure that CEC is accountable and that CEC has adequate systems audit and control procedures in place to ensure that EVMs as computer systems function efficiently and effectively to provide confidence to the sovereign voters that the exercise of their votes which is the most sacrosanct duty is not compromised in any manner. Like any computer network, EVMs should be subjected to periodic and regular systems audit which is the global norm for all computer networks to ensure their security, authentication, accessibility and prevention of frauds. Bringing EVMs under the ambit of Information Technology Act 2000 will provide the needed confidence to the Indian electorates that CEC as a functionary under the Constitution, is not beyond accountability.

Two types of EVMs are being used by CEC: one with timer stamping facility and one without. There should be uniformity in the systems used for the most sacred function in a democracy: free and fair elections. Any violation recorded should declare EVMs unconstitutional.

Annexure 3.1

Excerpts from Central Election Commission Website on the Nature of EVMs*

Q1. What is an Electronic Voting Machine? In what way its functioning is different from the conventional system of voting?

Ans. An Electronic Voting Machine consists of two Units — a Control Unit and a Balloting Unit — joined by a five-meter cable. The Control Unit is with the Presiding Officer or a Polling Officer and the Balloting Unit is placed inside the voting compartment. Instead of issuing a ballot paper, the Polling Officer in-charge of the Control Unit will press the Ballot Button. This will enable the voter to cast his vote by pressing the blue button on the Balloting Unit against the candidate and symbol of his choice.

Q2. When was the EVM first introduced in elections?

Ans. EVMs manufactured in 1989-90 were used on experimental basis for the first time in 16 Assembly Constituencies in the States of Madhya Pradesh (5), Rajasthan (5) and NCT of Delhi (6) at the General Elections to the respective Legislative Assemblies held in November, 1998.

. . . .

Q16. How long the Control Unit stores the result in its memory?

Ans. The Control Unit can store the result in its memory for 10 years and even more . . . .

. . . .

Q21. Is it possible to programme the EVMs in such a way that initially, say up to 100 votes, votes will be recorded exactly in the

---

* http: //eci.nic.in/eci_main/faq/evm.asp

same way as the "blue buttons" are pressed, but thereafter, votes will be recorded only in favour of one particular candidate irrespective of whether the "blue button" against that candidate or any other candidate is pressed?

Ans. The microchip used in EVMs is sealed at the time of import. It cannot be opened and any rewriting of programme can be done by anyone without damaging the chip. There is, therefore, absolutely no chance of programming the EVMs in a particular way to select any particular candidate or political party.

Annexure 3.2

Excerpts from Information Technology Act, 2000

Preamble

An Act to provide legal recognition for transactions carried out by means of electronic date interchange and other means of electronic communication, commonly referred to as "electronic commerce", which involve the use of alternative to paper-based methods of communication and storage of information to facilitate electronic filing of documents with the Government agencies and further to amend the Indian Penal Code, the India Evidence Act, 1872, the Banker's Books Evidence Act, 1891 and the Reserve Bank of India Act, 1934 and for matters connected therewith or incidental thereto;

Whereas the General Assembly of the United Nations by resolution A / RES / 51 / 162, date 30th January 1997 has adopted the Model Law on Electronic Commerce adopted by the United Nations Commission on International Trade Law;

AND WHREAS the said resolution recommends, *inter alia*, that all States give favourable consideration to the said Model Law when they enact or revise their laws, in view of the need for uniformity of the law applicable to alternatives to paper based methods of communication and storage of information;

AND WHEREAS it is considered necessary to give effect to the said resolution and to promote efficient delivery of Government services by means of reliable electronic records . . . .

Section 2: Definitions

. . . "computer" means electronic, magnetic, optical or other high-speed date processing device or system which performs logical, arithmetic and memory functions by manipulations of electronic, magnetic or optical impulses, and includes all input, output, processing, storage, computer software or communication facilities which are connected or relates to the computer in a computer system or computer network . . . .

"computer network" means the interconnection of one or more computers through.

(i) The use of satellite, microwave, terrestrial lime or other communication media; and
(ii) Terminals or a complex consisting of two or more interconnected computers whether or not the interconnection is continuously maintained; . . .

"computer system" means a device or collection of devices, including input and output support devices and excluding calculators which are not programmable and capable being used in conjunction with external files which contain computer programmes, electronic instructions, input data and output data that performs logic, arithmetic, data storage and retrieval, communication control and other functions.

Annexure 3.3

"EVM is Like a Super Calculator, Says Chawla"*

Electronic voting machines (EVMs) have come to stay and there is no question of the country reverting to the old system, Chief Election Commissioner Navin Chawla said on Saturday. Speaking to journalists here, he said: "Other nations have lauded India for declaring election results without delay by using the EVMs."

Asked about various parties referring to the ballot voting in the United States, he pointed out that it was federal system. The EVM was like a "super calculator" and its role and commands could not be altered, he said, adding the people accepted that the machines were tamper proof.

Recalling that doubts over the EVMs had been brought to the Election Commission's notice, Mr. Chawla said that since the proof of the pudding is in the eating, 100 machines from various States were placed before a number of invitees and they were asked to choose machines at random and demonstrate how they could be tampered with. None could prove that the EVM was untrustworthy.

Stating that the machines were being procured from Bharat Electronics and the Electronics Corporation of India, the CEC pointed out that these firms were catering for the needs of the defence sector and the Atomic Energy Commission.

After the recent Maharashtra Assembly elections, a candidate said he would accept the verdict only if the votes were counted four times. It was done and there was no variation in the vote count.

To another query, he said the controversy surrounding EVMs was laid to rest. "As head of the Commission I am convinced one thousand per cent about its use."**

---

* News Report in *The Hindu*, 2 January 2010.

** http://www.thehindu.com/2010/01/03/stories/2010010360340800.htm

Annexure 3.4

A Remote Wireless Manipulation of EVM

Since the early days of electronic devices such as Read Only Memory (ROM) chips, there have been dramatic advances including wireless technologies.

UC SanDiego Professor writes about having been able to reverse engineer the software of (American) EVMs, without opening them up at all. His programming style suggest that there have been many changes in the capability of software hackers.

The Possibility of Embedding Wireless Feature in the Chip

The first question is how will we know, if a chip contains wireless feature or not? It is impossible to find the architecture of the chip, after it is manufactured. This wireless feature can be made passive, so that it gets activated only upon receiving a specific signal in a specific frequency.

A simple analogy is that, our mobile phone rings only if the call is intended for it. All the GSM waves are available to the mobile phone, but it activates only when a particular signal (corresponding to its mobile number or set code) is detected. IT rejects all other waves, even though it can read those.

In a similar case, the wireless feature will remain passive, unless activated by the known person. And this can be done, through satellite from any part of the world.

Or, it can be done at a distance of 200-300 metres outside the polling booth. The possibility is wide here.

Failure to Audit the Design Integrity of EVMs and Embedded Software

Beep sound can NEVER be a confirmation of the vote.

The EC claims that when a voter presses the particular party's button, there will be a beep sound to confirm his vote. But in practical perspective, a beep sound confirms only the pressing of the button, but it does not confirm whether the vote has been delivered to the particular party.

This is just like giving our vote to a third person, who in turns puts in to ballot box. We never know if that third person puts our vote correctly or he changes it and puts a different vote or he may not even deliver the vote itself.

So, direct and secret voting itself is violated, which is available in the ballot paper, where we know which party symbol we are marking, and we ourselves ensure the voting by directly putting the paper in the ballot box ourselves:

- Closed source proprietary design — If it is a mere calculator and completely secure, why the secrecy about its design and software, why not allow use of any EVMs that confirm to a standard? We do not restrict to using HP calculators and ban the use of any other calculator for number crunching.
- EVMs cannot work without elaborate supervised pre- and post-poll process involving observers, agents and security paper seals. This is a huge risk and cost. Like a calculator that cannot work unless scientists, teachers and examiners certify that the calculator is secure and not fraudulent.
- There is no verification of software on the EVM — no checksum or debug programmes to confirm identity and version of software — besides black-box testing. What can distinguish an authentic EVM from an unauthentic one?

An extraordinary statement was made by EC that from now on ECIL / BEL (makers of EVMs) will be asked to certify the EVMs supplied by them. It is amazing that such certification and audit by

EC did not occur for the more than 13 lakh EVMs presently in use and for the 2009 Lok Sabha elections.

Trojan Code

Secret trojan code embedded right at the manufacturing stage. This trojan can be activated, by combination of special keys known only to secret group of people. This trojan need not know the candidate or his serial number or his party symbol. What it needs is to know the exact button, to which the beneficiary party belongs to, so that it can either simulate that button press, or transfer votes from other buttons to the beneficiary party's button code.

This point is very important, because the Indiresan committee report claims that the candidate serial number is not known till two weeks of commencement of election. This is a false claim, because, candidate serial number is only for human reference, and all the internal workings are based on machine codes.

Even if candidate serial number claim is to be accepted, there should be a mechanism to feed or map the button to the serial number, and that can be done only by humans. Who are they?

Absence of Standards for EVM Data Storage and Retrieval

- There are no standards and procedures for data-storage, data-retrieval, archiving, data-transfer, data-verification. In fact the BEL and ECIL machines are not even compatible when it comes to obtaining, storing retrieving, archiving or transferring data. What is the standard? Why are there no third party designs? Who are the OEMs? This is like NTSC and PAL — only the manufacturers benefit.
- There is a manual process for reading the votes — Why is there no print-out of the votes recorded on the machine with the machine id? Why can the entire data not be transferred to public website instantaneously? Why must the form 17C and form 20 be manually filled? Why can it not be printed by the EVM?

Absence of EVM Audit Procedures

- There is no standard for maintaining a transaction trail and statutory independent audit by anyone who wishes to audit an EVM or entire constituencies. This is like allowing pass-books to be updated without entries in registers and without payment slips or cheque-book entries in the registers. This is like trusting the system because it runs, not because there is a mechanism to check for points of malfunction or misuse.

- There is no transaction slip to the voter. For the voter, the vote is untraceable once it is cast. This is like depositing money without a deposit slip. It is like a bank that has no pass-book updates or ways to check that the money is still in your account.

EC Gets Results on 6 May 2009 before Voting is Completed (Last Date of Polling 13 May)

- Coded "results" were available on the ECI website in the versions of the spreadsheet CandidateAC.xls downloaded between the 6th and 11th of May. They contained "results" for all but 47 of the 8071 candidate. If EVMs were secure with DEO / district collectors, and elections were not even held in many constituencies, how did the ECI have this data?
- Was this data not in control of the ECI? Was their site hacked? Or was data from various EVMs uploaded in advance?
- How can the ECI distinguish between real and dummy data?

EC in Violation of Supreme Court Order of 19 January 2009

- The existence of the poll results data as early as 6 May (one week before 13 May, the final date of polling) contravenes the Order passed by the Supreme Court on 19-01-2009, in writ petition (C) No. 207 of 2004th. (*See* http://eci.nic.in/press/current /pn140409.pdf reproduced below):

Election Commission of India
Nirvachan Sadan, Ashoka Road, New Delhi — 110 001
No. ECI / PN / 23 / 2009 Dated : 14th April, 2009

Press Note
Subject: Prohibition on Publication and Dissemination of Results of Opinion polls / Exit polls.

In pursuance of the Order passed by the Hon'ble Supreme Court on 19-01-2009, in writ petition (C) No. 207 of 2004, the Election Commission issued Guidelines, on 17th February, 09, to be followed in the matter of publication / dissemination of results of opinion polls and exit polls in connection with the current elections to the Lok Sabha and State Legislative Assemblies. As per the guidelines, result of opinion / exit polls carried out at any time, cannot be published, publicized or disseminated in any manner, during the period starting from 48 hours before the hour fixed for conclusion of poll in the first phase of election and till the conclusion of poll in the last phase of election. The period referred to in the guidelines starts from 3 PM today, the 14th April, 09 (as the hour fixed for conclusion of poll in some of the constituencies in the first phase of election on 16.4.09 is 3 PM), and will continue till the conclusion of poll in the last (the fifth) phase of election.

(K. F. Wilfred, Secretary)

Use of Genesys Software by EC to Consolidate Vote Counts — Counting of Votes Using Genesys Software

EC has not publicized, NOR audited the flow of information after the EVMs have been used for the polls. There are so many places along the route (not to mention the idea of using E-mails to collect vote totals!) where errors can creep in. (In fact, the Genesys programme mentioned by EC to Anupam and Nalapat has NOT been publicised. Has it been checked out by the technical group led by Indiresan?

If this data is generated as test / dummy data by "Genesys" software that collects and transfers data from districts to the ECI then:

- Why did this happen during the poll process?
- Why did the ECI not put up notice to the effect on its website?
- Why did it not react to the alert to this data sent to them on the 6th of May by NIC and Dr. Anupam Saraph?
- Why is there no response to date?
- Why is there no clarification on this?
- If the purpose of the test is to match names with votes, why were the names coded to match the order in which they appear on the EVM?

- If it is just meant to tally the match, why was the data changing for at least some constituencies in this period?

Votes polled by 108 winners in 2009 Lok Sabha polls tally with 6 May spreadsheet data of EC Nalapat's discovery of EC working with spreadsheets on 6 May when the final count and results were due only on 10 May. Prof. S. P. Modak has found that 108 constituency results match with the numbers used in the spreadsheets. This is a serious issue requiring CBI inquiry. EC cannot be allowed to brush this under the carpet; this is comparable to a cyber crime of fraudulent of use of ATMs of Banks. An external agency should audit the use of Genesys software for gathering info. On counted votes from the State Election Commission officials:

- Why do 108 winners tally with winners as per this data?
- Why do the ranks of 662 candidates match the finally declared?
- In many cases multiple ranks in the same constituency match — this is a highly non-random event considering each of the "n" candidates in a constituency would have "1 / n" chance of making it to any position and p positions matching is a low probability chance with probability 1 / (n)**p.
- If previous years data is used to generate "dummy data", why are there only 108 matches? Also where does the data for those who did not contest previously come from?
- Why was this data "sanitized" on the 15th of May?
- Why were the final results never uploaded onto the spreadsheet?
- Why was the link to the spreadsheet removed on the 15th of July when the media asked the ECI questions about it?

EC Has Not Replied to the Notes Sent by Anupam Saraph and Nalapat Madhav

- Why has the ECI not replied to the mails and minutes of the meeting with ECI sent to them by Dr. Anupam Saraph and Professor Madhav Nalapat?
- Why does the voters and votes polled data reported by the ECI in different documents on its own website differ significantly?

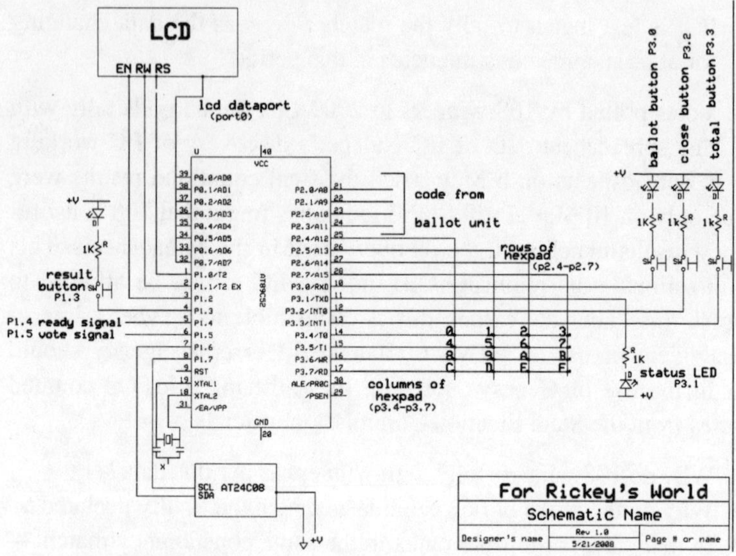

EC Contravenes Cyber Laws in India

SC should direct that EC be made accountable under the Information Technology Act 2000 since EC is using a computer / computer network / computer resource / computer system as defined in the Act.

EVMs are computers / computer networks / computer resource / computer system under the definitions included in The Information Technology Act, 2000 (No. 21 of 2000) of India http://www.legalserviceindia.com/cyber/itact.html (For the full text of the Act)

Amendments have also been made to the Indian Penal Code (45 of 1860) to recognize electronic records and to the Indian Evidence Act 1872 (1 of 1872) and Reserve Bank of India Act 1934 (2 of 1934).

In the Reserve Bank of India Act, 1934, in Section 58, in sub-section (2), after clause (p), the following clause shall be inserted, namely:

> "(pp) the regulation of fund transfer through electronic means between the banks or between the banks and other financial institutions referred to in clause (c) of section 45-1, including the laying down of the conditions subject to which banks and other financial

institutions shall participate in such fund transfers, the manner of such fund transfers and the rights and obligations of the participants in such fund transfers;".

This is an Act to provide legal recognition for transactions carried out by means of electronic data interchange and other means of electronic communication, commonly referred to as "electronic commerce", which involve the use of alternatives to paper-based methods of communication and storage of information, to facilitate electronic filing of documents with the Government agencies and further to amend the Indian Penal Code, the Indian Evidence Act, 1872, the Bankers' Books Evidence Act, 1891 and the Reserve Bank of India Act, 1934 and for matters connected therewith or incidental thereto:

1. (2) It shall extend to the whole of India and, save as otherwise provided in this Act, it applies also to any offence or contravention there under committed outside India by any person.

2. "computer" means any electronic magnetic, optical or other high-speed data processing device or system which performs logical, arithmetic, and memory functions by manipulations of electronic, magnetic or optical impulses, and includes all input, output, processing, storage, computer software, or communication facilities which are connected or related to the computer in a computer system or computer network;

(a) "Computer network" means the interconnection of one or more computers through:

(i) The use of satellite, microwave, terrestrial line or other communication media; and

(ii) Terminals or a complex consisting of two or more interconnected computers whether or not the interconnection is continuously maintained;

(b) "Computer resource" means computer, computer system, computer network, data, computer data base or software;

(c) "Computer system" means a device or collection of devices, including input and output support devices and excluding calculators which are not programmable and capable of being used in conjunction with external files, which contain computer programmes, electronic instructions, input data and output data, that performs logic, arithmetic, data storage and retrieval, communication control and other functions;

The act defines in Section 2 (ze) a "secure system" means computer hardware, software, and procedure that-

(a) Are reasonably secure from unauthorised access and misuse;

(b) Provide a reasonable level of reliability and correct operation;

(c) Are reasonably suited to performing the intended functions; and

(d) Adhere to generally accepted security procedures;

Sections 65 and 66 of the IT Act 2000 prescribe penalties for tampering / hacking:

65. Tampering with Computer Source Documents.

Whoever knowingly or intentionally conceals, destroys or alters or intentionally or knowingly causes another to conceal, destroy or alter any computer source code used for a computer, computer programme, computer system or computer network, when the computer source code is required to be kept or maintained by law for the time being in force, shall be punishable with imprisonment up to three years, or with fine which may extend up to two lakh rupees, or with both.

Explanation.— For the purposes of this section, "computer source code" means the listing of programmes, computer commands, design and layout and programme analysis of computer resource in any form.

66. Hacking with Computer System

(1) Whoever with the intent to cause or knowing that he is likely to cause wrongful loss or damage to the public or any person destroys or deletes or alters any information residing in a computer resource or diminishes its value or utility or affects it injuriously by any means, commits hack.

(2) Whoever commits hacking shall be punished with imprisonment up to three years, or with fine which may extend up to two lakh rupees, or with both.

Procedures Governing ATMs Which Require Printout of Transaction as an Audit Trail for the Customer Should be Followed in EVM Operations.

Just as an ATM produces a receipt, EVM should produce a receipt which can be deposited in a separate box for verification in cases of EVM malfunction / complaints. Secrecy of the ballot will not be vitiated. The voter is free to inform others of how he voted; there is no law prohibiting this freedom. He should also get a copy of the EVM receipt. Even as of now, since an EVM can accommodate only 3000 votes, secrecy of ballot has already been violated; it will be possible to know which ward voters voted for which candidates.

A note on cyber laws is provided in a separate document. Just as a bank is accountable for preventing potential ATM frauds, EC will have to be answerable to the possibility of crimes committed on EVMs which are computing devices. RBI regulates the operation of the ATMs of banks. Similar regulatory mechanism is needed for EVMs operated by EC. Elections are high-stake democratic exercises.

Why EVM Should be Declared Unconstitutional by the Supreme Court

Voter cannot be expected to be able to understand the systems audit requirements for complex computing devices. Elections as a public exercise should be simple and intelligible to the voter. This is the "simplicity" criterion on which German Supreme Court declared use of EVMs unconstitutional.

Non-Transparency of EC About Vote Counting

EC is not transparent about the election counting procedure. See also the episode about EC admitting the use of Genesys Software to maintain spreadsheets of election results. This software had been used to keep the count on 6 May itself even before the final counting date of 16 May in serious violation of all canons of propriety. EC has promised to explain this issue to Anupam Saraph and Nalapat. Response from EC still awaited as of August 2010.

Dangers of Erroneous Counting or Manipulated Counting or Tally of Votes

The possibility of changing the values at the last minute:

- All the votes are electronically stored, most probably in a flash memory. (Similar to pen drive). This memory should be rewritable, otherwise, the votes cannot be entered in this memory. The EC claims only the controlling unit is one time writable. But not the storage chip.
- When there is a mechanism to read the total number of votes, can't there be a secret mechanism to alter the reading?

In the Case of Chidambaram Episode, the EVMs Seem to Have Been Modified Somewhere in the Middle

To give an idea on how to change the values, we can refer to digital FM radios available now, where the frequency can be either incremented or decremented, just using two buttons.

The focus on Election Counting Machine:

- EVMs are NOT manually counted . . . rather, they are connected to a counting machine, which reads the bulk of EVM machines. Why can't the counting machine be hacked? Since the counting machine gives a consolidated total, it would be possible to change values through the counting machine, since what it displays tends to be the final result.
- Surely, EC has to provide a lot of answers instead of issuing Press Notes declaring that EVMs are tamper-proof. No one buy this declaration in this electronic, wireless age. Else, there would have been no need for an IT Act 2000 as a cyber law of India.

4

EVMs Can Be Rigged*

Sam Rajappa

One does not have to be an electronics engineer or a conspiracy theorist to claim the EVMs (electronic voting machines) are not infallible. But according to Navin B. Chawla, Chief Election Commissioner, the EVMs used in Indian elections are "totally infallible and tamperproof". Delivering a lecture on "Elections 2009: And the Road Ahead", in New Delhi on 3 August, he said the EVMs used by the EC were manufactured in two public sector companies, ECIL and BEL, and there was a thorough randomisation while sending them to various booths. "One does not know which machine is being sent to which state and who is the presiding officer. One cannot remove he chip in an EVM." Ergo it is infallible. He was more concerned about including "none-of-the-above" option in the EVMs to protect the identity of voters opting to register their protest vote. Under Rule 49-O of the Conduct of Election Rules, a register is provided to record the "none-of-the-above" option which, according to Chawla, failed to protect the identity of the voter.

While most of the advanced countries have rejected EVMs as they can be hacked, in India, most political parties barring the Congress and its allies have come to the realisation that the voting machines need further refinement to make them foolproof or the EC

* This article by Sam Rajappa, a journalist, originally appeared as an Edit Page Special, *The Statesman*, 8 August 2009, under the caption. "Chief Election Commissioner holds EVMs Infallible".

should go back to the days of ballot papers. Opposition leader L. K. Advani set the ball rolling by demanding the use of EVMs be suspended till doubts about their fallibility are cleared. The BJP demand was followed by the AIADMK, CPI (M), JD(S), LJP, Telugu Desam, and PMK, among others. There has been a spate of PILs in the Supreme Court and in High Courts against the use of EVMs in their present form. The AIADMK and its allies in Tamil Nadu have taken the unusual step of boycotting the five by-elections to the State Assembly due on 18 August. J. Jayalalitha, leader of the alliance, expressed no-confidence in the EC and the way in which it conducts elections, including the use of EVMs. She is among the first political leaders to detect flaws in the EVM. She wants the EC to declare the candidates of the ruling DMK and the Congress its ally, declared elected without going through the process of polling, for she is convinced the results would be no different no matter whom the people vote for.

Elections, to be free and fair, like Caesar's wife, must be above suspicion. Other than the use of questionable EVMs, the EC has so solution to curb the money power of political parties which had enjoyed power in the preceding five years. N. Gopalaswamy, who retired as CEC mid-way through the recent Lok Sabha election, lamented: "In three months the Election Commission cannot obliterate the massive money power acquired by politicians in 57 months." Maintaining the EVMs could not be hacked or tampered with, he admitted bogus voting was very much possible and very much prevalent. The EC need not plead helplessness in the face of money power of politicians. Section 123 of the Representation of the People Act empowers the EC to countermand elections in constituencies where the result is likely to be affected because of money power. Unfortunately, no Election Commissioner so far had made use of this provision to curb money power.

Two eminent professors of computer science, writing in the May 2009 issue of the respected *International Electrical and Electronic Journal* under the title "Trustworthy Voting", had concluded "while electronic voting machines offer a myriad of benefits, these cannot be reaped unless nine suggested safeguards are put in place for protecting the integrity of the outcome". None of these nine safeguards are in place in the Indian EVMs which ere certified as far superior to the European ones by the Tamil Nadu Chief Minister and president of the DMK, M. Karunanidhi. He is not known to be an expert in electronics. The Supreme Court in Germany ruled electronic voting unconstitutional in March this year because the average citizen could not be expected to understand the exact steps involved in the recording and tallying of votes. The Netherlands banned EVMs in October 2006 after a public-interest group produced a video showing how quickly these machines could be hacked without the voters or election officials being aware of it.

After losing in the contest in Madurai in the 1999 Lok Sabha election, the Janata Party president, Subramanian Swamy, was flooded with postcards from voters, particularly from the Cholavandan segment, his ancestral home, complaining their votes were not reflected in the counting. He then arranged a presentation before the three-member EC by Professor E. S. Sarma of the world renowned Massachusetts Institute of Technology in Cambridge, USA, an acknowledged expert in the field of Radio Frequency Identification, and Dr. Gitanjali Swamy of Harvard, whose doctoral dissertation from the University of California at Berkeley was on the subject of verification, i.e. how to ensure that machines are actually doing the work they were intended to do. M. S. Gill, then the CEC, and now Minister for Youth Affairs and Sports in the UPA government, was convinced that it was possible for one of the various persons having access to the EVMs at different points of time to plant a software programme that would have the effect of producing an election result in favour of a predetermined candidate or political party. He was advised that one way to reduce the risk of fraud was to have the EVMs print a paper trail of each vote as a backup which the voters could then deposit into a ballot box. In case of any dispute, the slip of paper would be available for authentication of the vote. This has been in vogue in 27 states in the USA since 2007. No follow-up action was taken by the EC.

Since then, public realisation of the drawbacks of the EVMs has become widespread. Chandrababu Naidu, leader of the Telugu Desam, with the help of experts, has prepared a software which could tamper with the ballots in the EVMs. He is convinced his party lost the Andhra Assembly election earlier this year due to tampering of EVMs. PILs against the use of EVMs are pending in the Kerala and the Madras High Courts. Meanwhile, the Supreme Court has acknowledged concerns raised by V. V. Rao in a PIL over technical glitches in EVMs but expressed the view the EC should inquire into the matter rather than the judiciary. A Bench comprising Chief Justice K. G. Balakrishnan, Justice P. Sathasivam and Justice Cyriac Joseph has directed the petitioner to approach the EC which, in consultation with political parties, could sort out the problems. "It is not possible to address the issue in a judicial forum," it ruled. It may be recalled that in 2004, the Supreme Court First Bench of Chief Justice V. N. Khare, Justice Babu and Justice Kapadia directed the EC to consider the technical flaws in the EVMs put forward by Professor Satinath Choudhary, a US-based software engineer, in a PIL. The EC failed to consider his representation. Last month, Omesh Saigal, a 1964-batch IAS officer who is an alumnus of IIT, Delhi, convincingly demonstrated before the EC how the EVMs could be hacked and results manipulated.

Recognised political parties, instead of moving the courts and holding demonstrations the riggability of EVMs before the EC, which had already made up its mind that the voting machines are infallible, should prepare a list of candidates who narrowly lost to the UPA in the recent Lok Sabha election and find out in how many booths they polled less than 10 votes. Every candidate of a recognised party would have not less than five workers per booth. With their wives, they would have contributed at least 10 votes in the booth for the candidate. Armed with affidavits from them about their votes the parties could approach High Courts and *prima facie* establish that the EVMs had been tampered with. The only way we the people can be sure that our votes have indeed gone to the candidates we voted for is paper ballots.

5

German Supreme Court Declares EVMs Unconstitutional

Dr. Till Jaeger*

Use of Voting Computers in 2005 Bundestag Election Unconstitutional**

The Federal Constitutional Court rendered judgement on two complaints concerning the scrutiny of an election, which were directed against the use of computer-controlled voting machines (so-called voting computers) in the 2005 Bundestag election of the 16th German Bundestag (see German press release no. 85 / 2008 of 25 September 2008). The Second Senate decided that the use of electronic voting machines requires that the essential steps of the voting and of the determination of the result can be examined by the citizen reliably and without any specialist knowledge of the subject. This requirement results from the principle of the public nature of elections (Article 38 in conjunction with Article 20.1 and 20.2 of the Basic Law (Grundgesetz — GG)), which prescribes that all essential steps of an election are subject to the possibility of public scrutiny unless other constitutional interests justify an exception.

---

* Advocate, Federal Constitutional Court, Germany Christinenstraße 18 / 19 10119, Berlin, Germany www.jbb.de jaeger@jbb.de

** [Federal Constitutional Court — Press Office
Press release no. 19 / 2009 of 3 March 2009
Judgement of 3 March 2009 — 2 BvC 3 / 07 and 2 BvC 4 / 07 –]

Accordingly it is, admittedly, constitutionally unobjectionable that § 35 of the Federal Electoral Act (Bundeswahlgesetz — BWG) permits the use of voting machines. However, the Federal Voting Machines Ordinance (Bundeswahlgeräteverordnung) is unconstitutional because it does not ensure that only such voting machines are permitted and used which meet the constitutional requirements of the principle of the public nature of elections. According to the decision of the Federal Constitutional Court, the computer-controlled voting machines used in the election of the 16th German Bundestag did not meet the requirements which the constitution places on the use of electronic voting machines. This, however, does not result in the dissolution of the Bundestag because for lack of any indications that voting machines malfunctioned or could have been manipulated, the protection of the continued existence of the elected parliament prevails over the electoral errors which have been ascertained. To the extent that the manner in which the German Bundestag's Committee for the Scrutiny of Elections conducted the proceedings was objected to, the complaint for the scrutiny of an election was unsuccessful.

In essence, the decision is based on the following considerations:

I. The objections to the errors of the proceedings for the scrutiny of elections which had been conducted before the German Bundestag were unsuccessful. Even though the duration of the proceedings between the lodging of the objection to the election and the German Bundestag's decision was more than a year, this is not yet a serious procedural error. The duration of the proceedings alone does not deprive the German Bundestag's decision of its foundation. Nor is the fact that the Committee for the Scrutiny of Elections refrained from conducting an oral hearing of the complainant's objection to the election, and also apart from this did not deliberate in public, a serious error which deprives the German Bundestag's decision of its foundation.

II. The principle of the public nature of elections, which results from the fundamental decisions of constitutional law in favour of democracy, the republic and the rule of law prescribes that all essential steps of an election are subject to the possibility of public scrutiny unless other constitutional interests justify an exception. Here, the examination of the voting and of the ascertainment of the election result attains special significance.

The use of voting machines which electronically record the voters' votes and electronically ascertain the election result only meets the constitutional requirements if the essential steps of the voting and of the ascertainment of the result can be examined reliably and without any specialist knowledge of the subject. While in a conventional election with ballot papers, manipulations or acts of electoral fraud are, under the framework conditions of the applicable provisions, at any rate only possible with considerable effort and with a very high risk of detection, which has a preventive effect, programming errors in the software or deliberate electoral fraud committed by manipulating the software of electronic voting machines can be recognised only with difficulty. The very wide-reaching effect of possible errors of the voting machines or of deliberate electoral fraud make special precautions necessary in order to safeguard the principle of the public nature of elections.

The voters themselves must be able to understand without detailed knowledge of computer technology whether their votes cast are recorded in an unadulterated manner as the basis of vote counting, or at any rate as the basis of a later recount. If the election result is determined through computer-controlled processing of the votes stored in an electronic memory, it is not sufficient if merely the result of the calculation process carried out in the voting machine can be taken note of by means of a summarising printout or an electronic display.

The legislature is not prevented from using electronic voting machines in elections if the possibility of a reliable examination of correctness, which is constitutionally prescribed, is safeguarded. A complementary examination by the voter, by the electoral bodies or the general public is possible for example with electronic voting machines in which the votes are recorded in another way beside electronic storage. In the case at hand, it need not be decided whether there are other technical possibilities which make it possible for the electorate to trust in the correctness of the procedure of the ascertainment of the election result in a way that is based on its retraceability, thus complying with the principle of the public nature of elections.

Limitations of the possibility for the citizens to examine the voting cannot be compensated by an official institution testing sample machines in the context of their engineering type licensing procedure, or the very voting machines which will be used in the elections before their being used, for their compliance with specific security requirements and for their technical integrity. Also an extensive entirety of other technical and organisational security measures alone is not suited to compensate a lack of the possibility of the essential steps of the electoral procedure being examined by the citizens. For the possibility of examining the essential steps of the election promotes justified trust in the regularity of the election only by the citizens themselves being able to reliably retrace the voting.

If computer-controlled voting machines are used, no contrary constitutional principles can be identified which could justify a far-reaching restriction on the public nature of the election, and thus on the possibility of examining the voting and the ascertainment of the result. The exclusion of ballots unwittingly being marked in an erroneous manner, of inadvertent counting errors and of erroneous interpretations of the voters' will in vote counting does not as such justify forgoing any kind of retraceability of the voting. The principle of the secrecy of the vote and the interest in a rapid clarification of the composition of the German Bundestag are also no contrary constitutional interests which could be invoked as the basis of a far-reaching restriction on the possibility of examining the voting and the ascertainment of the result. It is not constitutionally required hat the election result be available shortly after the closing of the polls. Apart from this, the past Bundestag elections have shown that also without the use of voting machines, the official provisional result can, as a general rule, be ascertained within a few hours.

III. While the authorisation to issue an ordinance, which is granted by § 35 BWG, does not meet with any overriding constitutional reservations, the Federal Voting Machines Ordinance is unconstitutional because it infringes the principle of the public nature of elections. The Federal Voting Machines Ordinance does not contain any regulations which ensure that only such voting machines are permitted and used which comply with the constitutional requirements placed on an effective examination of the voting and a reliable verifiability of the election result. The Federal Voting Machines Ordinance does not ensure that only such voting machines are used which make it possible to reliably examine, when the vote is cast, whether the vote has been recorded in an unadulterated manner. The ordinance also does not place any concrete requirements as regards its content and procedure on a reliable later examination of the ascertainment of the result. This deficiency cannot be remedied by means of an interpretation in conformity with the constitution.

IV. Also the use of the above-mentioned electronic voting machines in the election to the 16th German Bundestag infringes the public nature of the election. The voting machines did not make an effective examination of the voting possible because due to the fact that the votes were exclusively recorded electronically on a vote recording module, neither voters nor electoral boards nor citizens who were present at the polling station were able to verify the unadulterated recording of the votes cast. Also the essential steps of the ascertainment of the result could not be retraced by the public. It was not sufficient that the result of the calculation process carried out in the voting machine could be taken note of by means of a summarising printout or an electronic display.

V. The electoral errors which have been identified do not lead to a repetition of the election in the constituencies affected. The electoral error which results from the use of computer-controlled voting machines whose design was incompatible with the requirements placed on an effective possibility of examining the voting does not result in a declaration of partial invalidity of the election to the 16th German Bundestag even if it is assumed to be relevant to the allocation of seats. The interest in the protection of the continued existence of parliament, the composition of which was determined trusting in the constitutionality of the

Federal Voting Machines Ordinance, prevails over the electoral error because its possible implications on the composition of the 16th German Bundestag can be rated a marginal at most, for lack of any indications that voting machines malfunctioned or could have been manipulated, and because, also in view of the fact that the established infringement of the constitution took place when the legal situation had not been clarified yet, they do not make the continued existence of the elected parliament appear intolerable.*

German Federal Constitutional Court on EVMs

Background of the Judgement

Elections to the German Federal Parliament 2005:

- 2 million voters had to use voting computers
- Software security specialist Dr. Ulrich Wiesner and his father Prof. Wiesner made objections against the validity of the election for unconstitutional use of EVMs www.jbb.de
- EVMs were used since 1998
- A "Federal Voting Machine Ordinance" contained specific prerequisites for the deployment of EVMs
- German administration specialized in technical control of devices examined and approved a device type www.jbb.de

Proceedings

- German Parliament rejected the objections of Dr. Ulrich Wiesner and Prof. Wiesner in December 2006 — In January 2007, Dr. Wiesner filed a complaint in the German Federal Constitutional Court, the highest instance for decisions on the validity of elections in Germany — Complaint is available at www.ulrichwiesner.de (in German). The complete decision is

* http://www.bundesver-fassungsgericht.de/pressemitteilungen/bvg09-019en.html

available in English at (http://www.bundesverfass-ungsgericht.de/en/decisions/rs20090303_2bvc000307en.html).

- Compliant proceedings not a contradictory proceeding but a control of constitutionality
- De-facto opponent: German Home Office
- Oral hearing in October 2008
- Judgement published on 3 March 2009 www.jbb.deww.jbb.de
- Rationale of the Court
- Conclusion:

> "When electronic voting machines are deployed, it must be possible for the citizen to check the essential steps in the election act and in the ascertainment of the results reliably and without special expert knowledge."

- The "Federal Voting Machine Ordinance" was declared unconstitutional and EVMs are ruled out since then.
- Starting point: "constitutional principle of the public nature of elections" (= transparency of election) as a requirement of democracy:

The public nature of elections is a fundamental precondition for democratic political will-formation. It ensures the correctness and verifiability of the election events, and hence creates a major precondition for the well-founded trust of the citizen in the correct operation of the elections."

www.jbb.debb.de

The possibility of monitoring is crucial:

> "The democratic legitimacy of the elections demands that the election events be controllable so that manipulation can be ruled out or corrected and unjustified suspicion can be refuted. . . .
> Only if the electorate can reliably convince itself of the lawfulness of the transfer act, if the elections are therefore implemented "before the eyes of the public" is it possible to guarantee the trust of the sovereign in Parliament being composed in a manner corresponding to the will of the voters that is necessary for the functioning of democracy."

Exceptions have to be justified with constitutional interests:

> "The principle of the public nature of elections requires that all essential steps in the elections are subject to public examinability unless other constitutional interests justify an exception."

Efficiency of elections is not a constitutional interest.

The Court states strict preconditions for the deployment of EVMs:

- It is necessary that everyone may check the essential steps of the election without specific expert knowledge.
- EVMs (at least without paper trail) do not comply with this precondition.

The Court:

> "The voter himself or herself must be able to verify — also without a more detailed knowledge of computers — whether his or her vote as cast is recorded truthfully as a basis for counting or — if the votes are initially counted with technical support — at least as a basis for a subsequent re-count. It is not sufficient if he or she must rely on the functionality of the system without the possibility of personal inspection."

> "Equal viability must also apply to the election bodies and to interested citizens."

> "For this reason, a comprehensive bundle of other technical and organisational security measures (e.g., monitoring and safekeeping of the voting machines, comparability of the devices used with an officially checked sample at any time, criminal liability in respect of election falsifications and local organisation of the elections) is also not suited by itself to compensate for a lack of controllability of the essential steps in the election procedure by the citizen."

Conclusion

EVMs without an additional paper receipt are unconstitutional:

- The democratic principle asks for transparency of the voting act.
- Each citizen must be able to verify the correct counting of the votes.
- JBB Rechtsanwälte.
  (*See* Full text of English translation in Annexure 5.1).

Annexure 5.1

German Supreme Court Judgement Holding EVMs Unconstitutional

[Zitierung: BVerfG, 2 BvC 3 / 07 vom 3.3.2009, Absatz-Nr. (1-166), (http://www.bverfg.de/entscheidungen/rs20090303_2bvc000307en.html) Frei für den nicht gewerblichen Gebrauch. Kommerzielle Nutzung nur mit Zustimmung des Gerichts.]

Head Notes

1. The principle of the public nature of elections emerging from Article 38 in conjunction with Article 20.1 and 20.2 of the Basic Law (Grundgesetz — GG) requires that all essential steps in the elections are subject to public examinability unless other constitutional interests justify an exception.
2. When electronic voting machines are deployed, it must be possible for the citizen to check the essential steps in the election act and in the ascertainment of the results reliably and without special expert knowledge.

Judgement of the Second Senate of 3 March 2009 on the basis of the oral hearing of 28 October 2008 — 2 BvC 3 / 07, 2 BvC 4 / 07 — in the proceedings regarding the complaints requesting the scrutiny of an election

I. of Dr. W . . .

— authorised representative:

1. Prof. Dr. . . .,
2. lawyers . . .

— the resolution of the German *against* Bundestag of 14 December 2006 — WP 145 / 05 — (Bundestag document (Bundestagsdrucksache — BTDrucks) 16 / 3600) — 2 BvC 3 / 07 —,

II. of Prof. Dr. W . . .

— authorised representative:

Prof. Dr. . . .

— the resolution of the German *against* Bundestag of 14 December 2006 — WP 108 / 05 — (Bundestag document 16 / 3600) — 2 BvC 4 / 07 —.

Ruling

1. The Ordinance on the Deployment of Voting Machines in Elections to the German Bundestag and of the Members of the European Parliament from the Federal Republic of Germany (Federal Voting Machine Ordinance (Bundeswahlgeräteverordnung — BWahlGV)) of 3 September 1975 (Federal Law Gazette (Bundesgesetzblatt — BGBl) I p. 2459) in the version of the Ordinance Amending the Federal Voting Machine Ordinance and the European Election Code (Verordnung zur Änderung der Bundeswahlgeräteverordnung und der Europawahlordnung) of 20 April 1999 (Federal Law Gazette I p. 749) is not compatible with Article 38 in conjunction with Article 20.1 and 20.2 of the Basic Law insofar as it does not ensure monitoring that complies with the constitutional principle of the public nature of elections.
2. The use of the electronic voting machines of N. V. Nederlandsche Apparatenfabriek (Nedap) of type ESD1, hardware versions 01.02, 01.03 and 01.04, as well as of type ESD2, hardware version 01.01, in the elections to the 16th German Bundestag was not compatible with Article 38 in conjunction with Article 20.1 and 20.2 of the Basic Law.
3. The complaints requesting the scrutiny of an election are rejected in other respects.
4. The Federal Republic of Germany is ordered to reimburse to the complainant re 1. the full amount of the necessary expenses from these proceedings and to reimburse to the complainant re 2. three-quarters of his necessary expenses.

Grounds

A

The complaints requesting the scrutiny of an election relate to the permissibility of the deployment of computer-controlled voting machines, which are also referred to as electronic voting machines or "election computers", in the elections to the 16th German *Bundestag*.

I

1. Roughly two million persons eligible to vote in Brandenburg, Hesse, North Rhine-Westphalia, Rhineland-Palatinate and Saxony-Anhalt cast their votes in the elections to the 16th German *Bundestag* via computer-controlled voting machines which are manufactured by the Dutch company Nedap and have been sold in Germany since 1999 as a central component of the "Integral Election System" (IWS) of H. GmbH. The type designations of these voting machines are composed of a name for the device generation (ESD1 or ESD2), as well as in each case of a version number for the hardware (HW) and for the software (SW). The types ESD1 (HW 1.02; SW 2.02), ESD1 (HW 1.02; SW 2.07), ESD1 (HW 1.03; SW 3.08), ESD1 (HW 1.04; SW 3.08) and ESD2 (HW 1.01; SW 3.08) have so far been used in elections to the German *Bundestag*.

These voting machines are controlled via a microprocessor and a software program. The votes cast are exclusively stored on an electronic storage medium and are counted electronically by the voting machine at the end of the election day. After the electronic ascertainment of the results, the voting machine shows the total votes cast for the respective electoral proposals; the results can be printed out via a printer that is integrated into the voting machine. The software programme which controls the registration of the ballot and the ascertainment of the results is to be found on two electronic storage modules (so-called EPROMs; EPROM = Erasable Programmable Read-Only-Memory) which are installed in the device under a screwed-on cover and are secured by two seals applied by the manufacturer. The votes cast at the voting machine — including the linkages (first vote and connected second vote) — are stored on a removable cassette-like storage medium — the so-called vote storage module, also referred to as "electronic ballot box" (see Schönau, *Elektronische Demokratie*, 2007, p. 53). The data of the voting slips, the attribution of the individual keys to the electoral proposals, as well as the date of the election and the polling station, are also stored on the vote storage module.

The voting machines have a keypad ("the voter *tableau*") over which an insertion sheet is placed portraying a voting slip imitating the official voting slip. Above the key field one finds a display (LCD display) which guides the voter through the election procedure and enables him or her to examine her or her entries. The keypad and the LCD display are flanked by two vision-shielding panels on either side. On the reverse of the voting machine are the above mentioned printer and a slot for the vote storage module. The voting machines are linked with a control unit on the returning committee's table. The control unit shows the returning committee the casting of the votes by the respective voter such that the display of the number of voters increases by one. After the voter has cast his or her votes, the voting machine is blocked for further balloting until the returning committee releases it for the next voter.

An element of the "Integral Election System" sold by H. is a programming and reading out device which enables the local authority to prepare the vote storage modules in conjunction with a personal computer prior to the elections and to read out the ballot information from the storage module after the election and to make it available for further data processing. The storage modules can be read out once more after the election day with the aid of a voting machine. The software of the "Integral Election System" also makes it possible to print the stored votes at a computer as voting slips with the corresponding crosses.

An individual identification number of the individual voting machine, as well as the version numbers of the hardware and the software, and two checksums which are constituted by a checksum algorithm contained in the voting machine software, can be shown and printed on the voting machine. These data can be compared with the information on the nameplate of the voting machine and in the declaration of identity.

2. An attempt was already made in Germany in the nineteen-sixties to replace the manual counting of the voting slips linked to the traditional election event using more rational methods and by deploying voting machines. According to § 35.3 of the Federal Electoral Act (*Bundeswahlgesetz — BWG*) of 7 May 1956 (Federal Law Gazette I p. 383 — Federal Electoral Act), the Federal Minister of the Interior was able to permit officially authorised vote counting devices to be used instead of voting slips. The Ordinance on the Use of Vote Counting Devices in Elections to the German *Bundestag* (*Verordnung über die Verwendung von Stimmenzählgeräten bei Wahlen zum Deutschen Bundestag*) of 24 August 1961 (Federal Law Gazette I p. 1618) was handed down on this basis. § 35.3 of the Federal Electoral Act was rescinded by means of the Act Amending the Federal Electoral Act (*Gesetz zur Änderung des Bundeswahlgesetzes*) of 24 June 1975 (Federal Law Gazette I p. 1593), and replaced by a more detailed provision on "balloting with voting machines", which since the promulgation of the new version of the Federal Electoral Act of 1 September 1975 (Federal Law Gazette I p. 2325) can be found in § 35 of the Federal Electoral Act. The Ordinance on the Deployment of Voting Machines in Elections to the German Bundestag (Federal Voting Machine Ordinance) (*Bundeswahlgeräteverordnung — BWahlGV*) of 3 September 1975 (Federal Law Gazette I p. 2459) provided in § 1 that mechanically or electrically driven voting machines may be used in elections to the German *Bundestag* if their type is authorised and their use was approved.

On the basis of the Ordinance on the Use of Vote Counting Devices of 24 August 1961 (Federal Law Gazette I p. 1618) and of the Federal Voting Machine Ordinance of 3 September 1975 (Federal Law Gazette I p. 2459), voting machines were initially authorised and used in Germany which worked on the basis of (electro) mechanical counting devices (see Schreiber, *Handbuch des Wahlrechts zum Deutschen Bundestag*, 7th ed. 2002, *§ 35*, marginal no. 5). These voting machines worked mechanically; a count was mechanically increased by activating a button or by placing an election token in an opening allotted to the respective electoral proposal. They did not catch on since the cost of procuring, transporting, storing and maintaining the devices was compared to a relatively minor gain in time, and the devices could frequently only be deployed in elections with a small number of electoral proposals (see *Bundestag* document 8 / 94, p. 2).

These disadvantages were to be avoided by the deployment of electronic voting machines. In 1997, Nedap applied to the Federal Ministry of the Interior for a type approval for an electronic voting machine which it manufactured. The Federal Voting Machine Ordinance of 3 September 1975 (Federal Law Gazette I p. 2459), at that time most recently amended by Ordinance of 15 November 1989 (Federal Law Gazette I p. 1981) was not amenable to examine and approve such a device type. After the *Physikalisch-Technische Bundesanstalt*, referring to this circumstance in an examination report of 8 September 1998, had made a positive evaluation of the Nedap voting machine in technical terms and a test of the voting machine in Cologne had been assessed as satisfactory, the Federal Ministry of the Interior decided to make it possible to deploy computer-controlled voting machines in the European elections in June 1999. For this reason, amendments were also prepared to § 35 of the Federal Electoral Act and the Federal Voting Machine Ordinance for the deployment of computer-controlled voting machines in future *Bundestag* elections.

§ 35.1 of the Federal Electoral Act in the version promulgated on 23 July 1993 (Federal Law Gazette I p. 1288, 1594), most recently amended by Act of 1 July 1998 (Federal Law Gazette I p. 1698, 3431), applicable at that time was worded as follows:

Voting machines with separate counting devices may be used in place of voting slips, election envelopes and ballot boxes to make the casting and counting of the votes easier.

The words "with separate counting devices" were deleted with the Act on General and Representative Election Statistics in Elections to the German Bundestag and in the Election of Members of the European Parliament from the Federal Republic of Germany (*Gesetz über die allgemeine und die repräsentative Wahlstatistik bei der Wahl zum Deutschen Bundestag und bei der Wahl der Abgeordneten des Europäischen Parlaments aus der Bundesrepublik Deutschland*) of 21 May 1999 (Federal Law Gazette I p. 1023). The amendment to § 35 of the Federal Electoral Act was regarded as being necessary in order to be able to adjust the Federal Voting Machine Ordinance to technical developments in voting machines (see *Bundestag* document 14 / 401, p. 5).

The Ordinance Amending the Federal Voting Machine Ordinance and the European Election Code of 20 April 1999 (Federal Law Gazette I p. 749) already entered into force on 24 April 1999 and amended a large number of provisions of the Federal Voting Machine Ordinance in order to create the preconditions for the deployment of computer-controlled voting machines. The words "including computer-controlled" were added in § 1 of the Federal Voting Machine Ordinance after the words "electrically driven". Further amendments were effected where the Federal Voting Machine Ordinance had previously used the term "counting devices". § 2.6 of the Federal Voting Machine Ordinance was added, obliging the manufacturer to enclose a declaration of identity.

3. § 35 of the Federal Electoral Act applied to the elections to the 16th German *Bundestag*, in the version of the Federal Electoral Act promulgated on 23 July 1993 (Federal Law Gazette I p. 1288, corrected p. 1594), most recently amended by the Eighth Competence Adjustment Ordinance (*Achte Zuständigkeitsanpassungsverordnung*) of 25 November 2003 (Federal Law Gazette I p. 2304).

The provision read as follows:

§ 35 Voting with voting machines

(1) Voting machines may be used in place of voting slips and ballot boxes to make it easier to cast and count the votes.

(2) Voting machines within the meaning of subsection 1 must guarantee that the ballot remains secret. Their type must be authorised for use in elections to the German Bundestag officially for individual elections or generally. The Federal Ministry of the Interior shall decide on authorisation on request by the manufacturer of the voting machine. The use of an officially authorised

voting machine shall require approval by the Federal Ministry of the Interior. Approval may be issued for individual elections or in general terms.

(3)The Federal Ministry of the Interior is herewith empowered to hand down by means of a legal ordinance which shall not require the consent of the Bundesrat more detailed provisions regarding:

1. The preconditions for the official approval of the type of voting machine, as well as for the withdrawal and revocation of approval,
2. The procedure for the official approval of the type,
3. The procedure for the examination of a voting machine for construction corresponding to the officially approved type,
4. The public testing of a voting machine prior to its use,
5. The procedure for the official authorisation of the use, as well as for the withdrawal and revocation of the authorisation,
6. The particularities related to the elections caused by the use of voting machines.

The legal ordinance shall be handed down in agreement with the Federal Ministry of Economics and Labour in cases falling under nos. 1 and 3.

(4) § 33.1 sentence 1 and § 33.2 shall apply mutatis mutandis to the operation of a voting machine.

The provisions of the Federal Voting Machine Ordinance of 3 September 1975 (Federal Law Gazette I p. 2459), which were most recently amended by ordinance of 20 April 1999 (Federal Law Gazette I p. 749), relevant to the proceedings at hand, relate to the approval of voting machines and their deployment in elections. The voting machines require a type approval and a use authorisation (see § 1 of the Federal Voting Machine Ordinance). According to § 2.2 sentence 1 of the Federal Voting Machine Ordinance, the type approval may be granted if the voting machine corresponds to the Guidelines for the Construction of Voting Machines (Richtlinien für die Bauart von Wahlgeräten) according to Annex 1 to the Federal Voting Machine Ordinance. These guidelines regulate in particular the technical requirements to be made on the voting machines, and contain detailed stipulations for the identification, technical structure and functioning of the voting machines. Statements are made in this context on the portrayal of the electoral proposals, on operation and operability, on the ballot, on the storage of votes and on the creation of backups. The examination of the compliance of the voting machine with the above guidelines is a matter for the Physikalisch-Technische Bundesanstalt.

The use of approved-type voting machines requires authorisation prior to each election (§ 4.1 sentence 1 of the Federal Voting Machine Ordinance). Only those voting machines may be used which, once the election date has been set, have been examined by the manufacturer or the local authority using the operating manuals and maintenance regulations and with regard to which it has been ascertained that they are functional (§ 7.1 sentence 1 of the Federal Voting Machine Ordinance). In the constituencies in which voting machines are used, the local authority is to familiarise the head of the returning committee and his or her deputies with the voting machines prior to the elections and to familiarise them with their operation (§ 7.3 of the Federal Voting Machine Ordinance). Prior to the commencement of the election act, the local authority assigns the devices to the head of the returning committee with the necessary operating manuals and the declaration of the manufacturer according to § 2.6 of the Federal Voting Machine Ordinance that the device is constructed identically to the tested, approved type sample (see § 8 of the Federal Voting Machine Ordinance). Prior to the commencement of the ballot, the returning committee must ascertain amongst other things that the counting and storage devices are set to zero or have been erased (§ 10.1 no. 3 of the Federal Voting Machine Ordinance) and must close the voting machine needed (§ 10.2 of the Federal Voting Machine Ordinance). Prior to reading the displays of the votes counted by a voting machine, the number of the ballot records in the voter list is to be added to the number of election slips taken in and compared with the number of votes displayed (§ 13 of the Federal Voting Machine Ordinance). Deviations are to be noted and explained in the election record (§ 13 sentence 3 of the Federal Voting Machine Ordinance). If the total of the counter results displayed does not tally with the number of the total votes cast as displayed, the returning committee must show the difference and note it in the election record (§ 14.5 of the Federal Voting Machine Ordinance). The head of the returning committee, the local authority and the district returning officer must ensure on completing the tasks of the returning committee and returning the voting machines that the voting machines used or the vote storage devices removed from them and the election record with the Annexes are not made available to unauthorised parties until the *Land* (state) returning officer has revoked the blocking and sealing of the voting machines and of the vote storage devices (see § 16.2 and § 17.3 of the Federal Voting Machine Ordinance).

4. The Federal Ministry of the Interior issued type approvals for the voting machines used in the elections to the 16th German *Bundestag*. On 15 August 2005, it announced the authorisation of the use of computer-controlled voting machines made by Nedap in the elections to the 16th German *Bundestag* with details on hardware versions, storage module types and software versions (Federal Gazette (*Bundesanzeiger*) no. 158 of 23 August 2005, pp. 12747-12748). Invoking company secrets of Nedap, the Ministry however refused to make available to the interested public documents which Nedap had provided to the *Physikalisch-Technische Bundesanstalt* for the examination of the samples, or test reports of the *Physikalisch-Technische Bundesanstalt*.

5. The decision as to whether voting machines are acquired, and in which constituencies they are used, is a matter for the towns and local authorities. As a reason for the acquisition and the deployment of voting machines, in addition to the more rapid calculation of the election result and to the anticipated cost savings, it is stated that it is virtually impossible to inadvertently cast invalid votes; cases of doubt as to the validity of individual votes because of ambiguous markings on the voting slip and unintended errors in counting the votes are said to be virtually ruled out (see Schreiber, *Handbuch des Wahlrechts zum Deutschen Bundestag*, 7th ed. 2002, *§ 35*, marginal no. 2). The recruitment of voluntary election assistants is also said to be made much easier because less time is needed to ascertain the election result (see Schönau, *Elektronische Demokratie*, 2007, p. 50). These advantages are said to be evident in particular in local elections, which in many *Länder* (states) were said to have been

made more complex because of possibilities of cumulative voting and voting for candidates from different party lists.

II

1. With their complaints requesting the scrutiny of an election, both complainants target the Federal Electoral Act and the Federal Voting Machine Ordinance insofar as they facilitate the deployment of computer-controlled voting machines. They complain of the authorisation of the use and deployment of the voting machines; furthermore, the type approvals which were issued for the Nedap voting machines used in the *Bundestag* election are said to be unlawful. The complainant re 2. complains over and above this that the proceedings of the German *Bundestag* suffered from a number of faults.

a) aa) The complainant re 1. objected to the result of the elections to the 16th German *Bundestag* in 30 constituencies in Brandenburg, Hesse, North Rhine-Westphalia, Rhineland-Palatinate and Saxony-Anhalt referred to in greater detail. He moved to ascertain the constituencies in which computer-controlled voting machines had been used, and the number of the votes cast with these voting machines, and to repeat the elections in the constituencies concerned. The deployment of computer-controlled voting machines was said to have violated the principle of the public nature of elections and the principle of the official nature of elections. Over and above this, the voting machines were said not to be compatible with the Guidelines for the Construction of Voting Machines.

The principle of the public nature of elections was said to guarantee the proper implementation of the elections and the correct constitution of Parliament. The monitoring of the election act was said to have to encompass above all ensuring that the marking of the vote took place secretly and that the votes cast by the voters were inserted into the ballot box without a change, that the votes were not subsequently altered and that only the votes from the ballot box were counted at the end of the election. In the deployment of the voting machines complained of, effective monitoring by the public and by the returning committee were said to be prevented since a major part of the election act and the investigation and ascertainment of the election result were said to take place inside the voting machine.

If voting machines were deployed, it was said to only replace the public nature of elections possible in an election with voting slips if equivalent and publicly verifiable control mechanisms existed, such as a paper record of the votes cast printed by the voting machine which the voter could inspect. Corresponding control possibilities were however said not to be available to the public in deployment of the Nedap voting machines.

It was said not to be possible for the public to check the trustworthiness of the software installed in the voting machines. The examination by the *Physikalisch-Technische Bundesanstalt* and the type approval were said not to have taken place publicly; also, the voting machines were said not to be made available to the interested public for independent examination. The source code software of the voting machines was said not to be open. Ultimately, it was said also not to be possible to examine whether the copies of the software used in the polling stations were identical to the sample examined by the *Physikalisch-Technische Bundesanstalt* and whether they were free of manipulations. It was said to be possible to effect authentication by a chain of characters ("hash value") being calculated for each original programme and the copy and then compared, so that agreement between the two values was said to document the authenticity of the software. This was however said not to be reliably guaranteed in the voting machines which were the subject of the complaint since the checksums displayed and printed when the device was launched were calculated by the software installed in the voting machine itself, so that it was alleged not to be ruled out that the calculation of the checksums provided the expected chain of characters because of a prior deliberate manipulation of the software.

The particular danger in computer-controlled voting machines was said to lie in the fact that elections could be much more effectively influenced via manipulation of the software by the device manufacturer than in ballot box elections. For instance, it was said to be possible for faulty software to allot a certain share of the votes cast to a certain party regardless of the election decision by the respective voter or for the total votes cast to be divided among the parties standing for election according to a set proportion. Manipulations were said to be possible both by politically or financially motivated "insiders", in particular employees of the manufacturer, and by external third parties who gained access to the computers used by the manufacturer (for instance via viruses or trojans); they were said with regard to the complexity of the software used not always to be discovered even in careful quality control effected by the manufacturer. Although it was said to be necessary to prevent unauthorised access to the devices between the elections through suitable security measures, no such monitoring was said to take place in Germany; there were also said to be no suitable regulations in force that were able to guarantee protected storage of the voting machines.

It was said that the proceedings for the examination of the type sample by the *Physikalisch-Technische Bundesanstalt* and the approval of the type by the Federal Ministry of the Interior should be public as a part of the preparations for the elections. Any interests of the manufacturer in protecting its business secrets should be subordinate to the principle of democracy. For a lack of a possibility to check the device independently, the publication of the control documents and reports of the *Physikalisch-Technische Bundesanstalt* and of the source code of the voting machine software was said to be the only possibility in order to be able to judge the integrity of the elections. The non-publication of the control reports and documents and of the source code was hence said to constitute an electoral error.

It was said not to be compatible with the "principle of the official nature of the elections" that the functionality of the voting machines could only be examined by the manufacturer (§ 7.1 of the Federal Voting Machine Ordinance), and that there was no official control of freedom from manipulation of the voting machines. Over and above the declaration of identity, there was said to be no authentication of the software implemented on the individual voting machines, so that the election bodies had to rely on effective quality assurance by the manufacturer and on there being no manipulation after the examination had been carried out by the manufacturer. The tests carried out by the district returning officer in the context of preparation for the election and by the returning committee in the polling station were said not to be suited to recognise any manipulations.

The voting machines were said not to be compatible with the "Guidelines for the Construction of Voting Machines" (Annex 1 to § 2 of the Federal Voting Machine Ordinance). They neither complied with the general state-of-the-art, nor were they constructed in compliance with the rules of technology for systems with grievous consequences in case of misconduct (letter B no. 2.1subsection 1 of the Guidelines for the Construction of Voting Machines). In contravention of to letter B no. 1 item 2 of the Guidelines for the Construction of Voting Machines, the software used was said not to be clearly identifiable.

It is also said to be objectionable that § 35 of the Federal Electoral Act only calls for the ballot to be held in secret, but not for adherence to the other electoral principles. The examinability of the election result provided for in Article 41 of the Basic Law was said to be undermined if as a result of the type it were no longer to be possible to establish whether the outcome of the election had been reached lawfully.

bb) The complainant re 2. Also submitted an objection to the elections to the 16th German Bundestag.

He takes the view that the deployment of the computer-controlled voting machines in at least 1,921 polling districts and 39 constituencies in five Länder had violated the principle of democracy, the principle of the rule of law and the principles of the public and official nature of elections. The deployment of the voting machines was said to violate the Federal Electoral Act and the Federal Voting Machine Ordinance from multiple points of view. Neither § 35 of the Federal Electoral Act, nor the Federal Voting Machine Ordinance, were said to comply with the constitutional principles of the law on elections of the public and official nature of elections.

The complainant re 2. moved *inter alia* for a finding that the election results in the constituencies designated by the complainant re 1., in the constituencies that were manifest from a "Customer overview [of Nedap] on the 2005 *Bundestag* election" provided by the Federal Statistical Office and in all other constituencies in which voting machines of the impugned nature might have been deployed, had come about unlawfully and were hence allegedly invalid. It was said that the elections needed to be repeated in these constituencies. Furthermore, the complainant re 2. applied for the publication of the examination documents of the *Physikalisch-Technische Bundesanstalt* regarding the voting machines to which the complaint referred, as well as for the holding of an oral hearing as soon as possible and the summons of specific witnesses and experts.

The more detailed statements of the complainant re 2. correspond to the objection submitted by the complainant re 1.

cc) The Federal Ministry of the Interior moved to reject the objections.

The public nature of the ballot was said to have been guaranteed in the deployment of the voting machines. The public was said to be able to check that only entitled voters were granted access to the voting booth. The returning committee was able to check by reading the control unit that each voter had in fact voted and had only done so once. Moreover, it was said that the principle of the public nature of elections was not guaranteed without restriction. It was said to be in conflict with the goal of forming a viable people's representation in a short time. The Federal Electoral Act was said to attach greater significance to the goal of elections being held in good time and to ascertaining the outcome of the election within a reasonable time than to detailed monitoring by the public.

The public nature of the vote counting was said to have been guaranteed. The public was said to be able to check how the result of the constituency ascertained by the voting machine on conclusion of the election act was printed by the returning committee and included in the election record. The returning committee and each election observer were said to be able to compare the ballot records in the voter register and the valid and invalid first and second votes registered by the voting machine, and hence to ascertain whether the device had covered and added all the votes cast. It was said to be not possible to physically cover the individual votes; a totalling procedure which was verifiable for the public was however said not to be necessary since protection against falsification of the election result was said to be ensured by a number of other measures guaranteeing the reliability of the result as with ballot box elections. For instance, the voting machine was examined thoroughly prior to being approved by the *Physikalisch-Technische Bundesanstalt*. Comprehensive monitoring by local authorities and returning committees also took place in the run-up to the elections. The local ascertainment of the results was said to guarantee that manipulations on the part of individuals could at most impact the outcome of the election in the respective constituency.

Public monitoring was said to be only one factor among many in order to prevent irregularities in the elections, albeit an important one. No measure was said to be able to prevent manipulations or unintentional falsification of the election result by itself. All measures together were however said to guarantee very broad protection of the elections against election falsifications.

Since the principle of the public nature of elections had not been violated, it was said not to be necessary to bring forward the public nature of elections by publishing the control results of the *Physikalisch-Technische Bundesanstalt* and the source code for the voting machine software. The fundamentally public nature of the preparations for the election and of the election itself could be restricted for reasons of the protection of private data or of operational and business secrets. The type approval, the examinations of the voting machines by the *Physikalisch-Technische Bundesanstalt*, as well as the conclusive examination by the local authorities, were said to replace monitoring by the public in this respect.

The paper record called for by the complainants for subsequent checking of the storage of the votes was said to be by no means non-contentious in expert circles because of its disadvantages. It was said that such a record could be manipulated just like any paper product. Further, it was impossible for a paper record to eliminate a lack of trust in the viability of the voting machine since it was created by the voting machine.

Since the preparation and implementation of the elections were said to be public tasks, it was said to be irrelevant whether this was actually expressed in a "principle of the official nature of the elections". It was only required that the state bodies provided the facilities and resources and took responsibility for organising the elections. It was said to be unobjectionable that private individuals effected individual actions; in this respect, the state bodies only had to carry out the monitoring required. For instance, the official voting slips were printed by private printers and the election notifications and postal voting documents were sent via private postal companies. It was said to always have been sufficient that the election authority classed the enterprises commissioned as trustworthy in each case. The same was said to apply to the manufacture and supply of voting machines with a declaration of identity of the manufacturer.

The voting machines were said to be compatible with the Guidelines for the Construction of Voting Machines. The voting machine software was said to be identifiable at any time by virtue of a comparison of the version number and the checksums with the information contained in the declaration of identity. Also the authenticity of the software was said to be guaranteed by a combination of protective measures.

Certainly, any electoral errors were said not to be relevant to mandates. Not concrete information had been put forward indicating that different election results had been achieved in specific polling stations because of the deployment of voting machines than would have been the case with a ballot box election.

dd) The German *Bundestag* rejected the election objections by resolution of 14 December 2006. The resolution recommendation of the Committee for the Scrutiny of Elections of 30 November 2006 (*Bundestag* document 16 / 3600, Annexes 1 and 2) considered the objections of both complainants to be manifestly unfounded.

The constitutionality of individual provisions of electoral law was said not to be amenable to a review by the German *Bundestag* since the German *Bundestag* and the Committee for the Scrutiny of Elections were not called on to find provisions of electoral law unconstitutional.

The deployment of the voting machines was said to have violated neither the concrete form given to the principle of the public nature of elections in non-constitutional law (§§ 10 and 31 of the Federal Electoral Act; § 54 of the Federal Electoral Code (*Bundeswahlordnung — BWO*), nor a principle of the public nature of elections going beyond this. The principle of the public nature of elections was said certainly not to entail each individual act being subject to an individual check. The public nature of the ballot was also said to be heavily restricted in postal voting. The election was said to be operated in the voting machines which were the subject of the complaint in principle in the same manner as in the ballot box election. Although marking of the voting slip and the ballot were carried out on one single device in the voting booth, the act of balloting was said to be transparent for the returning committee and the public since only the voter who had submitted his or her election notification card was able to vote using the voting machine.

In legal reality, when it came to the deployment of voting machines the concrete election act of voting was said to be in a conflict of interests between the principle of secret elections and that of the public nature of elections. It was said to be acceptable against this background that in the deployment of computer-controlled voting machines each sub-act of vote registration was not transparent to all. It was said to be one of the particularities of the advance in technology that one could presume that the systems deployed were viable if they had been examined in a special procedure prior to their deployment. This was said to be all the more valid given that the necessary monitoring took place in all other procedural steps, and hence the results that were obtained could be examined to determine their plausibility. The only decisive aspect was said to be whether the public had the fundamental possibility to become convinced of the viability of the election procedure. This was said to be accounted for by voting with voting machines: In particular, the public was able to check the printout of the result of the constituency ascertained by the voting machine and the transfer of the result into the election record, and hence the counting as a whole. By means of the comparison of the ballot records in the register of voters with the valid and invalid first and second votes registered by the device, as prescribed by § 14 of the Federal Voting Machine Ordinance, it was said also to be possible to check whether the voting machine had recorded all the votes and added them correctly. All the stored votes could be printed out as voting slips with the corresponding crosses and subsequently counted by hand.

The proceedings for type approval were said not to give rise to an election error. There was also said not to be a right to inspect the source code of the voting machine software with regard to the principle of the public nature of elections since the protection of the operational secrets of the manufacturer of the voting machines was said to outweigh the interest of the public in revealing the source code.

According to the convincing descriptions contained in the statement made by the Federal Ministry of the Interior, the voting machines which were the subject of the complaint were said to have complied with the provisions of the Federal Voting Machine Ordinance and with the Guidelines for the Construction of Voting Machines. According to the statements of the Federal Ministry of the Interior, manipulations were said to be theoretically possible, but hardly conceivable in practice. There were said to be no indications of deliberate manipulations or accidental alterations to the voting machines used in the *Bundestag* election forming the subject of the complaint. Even if none of the security measures mentioned were able by themselves to prevent manipulations, all the measures together were said to guarantee a very high degree of security against manipulation of the voting machines.

Where the complainant was complaining about a shift of state tasks towards private parties, this was said not to constitute an electoral error, even if the submission was assumed to be correct. In particular, the fact that the preparation and implementation of elections was a public task did not force the conclusion to be drawn that all necessary acts may only be carried out by officials. The necessary state control was said to be ensured.

Since no electoral error was therefore ascertainable, it was said not to be necessary to investigate any impact on the result of the ballot and on the distribution of seats in the German *Bundestag*. No oral hearing was set regarding the objection of the complainant re 2. according to § 6.1a no. 3 of the Law on the Scrutiny of Elections (*Wahlprüfungsgesetz –WahlPrüfG*), old version.

b) Both complainants have submitted a complaint requesting the scrutiny of an election to the Federal Constitutional Court (*Bundesverfassungsgericht*).

aa) The complainant re 1. moves to rescind the resolution of the German *Bundestag* of 14 December 2006 and to declare the elections to the 16th German *Bundestag* invalid in the constituencies referred to in the objection procedure insofar as computer-controlled voting machines were used there, and to order a repeat of the elections with voting slips and ballot boxes. Alternatively, he moves for a finding that the use of software-controlled voting machines in elections to the German *Bundestag* is not compatible with the Basic Law, furthermore as an alternative that the deployment of voting machines is not compatible with the Basic Law unless the transparency of the elections for the public, the examinability of the correctness of the election result and security against manipulation is guaranteed in a manner corresponding to elections with voting slips and ballot boxes.

The complainant re 1. repeats and expands his submission from the objection procedure, and submits the following as a supplement:

The deployment of the electronic voting machines, because of their technical and constructional security faults, was said to have violated the principles of electoral law set out in Article 38 of the Basic Law, the unwritten constitutional principles within electoral law of the public and official nature of elections, as well as the non-constitutional provisions of electoral law.

The public nature of the elections was also said to have been violated by virtue of the fact that the monitoring had been shifted to a non-public approval procedure and the publication of the examination results, examination documents, construction characteristics and of the source code of the devices had been refused. An evaluation of the votes cast that was verifiable by the public was said not to be possible because the individual votes could not be physically recorded.

The Federal Voting Machine Ordinance was said to contain serious faults insofar as it built on the principle of the declaration of identity; for there was said to be no monitoring as to whether the devices actually used corresponded to the software and hardware checked by the *Physikalisch-Technische Bundesanstalt*.

It was said not to be compatible with the principle of official nature of the implementation of the election for the state election authorities to relinquish control over the entire course of events, including the technical details. Democracy and the rule of law were said rather to demand that the entire election events, ranging into the ramifications of the technical details, could be traced both by state bodies and by the people. The design of the election procedure, the monitoring and the parliamentary and judicial examinability of the election results, were said to be subject to the state's reserve as core state tasks.

The technical and constructional security faults in the voting machines were said to violate the principles of electoral law as to the freedom, equality and secrecy of the elections. If votes were diverted, electronically "caught" and "spied on", the freedom of the elections was said to be placed at risk. Equality was also said to be affected if it was not sure whether the vote that had been cast had been counted at all, and if so whether it was counted correctly. What is more, it was said that the secrecy of elections could suffer damage were manipulations to occur. It was said to be sufficient for a violation of the principles of electoral law that a situation had been created by the deployment of electronic voting machines in which the errors described were possible.

The restrictions of the principles of electoral law were said not to be justified by contrary constitutional provisions. Nedap's company secrecy interests that are protected by fundamental rights had to be subordinated to the interest of the public in information and to the public monitoring which was fundamental to democracy. The gain in democracy (rapidity of ascertaining the election results and increased level of security of the election procedure), linked with the deployment of computer-controlled voting machines, was also said to be unable to justify the impairment of public elections.

The election errors were said to be relevant to mandates. Major alterations were said to be possible in the mandate structure because of the major part of the votes affected by the election errors. The complainant re 1. was said not to bear the burden of proof for the elections having led to a different result without voting machines than had in fact been the case in the constituencies in which voting machines had been deployed. For the election errors which had been complained of, in particular the violation of the principle of the public nature of elections, were said to have eliminated the actual possibility to demonstrate a manipulation in concrete terms.

bb) The complainant re 2. is essentially moving to rescind the rejection of his objection by the German *Bundestag* and to repeat the elections in the constituencies designated in the written objection of 15 October 2005, as well as basically to establish the unconstitutionality of § 35 of the Federal Electoral Act and the Federal Voting Machine Ordinance.

The complainant re 2. challenges both the constitutionality of the legal basis for the deployment of computer-controlled voting machines (§ 35 of the Federal Electoral Act and the Federal Voting Machine Ordinance), and the concrete deployment of the Nedap voting machines in the elections to the 16th German *Bundestag*. The electronic voting machines used were said to violate as to their construction and functioning the principles of electoral law of the public and official nature of elections and Article 38.1 sentence 1 of the Basic Law, as well as the Federal Voting Machine Ordinance. The procedures for the approval of the voting machines by the *Physikalisch-Technische Bundesanstalt* and the Federal Ministry of the Interior which were the subject of complaint were also said not to comply with the principles of democracy and the rule of law, as well as with the principles of electoral law of the public nature of elections and the sovereign implementation of elections.

As grounds, the complainant re 2. repeats the arguments that he already submitted in the objection procedure before the German *Bundestag*. He additionally alleges that the equality of elections had been violated by differing treatment of voting slip voters and voting machine voters since the principles of democracy and the rule of law, as well as of the public and official nature of the elections, were said to apply to the same degree to voting slip voters and to voting machine voters, and that the legislature had not provided legal provisions for the deployment of the electronic voting machines which were identical and equivalent to those in the Federal Electoral Code for voting slip elections. Insofar as it was not possible to rule out that because of the technical shortcomings of the voting machines there might be discrepancies between the ballot intended by voters and the ballot registered by the voting machine, the principle of equality between "successful" and "unsuccessful" voters was said to have been violated.

He also objects to the proceedings before the German *Bundestag*. The length of the proceedings was said not to be acceptable. The German *Bundestag* was said to have taken its decision on the basis of an insufficiently verified set of facts. The impugned resolution of the German *Bundestag* was said to have not come into being effectively for a lack of a quorum since 40 Members at most had attended the ballot. The deliberations of the Committee for the Scrutiny of Elections were said to have taken place in camera. The Rules of Procedure of the German Bundestag (*Geschäftsordnung des Deutschen Bundestages — GO-BT*) were said to be unconstitutional because they had not provided for the hearings, deliberations and rulings of the committee in the election scrutiny procedure to be held in public. Despite an explicit motion, no date had been set for an oral hearing.

2. The complaints requesting the scrutiny of an election were served on the German *Bundestag*, the *Bundesrat*, the Federal Government, all *Länder* Governments, the federal associations of the parties represented in the German *Bundestag* (CDU, SPD, The Greens, FDP, Linkspartei, CSU) and the federal returning officer. The *Physikalisch-Technische Bundesanstalt* and the Federal Office for Information Security were afforded the opportunity according to § 27a of the Federal Constitutional Court Act (*Bundesverfassungsgerichtsgesetz — BVerfGG*) to make a statement on the technical questions that had been put forward.

(a) The federal returning officer considers the deployment of the electronic voting machines to be lawful.

(b) The Federal Ministry of the Interior has extended and supplemented its statements from the objection procedure before the German *Bundestag* on the use of the voting machines allegedly having been constitutional and lawful.

The public nature of elections was said to be overstretched if it were to be demanded that anyone should be able to verify the entire election events, including the preparations for the election, right down into the ramifications of the technical details and the entire state activity in an election, including the type approval of the voting machines, and that the other preparatory work of the election bodies and other institutions were subject to public monitoring.

The local organisation was said to be one of the most important means to prevent manipulations in the use of voting machines. Since the local authorities decided on their own responsibility on the acquisition of the voting machines and were said to be responsible for the proper storage of the voting machines, and for their examination prior to deployment, manipulation of the voting machines was said to require, in addition to the appropriate technical skills, a knowledge of the manner in which each individual local authority stored the voting machines and how the security measures could be overcome. The local organisation was said to also include the ascertainment of the results in the respective polling station. This meant that it was not possible to manipulate the voting machine during transportation. Impacts of any irregularities were hence restricted to the election result in the respective constituency.

(c) The *Physikalisch-Technische Bundesanstalt* explained the examination concept on which the type sample check was based, and stated that the security requirements should be judged in the context of the implantation of the voting machines into the proven processes in traditional elections. The arguments of the complainant were said not to take this into account.

3. (a) The Chaos Computer Club e.V. refers in its statement to an examination of the security and manipulability of Nedap election computers which was implemented in 2006 in cooperation with the Dutch initiative "We do not trust voting computers" ("*Wij vertrouwen stemcomputers niet*"). The software and the hardware of the Dutch ES3B type, which in the view of the study's authors differed only slightly from the ESD 1 and ESD 2 types used in Germany, was said to have been susceptible to manipulation with relatively little effort. The test indicates that the processes and programming methods analysed by reconstructing the source code of the voting machine were trivial and only constituted the state-of-the-art of the early nineteen-nineties.

The voting machines could be manipulated by the votes cast for an electoral proposal being altered prior to their storage, so that they would be stored on the vote storage module as votes cast for another party. This was said not to require any knowledge of the list place of the party or of the candidate. A further manipulation variant was said to consist in already providing for a preset percentage final result for a specific electoral proposal prior to commencement of the elections without this coming to light in a test election. It was said to be possible in practice to exchange the software without encountering difficulties. The storage media could be removed from the voting machine, read out, deleted and re-programmed using widely available tools. A person with a modicum of technical knowledge could exchange a storage medium within less than five minutes after brief training; someone with experience could have effected a swap in about one minute. Manipulations to the hardware were also simple without this being identifiable by any testing procedure used or proposed by Nedap or by the *Physikalisch-Technische Bundesanstalt*.

All in all, the tests had shown that the Nedap voting machines did not meet the requirements of the Federal Voting Machine Ordinance. The dynamics of the development in the potential for attack and manipulation were said to constitute one of the main risk factors of computer-aided election procedures. In contradistinction to established procedures, it was possible at any time for attack methods to be developed which were as yet unknown and the consequences of which were not foreseeable which remained unrecognised and made it possible to falsify an election. None of the fundamental difficulties in the use of computer-controlled voting machines was said to be solvable by technical means with sufficient reliability since greater technical security measures would of necessity lead to more complex systems which could be examined by even fewer people.

(b) The Federal Ministry of the Interior takes the view that the statement of the Chaos Computer Club showed all in all an over-evaluation of technical security requirements as to the voting machines. There was said to be no way to guarantee absolute security against falsification in elections. Ballot box election and postal voting was said to be theoretically susceptible to manipulation in a similar way to elections with voting machines. Any technical security measure could be circumvented with the corresponding effort.

The criticised manipulation possibilities still in existence despite a protected environment were said not to differ from the risks also existing in classical elections. The existing regulations were said to be adequate.

4. In the oral hearing, the Senate furthermore heard Dr. Jörn Müller-Quade, European Institute for Systems Security (*Europäisches Institut für Systemsicherheit*) in Karlsruhe, and Melanie Volkamer, Institute of IT-Security and Security Law (*Institut für IT-Sicherheit und Sicherheitsrecht*) of the University of Passau, as experts. Dr. Müller-Quade particularly made a statement on the question of whether and to what degree manipulation to the hardware or software could be discovered by subsequent examinations of the voting machines. Ms Volkamer explained how the concurrence of the software with the samples installed in the individual voting machines could be examined prior to the elections.

B

Insofar as the complainant re 2. objects to the proceedings before the German *Bundestag*, his complaint requesting the scrutiny of an election is unsuccessful.

The complaints requesting the scrutiny of an election are well-founded insofar as they complain about the Federal Voting Machines Ordinance permitting the use of computer-controlled voting machines without ensuring effective monitoring of the election act and effective subsequent monitoring of the ascertainment of the result. In this respect, there is a violation of the principle of the public nature of elections under Article 38 of the Basic Law in conjunction with Article 20.1 and 20.2 of the Basic Law. The use of Nedap's computer-controlled voting machines was also not compatible with the principle of the public nature of elections. Both election errors however do not lead to the elections being declared invalid in the constituencies designated by the complainant.

It can remain open whether the constructive characteristics of the voting machines, and hence also the type approvals and the use authorisation, were compatible with the requirements contained in the Federal Voting Machine Ordinance, and in particular in the Guidelines for the Construction of Voting Machines, and with the principles of electoral law under Article 38.1 sentence 1 of the Basic Law. The same applies as to the complaints that the voting machines used had not been subject to adequate official monitoring, that the examination of the samples by the *Physikalisch-Technische Bundesanstalt* and that the type approval procedure had not taken place in public, as well as that the examination reports and documents of the *Physikalisch-Technische Bundesanstalt*, and the source code of the voting machine software, had not been made available to the public.

I

The complaint requesting the scrutiny of an election of the complainant re 2. is unsuccessful insofar as the complainant complains of the length of the proceedings before the German *Bundestag* and that the Committee for the Scrutiny of Elections had not deliberated in public and wrongly had not set an oral hearing. The complaint that the German *Bundestag* had not been quorate on accepting the resolution recommendation of the Committee for the Scrutiny of Elections is also not well-founded.

In the context of the complaint proceedings, the Federal Constitutional Court reviews the impugned resolution of the German *Bundestag* in formal and substantive terms. Faults in the proceedings of the German *Bundestag*, as they are claimed by the complainant, can only be relevant to the complaint if they are material and deprive it of the basis for its decision (see Decisions of the Federal Constitutional Court (*Entscheidungen des Bundesverfassungsgerichts* — BVerfGE 89, 243 (249); 89, 291 (299)). No such procedural violations are recognisable here.

1. Even if the proceedings took more than one year between the submission of the objection to the election and the decision of the German *Bundestag*, this does not yet constitute a grievous procedural error. The length of the proceedings by itself does not remove the basis for the decision (see Federal Constitutional Court (*Bundesverfassungsgericht* — BVerfG, judgement of the Second Senate of 3 July 2008 — 2 BvC 1 / 07, 7 / 07 –, *Neue Zeitschrift für Verwaltungsrecht* — *NVwZ* 2008, p. 991 (992)).

2. The fact that the Committee for the Scrutiny of Elections refrained from holding an oral hearing on the complainant's objection to the election, and also deliberated in camera in other respects, also does not constitute a grievous error removing the basis for the decision of the German *Bundestag*.

(a) According to § 6.1a no. 3 of the Law on the Scrutiny of Elections in the version of 24 August 1965 (Federal Law Gazette I p. 977 (Law on the Scrutiny of Elections, *Wahlprüfungsgesetz — WahlPrG*, old version)), which applied at the time of the decision on the complainant's objection, the committee was able to refrain from holding an oral hearing if the preliminary review revealed that the objection was manifestly unfounded. Since the amendment of § 6.1 of the Law on the Scrutiny of Elections by the Act Amending the Law on the Scrutiny of Elections of 6 June 2008 (Federal Law Gazette I p. 994), a date for an oral hearing is only to be set if the preliminary examination reveals that this can be expected to further promote the proceedings.

An objection is manifestly unfounded if no aspect is recognisable at the time of the decision which may help it to succeed (see BVerfGE 89, 243 (250); 89, 291 (300)). The evaluation is not conditional on the unfoundedness of the appeal being evident; it may also be the result of a prior thorough examination (see BVerfGE 82, 316 (319-320) on the regulation of § 24 of the Federal Constitutional Court Act with identical content).

Even if there may be reasons according to the submission of the complaint suggesting that the objection was not manifestly unfounded, in particular with regard to compliance with the Guidelines for the Construction of Voting Machines, refraining from holding an oral hearing is certainly not so grievous that the decision of the German *Bundestag* would be deprived of its basis by these means. It based its decision primarily on the deployment of computer-controlled voting machines not violating the principle of the public nature of elections and the concrete non-constitutional provisions contained in electoral law. In this respect, the German *Bundestag* has addressed the complainants' arguments in detail and made a detailed statement on the questions raised. Where it deals with the question of the approval of the Nedap voting machines used in the *Bundestag* election, it takes as a basis the statement of the Federal Ministry of the Interior, according to which manipulations are theoretically possible but, because of the bundle of technical and organisational security measures, are ruled out to the same degree as in classical voting slip elections.

(b) In contradistinction to the view taken by the complainant re 2., the Committee for the Scrutiny of Elections was not obliged to deliberate in an open hearing.

The Law on the Scrutiny of Elections regulates in the provisions on oral hearings (§§ 6 et seq. of the Law on the Scrutiny of Elections) the preconditions under which the proceedings of the Committee for the Scrutiny of Elections are held in public. If an oral hearing is not waived, the hearing takes place in public. According to § 10.1 of the Law on the Scrutiny of Elections, the Committee for the Scrutiny of Elections deliberates in secret on the result of the oral hearing. According to the system of the Act, this applies in the same way if an oral hearing is waived. No constitutional aspects are evident which might oblige the legislature to enact any different regulation when legislating on the scrutiny of elections (Article 41.3 of the Basic Law).

3. The complaint of the complainant re 2. that the resolution of the German *Bundestag* of 14 December 2006 had allegedly not effectively come into being for a lack of a quorum is also unsuccessful. The German *Bundestag* decides with a simple majority on the recommendation for a resolution of the Committee for the Scrutiny of Elections (§ 13.1 sentence 1 of the Law on the Scrutiny of Elections). According to § 45.1 of the Rules of Procedure of the German Bundestag, the *Bundestag* is quorate if more than half of its members are present in the plenary. The *Bundestag* is regarded as being quorate regardless of the number of its members present until it is found to not be quorate in the proceedings prescribed in § 45.2 of the Rules of Procedure of the German Bundestag. This provision does not come up against any constitutional reservations (see BVerfGE 44, 308 (314 et seq.) on the provisions of § 49.2 of the Rules of Procedure of the German Bundestag, old version, the content of which is largely identical).

As is shown by the record of the session, the German *Bundestag* unanimously accepted the resolution recommendation of the Committee for the Scrutiny of Elections on 14 December 2006 (see Minutes of plenary proceedings 16 / 73, Stenographic Record p. 7259 B). It cannot be derived from the minutes how many delegates were present in the house when the ballot was held. There is no record that it had been doubted, or indeed ascertained, whether the German *Bundestag* was quorate. There is hence no indication that the Bundestag was not quorate.

II

1. In the context of a complaint requesting the scrutiny of an election according to § 13 no. 3 and § 48 of the Federal Constitutional Court Act, the Federal Constitutional Court has not only to guarantee compliance by the competent election bodies and the German Bundestag with the provisions of federal election law, but also to review whether the provisions of the Federal Electoral Act comply with the requirements of the constitution (see BVerfGE 16, 130 (135-136); BVerfG, judgement of the Second Senate of 3 July 2008 — 2 BvC 1 / 07, 7 / 07 —, Neue Zeitschrift für Verwaltungsrecht 2008, p. 991 (992)). This examination also covers the validity of legal ordinances.

2. The deployment of computer-controlled voting machines is in particular to be reviewed against the standard of the public nature of elections (Article 38 in conjunction with Article 20.1 and 20.2 of the Basic Law).

The public nature of elections is a fundamental precondition for democratic political will-formation. It ensures the correctness and verifiability of the election events, and hence creates a major precondition for the well-founded trust of the citizen in the correct operation of the elections. The state form of parliamentary democracy, in which the rule of the people is mediated by elections, in other words is not directly exercised, demands that the act of transferring state responsibility to parliamentarians is subject to special public monitoring. The fundamentally required public nature of the election procedure covers the electoral proposal procedure, the election act (broken regarding the ballot by the secret nature of elections) and the ascertainment of the election result (see BVerfG, judgement of the Second Senate of 3 July 2008 — 2 BvC 1 / 07, 7 / 07 –, *Neue Zeitschrift für Verwaltungsrecht* 2008, p. 991 (992) with further references).

(a) The basis for public elections is formed by the fundamental constitutional options for democracy, the republic and the rule of law (Article 38 in conjunction with Article 20.1 and 20.2 of the Basic Law).

(aa) In a representative democracy, the elections of the people's representation constitute the fundamental act of legitimisation. The ballot in the elections to the German *Bundestag* forms the major element of the process of will-forming from the people to the state bodies, and hence at the same time constitutes the basis for political integration. Compliance with the election principles applicable to this, and confidence in compliance with them, hence constitute preconditions for a viable democracy. Only by the possibility of monitoring whether the elections comply with the constitutional election principles is it possible to ensure that the delegation of state power to the people's representation, which forms the first and most important part of the uninterrupted legitimisation chain of the people to the bodies and office-holders entrusted with state tasks, does not suffer from a shortcoming. The democratic legitimacy of the elections demands that the election events be controllable so that manipulation can be ruled out or corrected and unjustified suspicion can be refuted. This is the only way to facilitate the well-founded trust of the sovereign in the correct formation of the representative body. The obligation incumbent on the legislature and on the executive to ensure that the election procedure is designed constitutionally and is implemented properly is not sufficient by itself to impart the necessary legitimacy. Only if the electorate can reliably convince itself of the lawfulness of the transfer act, if the elections are therefore implemented "before the eyes of the public" (see Schreiber, *Handbuch des Wahlrechts zum Deutschen Bundestag*, 7th ed. 2002, § 31 marginal no. 2) is it possible to guarantee the trust of the sovereign in Parliament being composed in a manner corresponding to the will of the voters that is necessary for the functioning of democracy and the democratic legitimacy of state decisions (see North Rhine / Westphalia Constitutional Court (*Verfassungsgerichtshof-Nordrhein-Westfalen* — NRW VerfGH), judgement of 19 March 1991 — VerfGH 10 / 90 –, *Neue Zeitschrift für Verwaltungsrecht* 1991, p. 1175 (1179); Hanßmann, *Möglichkeiten und Grenzen von Internetwahlen*, 2004, p. 184).

(bb) In a republic, elections are a matter for the entire people and a joint concern of all citizens. Consequently, the monitoring of the election procedure must also be a matter for and a task of the citizen. Each citizen must be able to comprehend and verify the central steps in the elections reliably and without any special prior technical knowledge.

(cc) The public nature of the elections is also anchored in the principle of the rule of law. The public nature of the state's exercise of power, which is based on the rule of law, serves its transparency and controllability. It is contingent on the citizen being able to perceive acts of the state bodies. This also applies as to the activities of the election bodies.

(b) The principle of the public nature of elections requires that all essential steps in the elections are subject to public examinability unless other constitutional interests justify an exception. Particular significance attaches here to the monitoring of the election act and to the ascertainment of the election result.

An election procedure in which the voter cannot reliably comprehend whether his or her vote is unfalsifiably recorded and included in the ascertainment of the election result, and how the total votes cast are assigned and counted, excludes central elements of the election procedure from public monitoring, and hence does not comply with the constitutional requirements.

(c) Despite the considerable value attaching to the constitutional principle of the public nature of elections, it does not ensue from this principle that all acts in connection with the ascertainment of the election result must take place with the involvement of the public so that a well-founded trust in the correctness of the elections can be created. For instance, activities of the district returning officer with which according to § 76.1 of the Federal Electoral Code the — public — ascertainment of the election result is prepared by the district election committee are not constitutionally obliged to be subject to the principle of the direct public nature of elections (see BVerfG, judgement of the Second Senate of 3 July 2008 — 2 BvC 1 / 07, 7 / 07 –, *Neue Zeitschrift für Verwaltungsrecht* 2008, p. 991 (992)).

(d) The requirements as to the examinability of the election events apply to the implementation of parliamentary elections regardless of the responsibility of the state bodies which have a constitutional structure (see BVerfGE 20, 56 (113); 41, 399 (414); Seifert, *Bundeswahlrecht*, 3rd ed. 1976, p. 130).

It is primarily a matter for the legislature to regulate how the retraceability of the essential steps in the election procedure is ensured. Article 38.3 of the Basic Law empowers and obliges the legislature to determine the details of the structure of electoral law (in particular the election system and the election procedure) and compliance with the principles of electoral law (see Magiera, in: Sachs, *GG*, 5th ed. 2009, *Art. 38*, marginal nos. 106 et seq. and 113 et seq.). The design of the technical aspects of the election events also falls within the regulatory mandate under Article 38.3 of the Basic Law (see Morlok, in: Dreier, *GG*, Vol. 2, 2nd ed. 2006, *Art. 38*, marginal no. 127), and hence the decision on deployment of voting machines and the determination of the more detailed preconditions for their deployment. Details may be regulated by means of a legal ordinance on the basis of a statutory authorisation (see Magiera, in: Sachs, *GG*, 5th ed. 2009, *Art. 38*, marginal no. 114).

The legislature is entitled to broad latitude when lending concrete shape to the principles of electoral law within which it must decide whether and to what degree deviations from individual principles of electoral law are justified in the interest of the uniformity of the entire election system and to ensure the state policy goals which they pursue (see BVerfGE 3, 19 (24-25); 59, 119 (124); 95, 335 (349)). The Federal Constitutional Court only reviews whether the legislature has remained within the boundaries of the latitude granted to it by the Basic Law, or whether it has violated a valid constitutional election principle by overstepping these boundaries. It is not a matter for the Court to find whether the legislature has found solutions which are expedient or desired in terms of legal policy within the latitude to which it is entitled (see BVerfGE 59, 119 (125)).

3. The deployment of voting machines which record the voters' votes in electronic form and ascertain the result of the election electronically is hence only compatible with the Basic Law subject to strict preconditions.

(a) When electronic voting machines are deployed, it must be possible to check the essential steps in the election act and in the ascertainment of the results reliably and without special expert knowledge.

The necessity of such monitoring emerges not lastly from the susceptibility to manipulation of electronic voting machines and their amenability to error. In these, the acceptance of the voters' votes and the calculation of the election result is based on a calculation act which cannot be examined from outside or by persons without special computer knowledge. Errors in the voting machine software are hence difficult to recognise. Over and above this, such errors can affect not only one individual election computer, but all the devices used. Whilst manipulations or election falsifications are virtually impossible in classical elections with voting slips under the conditions of the valid provisions, including the provisions on the public nature of elections — or at least are only possible with considerable effort and with a very high risk of discovery which has a preventive impact — a major impact may in principle be achieved with relatively little effort by encroachments on electronically controlled voting machines. Manipulations of individual voting machines can already influence not only individual voters' votes, but all votes cast with the aid of this device. The scope of the election errors which are caused by alterations and malfunctions of a single software programme affecting multiple devices is even wider. The major scope of the effect of possible errors in the voting machines or targeted election falsifications requires special precautions to be taken in order to comply with the principle of the public nature of elections.

(aa) The voter himself or herself must be able to verify — also without a more detailed knowledge of computers — whether his or her vote as cast is recorded truthfully as a basis for counting or — if the votes are initially counted with technical support — at least as a basis for a subsequent re-count. It is not sufficient if he or she must rely on the functionality of the system without the possibility of personal inspection. It is hence inadequate if he or she is exclusively informed by an electronic display that his or her ballot has been registered. This does not facilitate sufficient monitoring by the voter. Equal viability must also apply to the election bodies and to interested citizens.

The consequence of this is that the votes may not be stored exclusively on an electronic storage medium after the ballot. The voter may not be required to trust solely in the technical integrity of the system after the electronic ballot. If the election result is ascertained by computer-controlled processing of the votes stored in an electronic storage medium, it is not sufficient if only the result of the calculation process as implemented in the voting machine can be taken note of using a summary paper printout or an electronic display. By these means, voters and election bodies can only examine whether the voting machine has processed as many votes as voters have been admitted to operate the voting machine in the elections. It is not easily recognisable in such cases whether there have been programming errors in the software or targeted election falsifications through manipulation of the software or of the voting machines.

(bb) The legislature is not prevented from using electronic voting machines in the elections if the constitutionally required possibility of a reliable correctness check is ensured. In particular, voting machines are conceivable in which the votes are recorded elsewhere in addition to electronic storage. This is for instance possible with electronic voting machines which print out a visible paper report of the vote cast for the respective voter, in addition to electronic recording of the vote, which can be checked prior to the final ballot and is then collected to facilitate subsequent checking. Monitoring that is independent of the electronic vote record also remains possible when systems are deployed in which the voter marks a voting slip and the election decision is recorded simultaneously (for instance with a "digital election pen", see on this Schiedermair, *Juristenzeitung* 2007, p. 162 (170)), or subsequently (e.g. by a voting slip scanner; see on this Schönau, *Elektronische Demokratie*, 2007, pp. 51-52; Khorrami, *Bundestagswahlen per Internet*, 2006, p. 30) by electronic means in order to evaluate these by electronic means at the end of the election day.

It is certainly ensured in these cases that the voters are in charge of their ballot and that the result of the election can be reliably checked by the election authorities or by interested citizens without any special prior technical knowledge. Whether there are still other technical possibilities which create trust on the part of the electorate in the correctness of the proceedings in ascertaining the election result based on verifiability, and which hence comply with the principle of the public nature of elections, need not be decided here.

(b) Restrictions on possibilities for citizens to monitor the election events cannot be compensated for by sample devices in the context of the type approval procedure or in the selection of the voting machines specifically used in the elections prior to their deployment being subjected to verification by an official institution as to their compliance with certain security requirements and their proper technical performance. The monitoring of the essential steps in the election promotes well-founded trust in the correctness of the election certainly in the necessary manner that the citizen himself or herself can reliably verify the election event.

For this reason, a comprehensive bundle of other technical and organisational security measures (e.g. monitoring and safekeeping of the voting machines, comparability of the devices used with an officially checked sample at any time, criminal liability in respect of election falsifications and local organisation of the elections) is also not suited by itself to compensate for a lack of controllability of the essential steps in the election procedure by the citizen.

Accordingly, neither participation by the interested public in procedures of the examination or approval of voting machines, nor a publication of examination reports or construction characteristics (including the source code of the software with computer-controlled voting machines) makes a major contribution towards ensuring the constitutionally required level of controllability and verifiability of the election events. Technical examinations and official approval procedures, which in any case can only be expertly evaluated by interested specialists, relate to a stage in the proceedings which is far in advance of the ballot. The participation of the public in order to achieve the required reliable monitoring of the election events is hence likely to require other additional precautions.

(c) The legislature can permit exceptions to the principle of the public nature of elections to a restricted degree in order to bring other constitutional interests to fruition, in particular the written principles of electoral law from Article 38.1 sentence 1 of the Basic Law. For instance, restrictions of public monitoring of the ballot with postal voting (§ 36 of the Federal Electoral Act) can be justified with the aim of achieving as comprehensive participation in the elections as possible, thereby complying with the principle of generality of elections (see BVerfGE 21, 200 (205); 59, 119 (125)). When deploying computer-controlled voting machines, however, no contrary constitutional principles are recognisable which are able to justify a broad restriction of the public nature of elections and hence the controllability of the election act and the ascertainment of the results.

(aa) Where the deployment of computer-controlled voting machines aims to rule out inadvertent incorrect markings on voting slips, unwanted invalid ballots, unintentional counting errors or incorrect interpretations of the voters' intention when votes are counted (see Schreiber, *Handbuch des Wahlrechts zum Deutschen Bundestag*, 7th ed. 2002, *§ 35*, marginal no. 2) which repeatedly occur in classical elections with voting slips, this serves the interest of the implementation of the equality of elections under Article 38.1 sentence 1 of the Basic Law. What weight attaches to this purpose can however be left open. It certainly does not justify by itself forgoing any type of verifiability of the election act. Unintentional counting errors or incorrect interpretations of the voters' intention can also be ruled out by voting machines if supplementary monitoring by the voter, the election bodies or the public is made possible in addition to electronic recording and counting of the votes. Corresponding monitoring is for instance possible with electronic voting machines which record the votes not only in electronic form in the voting machine, but at the same time in a form which is independent of this (see II. 3. a) bb above). Apart from this, user errors — such as pushing the "invalid" key presuming that this made it possible to correct an erroneous entry — cannot be ruled out in the voting machines approved for the elections to the 16th German *Bundestag*.

(bb) The principle of the secrecy of elections certainly does not constitute a counter constitutional principle which can be used as a basis for a broad restriction of the controllability of the election act and of the ascertainment of the results. There is no "conflict of interest" between the principle of secret elections and the principle of the public nature of elections which might justify such restrictions (*Bundestag* document 16 / 3600, Annex 1, p. 20).

The principle of secret elections guarantees that the voter alone is aware of the content of his or her election decision, and obliges the legislature to take the necessary steps to protect the election secret (see H.H. Klein, in: Maunz / Dürig, *GG, Art. 38*, marginal no. 110 [March 2007]; Pieroth, *Juristische Schulung — JuS* 1991, p. 89 (91)). The secrecy of elections constitutes the most important institutional protection of the freedom of elections (see BVerfGE 99, 1 (13)). In historic terms, secret elections may have been a caesura in the public nature of the election procedure because they renounced the open ballot in order to protect the freedom of election (see Breidenbach / Blankenagel, *Rechtliche Probleme von Internetwahlen*, Berlin 2000, pp. 34-35). Under the regime of the Basic Law, which explicitly prescribes elections as secret in order to protect their freedom, however, the principle of the public nature of elections from the outset does not apply to the act of the ballot. If the public nature of the elections is not ruled out in order to enable the ballot to be cast unobserved, the election procedure is subject to the principle of the public nature of elections (see H.H. Klein, in: Maunz / Dürig, *GG, Art. 38*, marginal no. 113 [March 2007]; Seifert, *Bundeswahlrecht*, 3rd ed. 1976, *Art. 38*, marginal no. 35). Accordingly, the impact of the principle of secrecy of elections is not to restrict the principle of the public nature of elections for the ballot act. It also does not justify a restriction of public monitoring in the casting of the — previously secretly marked — vote carrier or in the ascertainment of the results. This already follows from the fact that it does not oppose additional precautions enabling the voter to monitor whether his or her vote is recorded in an unfalsified manner as a basis for a subsequent re-count.

(cc) Finally, the goal of being able to form a viable people's representation in a short period does not constitute a restriction of the principle of the public nature of elections in the deployment of computer-controlled voting machines. The clarification of the correct composition of the people's representation within a suitable period is one aspect which can be taken into account when shaping the election procedure and the election scrutiny procedure (see BVerfGE 85, 148 (159)). The matter of the assembly of a new *Bundestag* in good time (see Article 39.2 of the Basic Law) is however not endangered by sufficient precautions being taken to ensure public elections. There is no constitutional requirement for the election result to be available shortly after closing the polling stations. What is more, the past *Bundestag* elections have shown that the preliminary official final result of the elections can as a rule be submitted in a matter of hours, even without the deployment of voting machines. The interest in rapidly clarifying the composition of the German *Bundestag* is therefore not a constitutional interest that is suited to impose restrictions on the public nature of the election event.

4. The normative level on which the questions related to the deployment of voting machines are to be regulated is determined in line with the requirements of the parliamentary reservation and the requirements which are placed on the authorisation to issue legal ordinances (Article 80.1 sentence 2 of the Basic Law).

(a) The parliamentary reservation rooted in the principle of the rule of law and in the principle of democracy requires that the major decisions are to be taken by the legislature in fundamental normative areas, especially in the area of the exercise of fundamental rights, insofar as this is amenable to state regulation (see BVerfGE 49, 89 (126-127); 61, 260 (275); 80, 124 (132); 101, 1 (34)). The obligation to legislate relates here not only to the question of whether a certain article must be regulated by law at all, but also to how far these individual regulations have to go (see BVerfGE 101, 1 (34)).

According to Article 80.1 sentence 2 of the Basic Law, the content, purpose and scope of the authorisation to issue legal ordinances must be laid down in the statute concerned. The legislature itself must decide which questions are to be regulated by the legal ordinance, within what limits and with what goal (see BVerfGE 2, 307 (334); 5, 71 (76-77); 23, 62 (72)). The wording of the authorisation need not be formulated as precisely as possible; it must constitutionally only be sufficiently determined (see BVerfGE 55, 207 (226); 58, 257 (277); 62, 203 (209-210). It is sufficient if the limits of the authorisation are determinable by interpretation using the interpretation principles that are generally recognised; the goals of the statute, the context together with other provisions and the genesis of the statute are significant here (see BVerfGE 8, 274 (307); 23, 62 (73); 55, 207 (226-227); 80, 1 (20-21)). In detail, the requirements as to the level of determinedness depend on the particularities of the respective object of regulation and on the intensity of the measure (see BVerfGE 58, 257 (277-278); 62, 203 (210); 76, 130 (143)). Whilst less stringent requirements are to be made with circumstances that are highly varied and subject to rapid change, more stringent requirements apply to the degree of determinedness of the authorisation with those regulations which are linked to more intensive encroachments on legal positions which are protected by fundamental rights (see BVerfGE 58, 257 (278); 62, 203 (210)).

(b) Because of their particularities, regulations relating to the deployment of voting machines are reserved for parliamentary decision insofar as they relate to the major requirements for the deployment of such devices. This includes the decisions on the permissibility of the deployment of voting machines and the fundamental prerequisites for their deployment. These decisions cannot be left to the institution adopting the ordinance.

The more detailed preconditions for the approval of voting machines and the procedures to be complied with here, the details of the use of the voting machines in the elections and the guarantee of the principles of electoral law in the concrete deployment of voting machines, by contrast, do not require any detailed parliamentary regulation, but can be regulated by the institution adopting the ordinance. The respective requirements of the voting machines depend heavily on the nature of the respective voting machine, and hence do not already have to be legislated in detail at the level of the parliamentary statute. Thus, for instance, the requirements for the deployment of electronically operated voting machines differ from those for the deployment of exclusively mechanical voting machines. Because voting machines are subject to ongoing technical development, a rapid adjustment of the law is better guaranteed if the detailed regulations are transferred to the institution adopting the ordinance.

III

According to these standards, the authorisation to hand down ordinances contained in § 35 of the Federal Electoral Act does not give rise to any profound constitutional objections.

1. The parliamentary legislature was not obliged over and above the regulation contained in § 35 of the Federal Electoral Act to regulate the deployment of computer-controlled voting machines since the major questions in connection with the deployment of computer-controlled voting machines are determined in § 35 of the Federal Electoral Act. Where § 35 of the Federal Electoral Act authorises the adoption of the Federal Voting Machine Ordinance, the content, purpose and scope of the authorisation that has been issued is adequately regulated (Article 80.1 sentence 2 of the Basic Law).

The parliamentary legislature made the fundamental decision in § 35.1 of the Federal Electoral Act for the deployment of voting machines. By restricting the deployment of the voting machines to facilitating the casting and counting of votes, the legislature clearly determined the goal of the authorisation to issue ordinances. It made it clear by deleting the words "with separate counting devices" in 1999 that § 35 of the Federal Electoral Act also covers the deployment of computer-controlled voting machines.

The fundamental prerequisites for the deployment of the voting machines are named in § 35.2 sentences 2 to 5 and 35.3 of the Federal Electoral Act, in particular the official type approval and the official authorisation of the use of the voting machines. Of the constitutionally guaranteed election principles, only the secrecy of the ballot and the keeping of the secrecy of elections are explicitly spoken of in § 35.2 sentence 1 of the Federal Electoral Act. The other principles of electoral law are regulated in § 1.1 sentence 2 of the Federal Electoral Act. They therefore certainly also apply to the deployment of voting machines in the elections to the German *Bundestag*. Finally, the legislature provided in § 35.3 sentence 1 no. 6 of the Federal Electoral Act that the Federal Ministry of the Interior may regulate the particularities in connection with the elections brought about by the use of voting machines. This provision forms not only a sufficient normative basis in order to account for the constitutional particularities of the deployment of computer-controlled voting machines. It also makes it recognisable for citizens that an election with voting machines may entail modifications in comparison with the classical ballot box election. It is not constitutionally required that all details of the content of a legal ordinance can be derived from the respective basis for the authorisation. The latitude which can be granted to the institution adopting the ordinance in this respect is also to be measured accounting for the complexity of the material and the dynamics of development processes in voting machines. The parliamentary legislature is hence certainly not constitutionally obliged to make detailed regulations for the deployment of electronic voting machines.

2. § 35 of the Federal Electoral Act is compatible with the principle of the public nature of elections.

(a) It is not constitutionally objectionable that § 35.1 of the Federal Electoral Act permits voting machines "in place of voting slips and ballot boxes". For § 35.1 of the Federal Electoral Act does not rule out with this wording the approval and use of voting machines with control devices which record the votes in addition to (electronic) recording in the voting machine in a manner controlled by the voter. According to the systematic status of § 35.1 of the Federal Electoral Act, the words "in place of voting slips and ballot boxes" refer to the classical election procedure set out in § 34 of the Federal Electoral Act in which exclusively official voting slips and ballot boxes are used. § 35.1 of the Federal Electoral Act, by contrast, does not rule out the adoption of provisions which provide for devices for a verifiability of the election result that is independent of the electronic recording and evaluation of votes.

(b) It is unobjectionable for the principle of the public nature of elections contained in § 35 of the Federal Electoral Act to not be explicitly listed once more as a precondition for the authorisation and use of computer-controlled voting machines. These requirements emerge directly from the constitution, and hence are also binding on the institution adopting the ordinance in lending concrete form to § 35 of the Federal Electoral Act. Independently of this, it also emerges from other provisions of the Federal Electoral Act that the use of voting machines is only permissible if the principle of the public nature of elections is adhered to. § 31 of the Federal Electoral Act determines that the election act is public. § 35.3 sentence 1 no. 4 of the Federal Electoral Act permits regulations to be made on the open testing of a voting machine prior to its use.

IV

The Federal Voting Device Ordinance is unconstitutional on grounds of a violation of the principle of the public nature of elections from Article 38 in conjunction with Article 20.1 and 20.2 of the Basic Law. It does not already encounter legal reservations because the expansion of the area of application of the Federal Voting Device Ordinance to cover computer-controlled voting machines effected by the Ordinance Amending the Federal Voting Device Ordinance of 20 April 1999 (Federal Law Gazette I p. 749) had exceeded the framework of the provision on authorisation of § 35 of the Federal Electoral Act. The Federal Voting Machine Ordinance does not however contain any provisions ensuring that only those voting machines are approved and used which comply with the constitutional preconditions of the principle of the public nature of elections.

1. Insofar as the Ordinance Amending the Federal Voting Machine Ordinance of 20 April 1999 (Federal Law Gazette I p. 749) with effect from 24 April 1999 regulates the preconditions for the deployment of computer-controlled voting machines, it remains within the authorisation contained in the version of § 35 of the

Federal Electoral Act still applicable on 24 April 1999. The latter permitted the use of voting machines "with separate counting devices" (§ 35.1 of the Federal Electoral Act). The subsequent deletion of the words "with separate counting devices" was considered necessary "in order to adjust the Federal Voting Device Ordinance to technical developments in voting machines" (*Bundestag* document 14 / 401, p. 5). This exception from the legislative procedure to amend § 35.1 of the Federal Electoral Act cannot however exert a decisive influence on the interpretation of the provision in the version which it had prior to the amendment. The expansion of the area of application of the Federal Voting Machine Ordinance to cover computer-aided voting machines was compatible with the wording of this earlier version. The term "counting device" only requires that item numbers, flow volumes or other values are calculated and shown automatically (see Duden, *Das große Wörterbuch der deutschen Sprache*, 3rd ed. 1999). According to the wording, this therefore also covers electronic or software-controlled counting devices in computer-controlled voting machines. The characteristic "separate counting devices" is intended in the view of the institution adopting the ordinance to refer merely to the requirement of "independent counting of first and second votes"; such independent counting of first and second votes is also possible with computer-controlled voting machines using an electronic counting device. Even if the legislature was not yet able to consider deployment of microprocessor-controlled voting machines in the original version of § 35.1 of the Federal Electoral Act (see Breidenbach / Blankenagel, *Rechtliche Probleme von Internetwahlen*, Berlin 2000, p. 7), neither the wording nor the purpose of § 35 of the Federal Electoral Act in the version applicable on entry into force of the Ordinance Amending the Federal Voting Machine Ordinance on 24 April 1999 suggest that these voting machines were intended to be ruled out from the legislative authorisation of the institution adopting the ordinance.

2. The Federal Voting Machine Ordinance violates the principle of the public nature of elections under Article 38 in conjunction with Article 20.1 and 20.2 of the Basic Law because in the use of computer-controlled voting machines it guarantees neither effective

monitoring of the election act nor the reliable verifiability of the election result. This shortcoming cannot be remedied by means of an interpretation in conformity with the constitution.

(a) The public nature of elections requires in the deployment of computer-controlled voting machines that the essential steps in the election act and the ascertainment of the results can be reviewed reliably and without special expert knowledge. Such provisions are not contained in the Federal Voting Machine Ordinance.

It particularly does not emerge from the Federal Voting Machine Ordinance that only voting machines may be deployed which enable the voter in casting his or her vote to ensure reliable monitoring of whether his or her vote is recorded in an unfalsified manner. The ordinance also does not make any concrete content and procedural requirements as to reliable subsequent monitoring of the ascertainment of the results.

The obligation to seal computer-controlled voting machines and the containers in which the vote storage media are located after ascertaining the election result (§ 15.3 of the Federal Voting Machine Ordinance), as well as to ensure that the vote storage media are not accessible to unauthorised parties (§ 16.2 of the Federal Voting Machine Ordinance), is not sufficient in this respect. Even if the vote storage media can be read out once again at any time after the election day with the aid of a voting machine, the object of such a recount is only the electronically stored votes, with regard to which neither voters nor the returning committee can examine whether they were recorded without falsification. The citizen cannot examine the essential steps in the ascertainment of the results if the recount again takes place inside a voting machine.

In addition, the counting of the ballot records entered in the list of voters and of the election slips which have been accepted, as well as the comparison with the numbers for the total first and second votes at the voting machine shown (see § 13 of the Federal Voting Machine Ordinance) only facilitates monitoring as to whether the voting machine has processed as many votes as voters have been admitted for the operation of the voting machine. This does not guarantee the public monitoring of the essential steps in the election act and the ascertainment of the results.

(b) The Federal Voting Machine Ordinance cannot be interpreted in conformity with the constitution such that only voting machines may be deployed which comply with the principle of the public nature of elections.

An application of the Federal Voting Machine Ordinance in conformity with the constitution such that type approval and use authorisation may only be issued by the Federal Ministry of the Interior if effective monitoring of election acts and ascertainment of the results is guaranteed (see Schiedermair, *Juristenzeitung* — *JZ* 2007, p. 162 (170)) would overstep the boundaries of an interpretation in conformity with the constitution. In principle, the institution handing down the ordinance has various possibilities at its disposal to ensure that the central steps in ballot and vote counting can be checked. Since the Federal Voting Machine Ordinance in its current version does not make it possible to recognise what such monitoring should look like, there is no constitutionally required provision, and hence there are no adequate indications which an interpretation in conformity with the constitution could take as its starting point.

It must also be taken into consideration here that the Federal Ministry of the Interior, as the institution handing down the ordinance, as it has also clearly confirmed in its statements in the proceedings at hand, considers the possibilities for monitoring which are constitutionally necessary for effective monitoring of election acts and ascertainment of the results to be neither legally required nor expedient.

V

The computer-controlled voting machines used in the elections to the 16th German *Bundestag* also did not meet the requirements made by the constitution as to the use of electronic voting machines.

The use of the Nedap electronic voting machines of Type ESD1 hardware versions 01.02, 01.03 and 01.04, as well as of Type ESD2 hardware version 01.01, violates the principle of the public nature of elections (Article 38 in conjunction with Article 20.1 and 20.2 of the Basic Law) because these voting machines did not facilitate effective monitoring of the election act or the reliable verifiability of the election result.

The votes were exclusively recorded on an electronic storage medium after the ballot. Neither the voter nor the returning committees, nor the citizens present in the polling station, were able to check whether the votes cast were recorded by the voting machines without falsification. Using the display on the control unit, the returning committees could only recognise whether the voting machines registered a ballot, but not whether the votes were recorded by the voting machines without changing the content in any way. The voting machines did not provide a possibility to record the votes independently of the electronic record on the vote storage module enabling the respective voter to check his or her ballot.

The essential steps in the ascertainment of the results by the voting machines also could not be verified by the public. Since the ascertainment of the results exclusively formed the object of a data processing procedure running inside the voting machines, it was possible for neither the election bodies nor the citizens participating in the ascertainment of the results to verify whether the valid votes cast were correctly allotted to the electoral proposals and the votes accounted for by the individual electoral proposals in total were correctly ascertained. It was not sufficient that the result of the computing process implemented in the voting machine could be taken note of using a summary paper printout or an electronic display. A public examination by means of which the citizen could have reliably verified the ascertainment of the election result himself or herself without prior special technical knowledge was hence ruled out.

VI

It may remain open whether the further complaints are well-founded. The complainants complain amongst other things that the characteristics of the voting machines and of the software used do not meet the requirements of the Federal Voting Machine Ordinance, in particular the Guidelines for the Construction of Voting Machines (Annex 1 to § 2 of the Federal Voting Machine Ordinance). The voting machines used were also said not to have been subject to sufficient official monitoring and examination of the samples by the *Physikalisch-Technische Bundesanstalt*, and that the type approval procedure should have been designed differently. The complainants hence ultimately object to the deployment of the computer-controlled voting machines used in the elections to the 16th German *Bundestag*. Even if these complaints were well-founded, in addition to the finding of the violation of the principle of the public nature of elections from Article 38 in conjunction with Article 20.1 and 20.2 of the Basic Law, these election errors would not take on any particular weight.

VII

The election errors that were ascertained do not lead to the complaints requesting the scrutiny of an election being permitted or to the repetition of the elections in the constituencies designated.

1. The election error emerging from the fact that the type approvals for Nedap computer-controlled voting machines were granted, that the use of these voting machines in the elections to the 16th German *Bundestag* was approved and that the voting machines were indeed deployed in the elections without an effective legal basis, has no relevance to mandates. Approval and use of voting machines despite inadequate design of the legal basis do not lead as such to an influence on the election result.

2. The election error emerging from the fact that computer-controlled voting machines were approved and deployed the characteristics of which were not compatible with the requirements of effective verifiability of the election events, even if its relevance to mandates were to be assumed, does not lead to a partial declaration of invalidity of the elections to the 16th German *Bundestag*.

(a) In the cases in which an election error may have had an impact on the distribution of mandates in the *Bundestag*, the election scrutiny decision of the Federal Constitutional Court is subject to the principle of the least incisive encroachment. The decision may only go so far as is demanded by the election error that has been ascertained. In principle, the requirement of the protection of the status quo of an elected people's representation (see BVerfGE 89, 243 (253)), which finds its legal basis in the principle of democracy, must be weighed up with the impact of the election error that has been ascertained. Simple influences on the election carrying no weight whatever do not therefore lead to the invalidity of an election. The encroachment on the composition of an elected people's representation by a decision under the law that regulates the scrutiny of elections must be justified in light of the interest in conserving the elected people's representation (see BVerfG, judgement of the Second Senate of 3 July 2008 — 2 BvC 1 / 07, 7 / 07 –, *Neue Zeitschrift für Verwaltungsrecht* 2008, p. 991 (997) with further references). Even where an election error that is relevant to mandates can be restricted to certain mandates, in other words where the whole election did not have to be declared invalid, a weighing up is to be undertaken which may come out in favour of the interest in protecting the status quo.

(b) The interest in the protection of the status quo of the people's representation composed in trust in the constitutionality of the Federal Voting Machine Ordinance outweighs the election errors that have been ascertained. Given that there are no indications that voting machines worked incorrectly or might have been manipulated, and hence that the election result would have been different in the constituencies concerned without the deployment of the computer-controlled voting machines, its possible impact on the composition of the 16th German Bundestag can be regarded as marginal at most. Such uncertain impacts do not justify the partial declaration of the invalidity of the elections to the 16th German Bundestag applied for. It should also be taken into account here that the violation of the constitution that was ascertained did not take place with intent, but when the legal situation was still unclear. Under these circumstances, after the above there is no election error making the continuation of the elected people's representation appear untenable.

C

With regard to the fact that the complainants rightly complain of the unconstitutionality of the use of computer-controlled voting machines, the necessary expenses which they have incurred are to be refunded to them according to § 18 and 19 of the Law on the Scrutiny of Elections in conjunction with § 34a.3 of the Federal Constitutional Court Act in this respect. Accordingly, the complainant re 1. is to be refunded the necessary expenses in full, and the complainant re 2., whose complaints are partly unfounded, is to be refunded three-quarters of the necessary expenditure.

Judges:	Voßkuhle,	Broß,	Osterloh,	Di Fabio,	Melling-hoff,	Lubbe-Wolff,	Gerhardt,	Landau

(Source: http://www.bundesverfassungsgericht.de/en/decisions/ rs20090 303 _2 bvc000307en.html)

6

The Case for Banning EVMs

Dr. Anupam Saraph*

The case for banning the EVM rests on the following six main points:

1. There are lacunae in the technology implementation. Annexure 6.1 lists out the various lacunae in the entire electronic voting process. It highlights the various vulnerabilities that result from the existing technology — not just the political and operational process. These vulnerabilities result from the public databases, the private databases, the EVMs, the mechanics of tracking votes using technology, the secrecy of the process and the reform agenda.
2. There is mounting evidence highlighting the failure of transparency, verifiability and fidelity of the process. Annexure 6.2 lists out the various facts and artefacts that resulted during the 2009 Election for the 14th Lok Sabha in each of these areas and highlight the failure to ensure the transparency, verifiability and fidelity of the process.
3. The system is not designed to distinguish a machine vote from that cast by a human. Annexure 6.3 explains the inability to distinguish human votes from machine votes thus not being able to certify that the votes polled by a candidate as being the votes cast by voters for the candidate.

* Democracy activist, advisor on Strategy, Innovation, Systems Design, Scenario Development and Information Systems.

4. There are several ways to have machines (software) cast votes on EVMs. Annexure 6.4 lists a few of the many ways in which machine votes may be cast by an EVM.
5. EVMs have been rejected and declared unconstitutional in many countries. Annexure 6.5 lists some of the grounds for rejection of EVMs in other countries.
6. Currently there is no reform agenda for EVMs. Annexure 8.6 highlights the absence of any agenda to address any of the concerns raised here in the reform agenda.

From all of these there is not just an adequate, but overwhelming case to ban the EVMs.

Suggestions

1. Ban the use of current EVMs in their current form.
2. Direct the Election Commission to create an election reform agenda, in consultation with the petitioners Expert Committee that will ensure transparency, verifiability and fidelity of the voting process.
3. The reform to be vetted through an open and inclusive process like this by the Supreme Court in consultation with those experts and petitioners who have researched these issues in depth.
4. If the Election Commission were to use any digital technology to conduct elections it must put into the public domain all such software and hardware that is used for conducting, storing and managing election processes so that anyone can audit or improve it.
5. The Election Commission must have a Chief Information Officer to design, oversee and certify the information at every stage of the process.
6. The Election Commission must have a Chief Security Officer to design, oversee and certify the security of any electronic processes, all logs should be made public on publicly accessible locations.

(*Source:* http:// government.wikia.com/wiki/Case_to_ban_EVM)

Annexure 6.1

Lacunae in Electronic Voting Process

1. Lacunae in Private Databases

- The ECI does not have a CIO to design, oversee and certify the information at every stage of the process.
- It appears therefore that several independent vendors and agencies manage the process of maintaining the private databases that store the various database tables including constituency, polling centre and candidate information.
- This makes the entire digital information of the ECI open to question in terms of its authenticity, interpretation and fidelity.
- The ECI does not have a Chief Security Officer to design, oversee and certify the security of any electronic processes, there appears no process to ensure overall security of the entire information network.
- Unlike the names of the DEO and Observers, the ECI does not appear to make public the names and contact details of the organizations and individuals involved in creating, maintaining and archiving the databases.
- The ECI does not have any technical process overview that includes a system diagram of the network architecture particularly highlighting the locations of the routers, switches and security firewalls.
- This makes the entire process of collecting, storing and reading digital information of the ECI open to question in terms of its security, integrity and fidelity.
- There appears no audit process from a third party security auditor obtained prior to, during and after an election certifying the network, systems, database and application security.
- There appears no regular reporting of inspections of the log file of the database server as well as the routers / switches / firewalls that provide access to the machine(s).

- This makes the entire digital information a matter of faith on the honesty and integrity of the people, organizations and processes that manage and control parts of the whole. This is obviously not a sufficient basis to trust the information.

2. Lacunae in Public Databases

- There are too many Universal Resource Locators (URLs) on which the entire election process is run: http://eci.nic.in, http://eciresults.nic.in, individual state CEO sites, various District Collectorate websites.
- This results in too many versions of the same public information-for example voters lists, candidate lists, results as well as instructions for candidates and agents.
- The authenticity of any site is not certified and there is no way to resolve the authentic version in case of discrepancy of information on different locations.
- The source of the public data accessible on various parts of the ECI website are unspecified. For example the data of candidates listed on http://eci.nic.in/candidateinfo/frmcandidate.aspx including the downloadable excel spreadsheet do not specify where or how the information got there in the first place, its authenticity or contents.
- There is no way to access any daily archives of the data (assuming they are maintained) making it difficult to allow public audit and transparency of the way information changes on the site.
- There are no clarifications provided on the website or otherwise of any coding of data as for example existed on the entire spreadsheet on Candidate Information between 6th May and 15th May.
- There is no clarification to those querying or publicly about the presence of votes polled in a coded form in the same spreadsheet between the same dates.
- This is a serious breach of trust of the vital information of the election process.
- There is no consistency of update of information or any timetable to the effect: the result data is not accessible on the location displaying candidate information and the spreadsheet that had the votes polled information in coded form after election was

completed in phase 1, 2 and 3 but before the elections happened in phase 4 and 5.

- There is no public list of the names and contact details of the organizations and individuals involved in creating, maintaining and archiving the website and public databases. This is as important as saying who the observer and returning officers are.
- This makes all public information provided by the ECI questionable in terms of its source, date and authenticity.

3. Lacunae in EVM

- The process followed to programme the ballot units to various candidates names and map the votes to a data-store on the control unit is not publicly documented. The names of officials doing this mapping are not public. This is critical as this is amongst the important ways to ensure the vote to a candidate actually gets counted for the same candidate.
- The data-structure used to store the votes polled on the control units are not part of public domain information. How is every vote stored and what information is associated with each vote to be able to count it or even audit it if needed?
- The source-code and the pseudo-code of the programmes used to read the data-structure to display the votes are not part of public domain. This is a crucial part of the EVM as it actually can maintain the fidelity of votes. There is no way to know if this process was not compromised by reading or reporting alternate numbers than the actual votes polled.
- There is a lot of speculation about the version of EVM that was used at every polling centre. Different versions have been reported to have ability to store different information with the votes (e.g., time stamp). It is not what is altered in the EVM when such upgrades occur (hardware, software, memory). There is no information on how the program that reads the votes is upgraded after such changes. This casts a shadow on the veracity of the machines ability to certify if what-it-says is what-it-does.
- There are no publicly declared software or hardware that ensures the data-structures that store the vote information cannot be accessed, read or written except by "authorized" software. This

means anyone who can generate software that can access the data-structure will be able to read or write to it.

- Since it is unclear how the data-structure changes with an "up-grade" of the EVM, it could still be written onto by programmes that can gain access to it.
- There are almost a million EVMs. There is no publicly documented way used to ensure all EVMs confirm to standard specifications only.
- The names and contact details of the organizations involved in programming the ballot units to candidate names are not public.
- The names and contact details of the organizations involved in programming the control units to read candidate names are not public.
- There is no documentation of any other than the operational layer (use of the EVM) security and audit that can guarantee that this transfer, storage and reading of data is secure or has high fidelity.
- There are no known controls in the software that can certify that the votes are those cast from the "ballot unit" and not from other software or hardware sources. There are no controls can certify that they have not been transformed in transmission or reading.
- There is no clarification from the ECI about the "coded spreadsheets". It is both possible and plausible that the data was coded to write onto the data structure of the EVM.
- There is no known digital database of "unit" wise votes is maintained to identify the unique votes read off each "unit".
- This makes the votes "polled" as read from the EVM completely a matter of trust in the people, organizations and processes and is not verifiable or auditable by the voters themselves or even at an aggregate level by analysts, candidates or independent auditors. This jeopardizes the very basis of democratic transparency.

4. Lacunae in Tracking Votes

- There is no electronic mechanism to track a vote to a unique polling centre and EVM. This makes it difficult to audit any vote and certify its genuineness.
- The process of randomization of EVM distribution is manual and not truly random. The EVMs assigned to a DEO are known.

- The EVM cannot store information about the polling centre it was deployed and can easily be substituted elsewhere.
- In case of discrepancy of the serial numbers that are manually recorded it is solely the discretion of the RO to decide if malpractice has occurred or clerical error has occurred.
- The EVM cannot store any record of the actual candidate or party whose votes are stored. It only has counters in memory locations that are manually mapped to a candidate.
- These facts make vulnerable the ability of tracking the votes as well as certifying them down to the polling booth and candidate by a third party audit process.

5. Secrecy about Process

- The ECI has not made the processes and operations that affect these questions public. These are questions that affect the very fabric of democracy and have nothing to do with the political process of voting.
- The ECI has not clarified on queries raised by various people.
- Copies of all filled Form 17C, 20 to be provided are not made public.
- This makes the entire democratic process vulnerable to mistrust and questioning. It gives rise to speculation and loss of faith in the ECI.

6. Reforms

- There is currently no agenda to devise alternative mechanisms to allow electronic voting to distinguish human votes (those cast by people through voting) from machine votes (those cast by software or hardware malfunction or compromise).
- No "Democracy Test" has been designed or used by the ECI that will help certify that the democratic process is not compromised in any of the technology steps and the votes that count are people votes.
- Currently there is no reform agenda to build a "vote bank" that would store the votes of every voter, available for recall or transfer that could help voters to ensure their vote continues to be counted- like the online banking enabling account holders to

deposit, withdraw or transfer money and also know their money still counts.

- This makes the entire election process remain a "black-box" to the voter. There is no mechanism to enhance democracy and the voters right to franchise, there is only automation that can hijack the right to franchise. This is a very serious vulnerability in ensuring democracy and its evolution will move in the right direction.

(*Source:* http:// government.wikia.com/wiki/EVM_Annexure_I)

Annexure 6.2

Artefacts and Data that Point to Failures in Ensuring Transparency, Verifiability and Fidelity of the Process in the 2009 Lok Sabha Elections

1. Private Database

- The data in the public databases is a result of the private databases maintained by the ECI. The strange observations noted in public databases implies failure to ensure security of the private databases.

2. Public Database

- Candidate information files downloaded on 6th May 2009, 7th May 2009, 11th May 2009 from the downloadable Candidate AC file at (http:// eci.nic.in/candidateinfo/frmcandidate.aspx). On each of these days the downloaded file has coded candidate names, party names and votes polled data for all 8070 candidates in all phases of elections including phase 4 and 5 where voting is yet to happen.
- The "votes polled" data in the CandidateAC file downloaded on the three days is different.
- The CandidateAC file containing candidate information downloaded on 16th May 2009, 19th May 2009, 20th May 2009 and 22nd May 2009 till date have encoded candidate names, party names and no votes polled.
- There is no explanation provided by the ECI about the coding that took place for a few days.
- Election results presented on a different site: (http://ecireults.nic.in) on 17th May 2009 in the form of a PDF file declaring the winners only.
- Results also made available on http:eci.nic.in/results on the 31st May 2009.

- "All Candidates Votes Polled" file available from 3rd June 2009 at (http://ec.nic.in/Analysis) but the Candidate AC files are not updated. This file is of a different structure and size than the Candidate AC files downloaded from (http://eci.nic.in/candid ateinfo/frmcandidate.aspx) between the 6th of May to date.
- Rajasthan is a state which BJP had let loose and fell in the hands of the Congress, 7,71,160 Ajmer, 7,62,694 Alwar, 7,68,753 Banswara, 7,85,199 Barmer, 5,60,691 Bharatpur, 7,54,457 Bhilwara, 5,69,804 Bikaner, 7,94,800 Chittorgarh, 8,02,467 Churu, 8,41,355 Dausa, 909629 Ganganagar, 8,12,901 Jaipur, 6,86,585 Jaipur Rural, 5,77,606 Jalore, 8,71,864 Jhalawar-Baran, 6,01,887 Jhunjhunu, 6,81,401 Jodhpur, 4,87,118 Karouli-Dholpur, 6,81,806 Kota, 6,09,879 Nagaur, 7,22,870 Pali, 5,90,981 Rajsamand, 7,25,265 Sikar, 8,02,111 Tonk — Sawai Madhopur, 7,58,240 Udaipur or 17,93,1523 Total. As my previous posts This time too I relayed upon the election commissions document and data. The poll percentage document gives the number of electors and the number of people participated in the election process (http://eci.nic.in/press/Poll_Percentage_GE2009.pdf). The next details I gave above is compiled from the results published in election commissions site (http://eci.nic.in/results/frm PCWise Result.aspx). Here comes the difference 17,93,1523 — 17,90, 6126 = 25,397 votes (twenty five thousand three hundred and ninety seven).
- Re: Tamil Nadu Results — Some shocking Revelations by Shreesmani on Thursday 28 May 2009 5:37 p.m. The Lok Sabha results. The Files used for verification (http://eci.nic.in/press/ Poll_Percentage_GE2009.pdf) and (http://eci.nic.in/press/ data_ phaseV.pdf). There are some conflicting details (I'll give it to you below). No. of Electors 58,87,628 Before polls (http://eci. nic.in/press/data_phaseV.pdf). No. of Electors 57,94,398. After Results (http://eci.nic.in/press/Poll_Percentage_GE2009.pdf). How did it drop, where did the 93230 Electors go? Just in a weeks time !!! Which one should we believe? Both the documents are authentic because both are downloaded from election commission website. When referring the (http://eci.nic.in/press /PollPercentageGE2009.pdf) (verify clearly). Total votes polled

is in the 5th phase is 31,59,889 but the total no of votes polled in all phases is 31,26,758 which has the negative difference of 13,297 (total votes is less than the votes of 5th phase), even a 2 std student could figure the error.

- (In Uttaranchal the polls are conducted only in the 5th phase). Now as per the election commission total no. of votes polled is (1.) 31,59,889 (2.) 31,26,758. When adding the total no. of votes each contestant from each constituency we get (1.) 3,14,0045 the differences will be any way 19,844 or "-13,287" (yes its a negative number which nobody can believe.) I don't know which one to believe, any one from this forum or the moderator please explain. 4,80,757 Almora, 5,33,568 Garhwal, 7,87,963 Hardwar, 7,53,682 Nanital-Udhamsingh Nagar, 5,84,075 Tehri Garhwal, 3,14,0045 Total.

(*Source:* http://lkadvani.in/forum/viewtopic.php?f=2&t=5743&st- art=30)

3. EVM

- Cases of candidates who have a stronghold in a polling centre getting only 0-5 votes: (please list such examples)
- Polling centres reporting more votes than voters: (please list such examples)
- EVMs not reading during counting (please list such examples with the AC-PC nos. as well as the machine serial numbers of the EVMs)

4. Tracking Votes

- List the exit polls and results for each constituency
- List a few candidates analysis of the results based on their voters demography showing illogical or inconsistent traits
- List the Assembly and Parliamentary traits that contradict each other

5. Secrecy

- ECI was alerted on the 6th of May 2009 about the candidate information files downloaded from its website having coded information including votes polled for all candidates — no response from the ECI and the files continued to have coded information that changed on the three days it was downloaded.

- The ECI was reminded of the previous alert and requested to clarify the coding on the 30th of May 2008. There is no acknowledgement or response from the ECI.
- List other requests filed by various parties for information (e.g. info request filed by Mallika Sarabhai).

6. Reforms

- List here statements from the CEC on the reforms that point out that the reforms process is not an open and public process and is not reforming technology.

(*Source:* http://government.wikia.com/wiki/ EVM_Annexure_II)

Annexure 6.3

Inability to Distinguish Human Votes from Machine Votes

The votes cast by the voters are not *tagged or signed* in any way to indicate that they belong to a unique voter. They are simply used to increment a counter.

Imagine if you cannot track money in the bank account as money deposited through a source. If someone were to gain access to the counter on the banks computers called "your account" it would be possible for them to add unlimited money or have whatever you deposited vanish without any ability to track it or have a third party audit the banks books. That is why the principle of leaving a transaction trail is important in any audit process.

Now imagine a candidates "account" on the EVM. Unless there is a mechanism to track every transaction as an inflow or outflow of votes from a legitimate source, there is no transaction trail and no ability to audit the actual vote balance in the candidates account. The votes cast by humans are completely indistinguishable from any votes cast by a "Trojan" software or hardware.

This constitutes as a very serious design lapse on EVMs and renders them completely useless as a transparent, clean and hi-fidelity machines to be responsible for the democratic process and controlling trillions of rupee spending, multitude of laws imposed on people and huge tax and debt burdens built up for every individual in the country. Would you trust your money with a bank that cannot track transactions to your account?

Imagine when you deposit money to your account you hand it over without an acknowledgement about your transaction specifying which account you deposited it to. Would you then be able to claim, in case of dispute, that you had deposited money into that account?

Now when you deposit a vote to your candidate, do you get any acknowledgement about your deposit that you can use in case of dispute? Further is there any way for you to check out later if your vote did indeed count? Would you trust your money with a bank that does not provide you a passbook or a statement of your deposits and withdrawals? What makes you trust the EVM that writes your blank check to trillions of rupees and your liberty to live your life in your country?

Now imagine your bank reporting different number of depositors in different statements as well as different deposits of money. How comfortable does that make you about your bank, its processes to manage your money and the claims it makes about the safety, and inability of fraudsters to hack, your deposits?

Now our crucial vote bank fails not just to track depositors, the voters, but also the deposits, the votes! Note the number of voters reported by the ECI in different public databases for the 2009 elections differs by anything between 25,72,993 to 28,99,538 voters. The number of votes reported in different public databases differs by at least 1,722 votes. Do please audit the public databases down to each constituency yourself to confirm to yourself the inability of the vote bank to track the votes and voters. Evidently the ECI has little control of its databases. Evidently the ECI needs much more reform in its technology than just the EVM.

Isn't it time we did not bank democracy with unaccountable vote banks?

(*Source:* http:// government.wikia.com/wiki/EVM_Annexure_III)

Annexure 6.4

Ability to Create Machine Votes in a Multitude of Ways

1. About 2,00,000 EVMs were acquired in January 2009 with modified programmes (for date / time stamping); thus two types of EVMs were used, the old units without date / time stamping (about 11 lakh of them) and the rest with the new "improvised" feature claimed by BEL, the company which made the program change.
2. With this programme change, an entry programme is provided for any programmer to modify the PROM (Programmable Read Only memory) since time is determined outside of the balloting unit and thus beyond the control of the EVM system.
3. A selective rigging of these 2,00,000 EVMs would be adequate to impact the results in about 70 constituencies (say, those won in UP by Congress, those lost by opposition in Tamil Nadu or Uttarakhand or Punjab, those won by BJD in Orissa). A remote control was possible to record, say, four votes for the desired party for every vote polled by any opposing party.
4 EC had also lost control over the EVM system because BEL, ECI contracted to make the systems had subcontracted the work to private contractors. No credible claims have been made by CEC about the systems audit conducted on the acquired EVMs and during the electoral process. CEC has clearly goofed up relying upon a scrappy Indiresan Committee report (just compare it with the professionalism with which system auditors audited the EVMs in USA).
5. India's e-elections rigged? Saturday, 4 July 2009, New Delhi: The Indian Election Commission (EC) could be sitting on a major election-rigging scandal, following a presentation on Friday showing how the software used in the electronic voting machines (EVMs) can be manipulated. Omesh Saigal, an engineering

graduate and former Delhi chief secretary, stunned the EC with a presentation showing that the software used in the EVMs can be manipulated to favour a particular party or candidate. Following the presentation, Chief Election Commissioner (CEC) Navin Chawla ordered an inquiry into the possibility of such rigging during the recently concluded elections in India and Indian-held Kashmir (IHK). Deputy Election Commissioner Balakrishnan was asked to conduct the inquiry on the basis of a report handed over by Saigal to the CEC, along with the software he had developed to show how the e-voting machines could be rigged. Saigal, who is an Indian Institute of Technology (IIT), New Delhi alumni, demanded an urgent check of the programme that runs the EVMs used in elections since 2004. The demonstration showed that after just keying in a certain code, the EVMs put every fifth vote in favour of a certain candidate. In his letter to the CEC, Saigal alleged that the EVM software had not been checked by the EC since the machines were manufactured more than 6 to 7 years ago. He argued that the EC merely relied on the certificates provided by the manufacturers, the government-run Bharat Electronics Limited (BEL) and Electronics Corporation of India Limited (ECIL). He alleged that the two firms had subcontracted private parties who actually provided the certificates.
(*Source:* http//www.dailytimes.com)

6. Rigging possible through EVMs: Ex-bureaucrat Maneesh Chhibber posted online: Friday, 03 July 2009 at 0047 hrs New Delhi: A former civil servant has raised questions about the claims by the Election Commission of India (ECI) that the electronic voting machines (EVMs) can't be rigged or hacked. Omesh Saigal, who has served as Chief Secretary of Delhi and retired as Secretary to Government of India, had written to Chief Election Commissioner Navin Chawla, claiming that a detailed study conducted by him with the help of information technology experts had shown that rigging of EVMs is "possible and plausible". When contacted, Saigal told *The Indian Express* that he met Chawla on Wednesday to explain the methodology adopted by him for the study and its results. "It is an important issue as the fate of this country's democratic set-up hinges on the fairness of the elec-

tions. There shouldn't be an iota of doubt about the same," he said. Saigal also cited a study conducted by the Johns Hopkins University and Rice University, which established that if one gets to know the source code of an EVM, it is possible for a single person to cast unlimited ballots without detection. "To see if a similar fraud could be done in India, on my request a young programmer wrote a very simple programme which could skew the result if a pre-programmed code number was keyed in. A mock poll showed that every 5th vote after the first 10 would go in favour of a particular candidate. This poll was conducted in the presence of some eminent people, whose names have also been sent to the CEC. I intend to conduct this poll before the EC," Saigal said.

(*Source:* http:// www.indianexpress.com/story-print/484802/)

7. Can electronic voting machine subvert elections in India?

   (*Source:* http://rajeev.posterous.com/can-electronic-voting-machines-subvert-electi)

8. Elections be rigged through EVMs? From Our Delhi Bureau, New Delhi.

   Chief Election Commissioner Navin Chawla is sitting over a major scandal of a possible massive rigging of elections by manipulation of software of the Electronic Voting Machines (EVMs). But for the charge levelled by a former Delhi chief secretary five years senior to him in the IAS cadre, Chawla would have rejected such claims of rigging. Omesh Saigal, a 1964 batch IAS officer of the Union Territory, stunned him with a presentation to force him to order an inquiry into any possibility of such a rigging. Chawla is himself a Union Territory cadre IAS of 1969 batch. Deputy Election Commissioner Balakrishnan has been asked to conduct the inquiry on the basis of a report handed over by Saigal to the CEC, with a software he got developed to show how the elections can be rigged. Saigal, who is an IIT alumni, has demanded an urgent check of the programme that runs the EVMs used in elections since 2004. He demonstrated with his software that its manipulation ensured that one has to just key in a certain code number and that will ensure every fifth vote cast in a particular polling booth goes in favour of a certain candidate.

He got interested to find out truth about a score of news reports in Press and on the net about candidates and parties expressing suspicion about the EVMs not recording the votes correctly as he wanted to ascertain whether these EVMs meet the standard of national integrity or safeguards the sanctity of the democracy. In his letter to the CEC, Saigal alleged that the software written onto the EVMs has never been checked by the Election Commission ever since these machines were manufactured more than 6-7 years back. His contention is that the EC merely relied on the certificates supplied by the manufacturers, the government-run BEL and ECIL. He alleged that these government firms had sub-contracted private parties who actually provided these certificates. "A public software audit of these machines from time to time, especially after and before an election, was a must to retain the credibility of the elections," Saigal affirmed, demanding that for the sake of transparency names and ownerships of these private companies must be disclosed as also the details of the factories where they were actually manufactured. The records retained in the factories must also be immediately taken over by the Commission to prevent any tampering and to facilitate an audit, he said. He also pointed out how, after nearly two years of deliberation, Germany's Supreme Court ruled last March that e-voting was unconstitutional because the average citizen could not be expected to understand the exact steps involved in the recording and tallying of votes. Earlier, Ireland had given up e-voting for similar reasons. In the US too, after considerable controversy the Federal Election Commission has come up in 2005 with detailed voting system guidelines which run into more than 400 pages. Saigal said it is noteworthy that not any of the safeguards mentioned in these guidelines is in place in India. Saigal said he had gone into all the safeguards built into the e-voting system in India with the help of former colleagues and IT experts and finds it both "possible and plausible" to rig these machines and get a crooked result. He says if the credibility of the electoral process is to be ensured, pre- and post-election checks of the software now fused onto the chips of the EVMs is a must. It is not that all the 10 lakh and odd machines used in the poll need to be checked. If we take only those booths where one of the candidates has received 75 per cent of the votes and in constituencies where the margin of the winner is less than 15,000, not more than 7,000-odd machines will need to be checked. Saigal argues in his report that "if we cannot do this we must revert to the paper ballot." The need for a fair, free and transparent polling system transcends any reasons anyone may have to the contrary, he added. Saigal says he organised a mock poll on a laptop to demonstrate how the results can be skewed by inserting a numerical code which is so simple. Just press F2, followed by the number of the favoured candidate. The demo showed that this code can be keyed in at any stage, even at the time of the poll by any voter. Those who attended the mock exercise included Ms. Asa Das, retired Secretary, Government of India, K. F. Fabian, retired IFS officer and former ambassador, Ravi Kathpalia, ex-controller general of accounts, and S. K. Agnihotri and Dr. Krishan Saigal, retired former chief secretaries of Assam. Saigal says at first glance, it does appear that there are adequate safeguards in place, as is mentioned in the FAQs on the Election Commission website, Returning Officers manual and details given in the website of the manufacturer, BEL. He, however, asserts in his letter to CEC that there are huge gaps in the safeguards. "Take the assurance of the manufacturer that "Programme codes once written and fused in this OTPROM (One Time Programmable Read Only Memory) cannot be read back or altered by anyone including the manufacturer". Does this mean that even the Election Commission, when it received the machines, did not check and has not checked since whether the programme fused in by the manufacturer did not have a secret code as a string like the one that we have prepared, Saigal asked. "If, as it seems, the EC is relying on the certificate given by the manufacturer, we have no protection whatsoever against the manufacturer itself preparing a programme like the one prepared by the undersigned and fusing it onto the chip / circuit board," he affirms. Once the election process begins, the EC claims total transparency in all its actions. First of all the machines are taken out of storage and sent to the Districts. Thereafter, according to a Government of India website, ". . . these machines are checked only by the engineers of the two PSUs before each election . . . ." Saigal says it is not clear what this "checking" is all about and whether these "engineers" are under the control of the EC. They use some "equipment" to prepare the machine by removing the result of the previous election and do not tamper or check the software chip in any way, the EC claims. "If this is all they do, why they need to come at all: surely the result could be deleted by simply pressing a button, which any official of EC could do! It is like you and me calling on Microsoft engineers to come in every time we need to permanently delete some programme from our desktops!" The EC claims that among the safeguards is the fact that randomisation is done at many levels so that it is impossible to find out which particular machine will go to which particular booth. Moreover, the order in which candidates are going to be listed in the electoral roll is known only a few days before the poll; so it is not possible for someone to rig the EVMs software to favour a particular candidate. Saigal, however, contests it. He says it is easy to say that randomisation will be of no help if the software is tricked. As for the fact that order of candidates is decided only a few days before the poll, with a specially prepared software the poll can be rigged at the time of the poll by any voter, he points out. "No, these safeguards are mere cosmetics; what we really need is a fool-proof method of checking whether the software in any / all machines has been corrupted through lapse of time or deliberate tampering or was so corrupted in the first place," the former Delhi chief secretary added. Saturday, July 04, 2009 New Delhi: The Indian Election Commission (EC) could be sitting on a major election-rigging scandal, following a presentation on Friday showing how the software used in the electronic voting machines (EVMs) can be manipulated. Omesh Saigal, an engineering graduate and former Delhi chief secretary, stunned the EC with a presentation showing that the software used in the EVMs can be manipulated to favour a particular party or candidate. Following the presentation, Chief Election Commissioner (CEC) Navin Chawla ordered an inquiry into the possibility of such rigging during the recently concluded elections in India and

Indian-held Kashmir (IHK). Deputy Election Commissioner Balakrishnan was asked to conduct the inquiry on the basis of a report handed over by Saigal to the CEC, along with the software he had developed to show how the e-voting machines could be rigged. Saigal, who is an Indian Institute of Technology (IIT), New Delhi alumni, demanded an urgent check of the programme that runs the EVMs used in elections since 2004. The demonstration showed that after just keying in a certain code, the EVMs put every fifth vote in favour of a certain candidate. In his letter to the CEC, Saigal alleged that the EVM software had not been checked by the EC since the machines were manufactured more than 6 to 7 years ago. He argued that the EC merely relied on the certificates provided by the manufacturers, the government-run Bharat Electronics Limited (BEL) and Electronics Corporation of India Limited (ECIL). He alleged that the two firms had subcontracted private parties who actually provided the certificates.

(*Source:* http://www.dailytimes.com.pk/default.asp?page=2009\074\story_4-7-2 009_ pg7_4)

See also:

- http://indianrealist.wordpress.com/2009/05/30/the-evm-fixing/
- http://jayasreesaranathan.blogspot.com/2009_05_01_archive. (html http://government.wikia.com/wiki/EVM_Annexure_IV).

Annexure 6.5

Grounds for Rejection of EVMs in Other Countries

Many countries have banned the use of electronic voting machines on different grounds. Interested readers can obtain detailed information from the following sources:

- http://warrenslocum.blogspot.com/2009/03/german-high-court-bans-e-voting-system.html
- http://www.bradblog.com/?p=6961
- http://www.concurringopinions.com/archives/2009/03/auf_wiedersehen.html
- http://www.bbvforums.org/forums/messages/77776/79587.html

See also:

- http://en.wikipedia.org/wiki/Federal_Constitutional_Court_of_Germany
- http://www.economist.com/displayStory.cfm?story_id=13376204
- http://www.bradblog.com/?cat=73
  http://government.wikia.com/wiki/EVM_Annexure_V.

Annexure 6.6

Failure of the Election Commission of India to Address the Concerns Raised about EVMs

1. Case for Election Reforms

The Election Commission must adapt clear norms to certify a democratic election process. Any programme on election reforms must therefore ensure:

- *The election is transparent*: no election is transparent if it does not provide for independent third party audits by anyone or uses closed standards and technologies to manage any part of the process.
- *The election is honest*: no election is honest or accountable if it denies (or requires court interventions or RTI applications for) a receipt to each voter and a poll-booth wise statement of voters, votes cast and votes received by each candidate to the public.
- *The election is fair*: no election is fair if it denies the right to track ones vote at least throughout the tenure of the elected body (if not for life).
- *The election is open*: no election is open unless it allows everyone the possibility to exercise franchise in a multitude of ways (by paper, by mobile, by ATM, by internet, by EVM, etc.) from a multitude of locations (anywhere in the world).
- *The election is people* centered: no election is people centered unless it allows the people a continued right and ability to shift their vote to an alternate candidate any time in the tenure of the elected body (or better for life).
- *The election must be a level-playing field*: no election is level-field unless it eliminates provides each candidate an identical opportunity to reach out to the community.

- *The election must be public*: no election is public unless it satisfies transparency, honesty, fairness, openness, is people centered and provides a level field.

By corollary an election fraud would repeatedly deny one or more of these.

(Soruce: http:// government.wikia.com/wiki/Requirements_from_the_ECI)

Elections to the Lok Sabha happened in India in April and May 2009. The data of various candidates could be obtained from the Election Commission of India's website. In order to track the elections and upload candidate and constituency information onto this wiki, we accessed this website and regularly downloaded the CandidateAC file from there:

- The first file was containing the list of candidates was obtained on 16th April 2009 from the Election Commission of India and was subsequently used to upload information onto wiki pages. You can download this version of the file from here. It is named: CandidateAC.xls Since the election was conducted in phases additional information had to be uploaded as it became available. On the 24th April 2009 we obtained an updated version of this file from the second list became available and the wiki pages were uploaded. You can obtain a copy of this file from here. It is named: CandidateAC-1.xls
- From the 6th of May, before the counting began or polling was complete, through the 15th of May the candidate information was incomprehensible as along with the votes polled data for all the candidates it appeared in "coded form" (You can download the various versions of the file under sequential names at the following locations: 6th May: CandidateAC-2.xls, Candidate AC-3.xls, 7th May: CandidateAC-4.xls,11th May: Candidate AC-5.xls, 15th May: CandidateAC-6.xls).
- The information available on 16th May, CandidateAC-7.xls, is not yet uploaded onto the wiki as votes polled data is not available to date (19th May 2009: CandidateAC-8.xls and 20th May: CandidateAC-9.xls).

This effort has resulted in several questions about the data and information systems of the Election Commission of India. Several people have reviewed this exercise and it has resulted in a case for technology reform of the entire Election Process.

2. Tracking the Elections 2009

Elections were held in 5 phases across India. The last phase of polling was completed on the 13th of May 2009. The counting of votes was to begin on the 16th of May 2009.

The data of various candidates could be obtained from the Election Commission of India's website. In order to track the elections and upload candidate and constituency information onto this wiki, we accessed this website and regularly downloaded the CandidateAC file from there. This spreadsheet had various columns containing information of all candidates including their political affiliations, age, address etc. There was also a column for "votes polled" and some "coding" called "DECODE (FINALISED,' YES', 'FINALISED',)".

By virtue of the Election Rules no votes polled data / exit poll was to be available before the 16th of May 2009, least of all on the Election Commission of India Website.

Unexpected Votes Data in Coded Spreadsheet

The excel spreadsheets on candidate information for all India downloaded from the ECI website between the 6th and 15th of May had "coded" Candidate Names, Party Names and votes polled. Despite repeated queries the ECI has not clarified the meaning of this data. This has resulted in widespread speculation and raised serious questions about the management and integrity of the democratic process.

3. Unclarified Questions

The serious questions being asked include:

Votes Polled?

- What was the coded data in the "votes polled" column in the versions of the spreadsheet downloaded between the 6th and 11th of May?

- Why were the spreadsheets between these dates "coded" all of a sudden?
- If the polling was not even complete how could "votes polled" data be available for all but 47 of the 8071 candidate?
- If EVMs were secure with DEO / district collectors, and elections were not even held in many constituencies, how was the data for 8023 candidates or all but 47 of the 8071 candidates available to the ECI on files downloaded between these dates?

Dummy Data?

- If the data in these files on the 6th was test / dummy data why does it change for some constituencies on the 6th, 7th and 11th May 2009?
- If data in these files was test / dummy data, how does it match the winners in 108 constituencies or 106 according to another analysis?
- If data in these files was test / dummy data, why was it not removed on the 7th after the NIC and ECI were intimated on the 6th? Why was there no explanation from NIC / ECI to date?

What Tests?

- If the data in these files was test / dummy data, what was it testing? Why was this test taking place during the polling period?
- What were the tests, and what were the results of the tests?
- If the data in these files is test / dummy data, why is real data not uploaded in this file to date, especially as it was removed on the 15th of May 2009?
- What tests were these that required only some data to keep changing and others to remain unchanging?
- Is there any way the ECI can distinguish test data from real data?

Incompetence or Intent?

- If the data on the ECI website resulted from pure error, why was it coded?
- If the data resulted from incompetence, is the result data not up in the same file for the same reason?

- If the data resulted from incompetence and these links are meaningful, why have the relevant links and the CandidateAC spreadsheet that contained the data been pulled off the website on July 15th?

Coding?

- What is the field "DECODE (FINALISED, 'YES', 'FINALISED',)" in these files and why does it change over time?

Can You Confirm if Your Vote Counted?

- Is there any mechanism by which the voters can go back and ensure that their vote is still counted? Something similar to going back to the bank and checking that the money is still accounted for?
- Besides a faith in the honesty of officials, integrity of the process and independence of the ECI, is there any other way to establish transparency and trust in an Election conducted by the ECI?
- Is there any test, audit that can certify that votes polled are those polled by the people and not a Trojan Horse or a machine? Like a reverse Turing Test, a Democracy Test?
- How can votes be certified by the ECI to be a true vote of the people of India?

Closed System?

- Is the source code of the entire electronic machinery "open-source"? Why not?
- If Electronic Voting Machines have been banned across the countries for their inability to distinguish between human and machine votes, why are they used in India?

What Reforms Do We Need?

- What is Election Reform needed to ensure Democracy is not only practiced and enhanced but is also auditable?

The Results?

The ECI have uploaded the individual vote data in a different file at a different location. You can compare the data in this file with the votes polled available on the 6th and 11th of May or look at the consolidated data file with some analysis assuming that the "votes polled" data in the earlier versions was not coded.

Unnecessary Confusion

Unfortunately, the ECI is using several different locations and different formats to convey election results:

- An analysis link that has results
- A results page
- A results page on a different URL: eciresults.nic.in
- A press release

This itself is raising questions about the information — Which is the real site? Which is the real data? What is the real ECI source? Why are many locations and formats needed?

If This is a Mistake, Why No Clarifications from the ECI?

On the 6th of May we had asked the ECI to clarify the following:

> "The queries are returning coded names. The spreadsheet is having votes polled for each candidate — Is this test data, a wrong file or actual votes polled?"

We have not yet heard from the ECI so we have sent a reminder on the 31st of May 2009 we have asked the ECI the following:

> "Can you kindly indicate what the data in the CandidateAC downloaded from http://
> eci.nic.in/candidateinfo/frmcandidate.aspx file between the 6th and 15th is? Why is the Final votes polled data not uploaded till date at this location? When do you plan to upload it?"

On the 7th of July 2009 we have sent another more detailed request for clarification.

We have not yet heard from the ECI. The ECI must act urgently to address these issues and restore faith in the democratic process.

Prof. Madhav Nalapat and Dr. Anupam Saraph 11:59, 31 May 2009 (UTC)

(*Source:* http://government.wikia.om/wiki/2009_Lok_Sabha_Data_Questions)

4. Voting Reforms: Options in an Imperfect World

Most voting practices across the world do not issue any receipts. The voter has no way to know if the vote cast was counted for the chosen candidate. There have been many arguments in favour of as well as against the issue of receipts.

A receipt is a confirmation, a proof of counting. It reinforces the value of the vote. It gives every voter the feeling of mattering.

The opponents of receipts have argued that they open up vote commerce: exchange of money for votes. Others have argued that voting process without receipts is also open to proxy by commerce.

In the world of business proxy voting is both common and legitimate as is the use of this system by lobbyists and interest groups to take over companies or change their directions. The compulsions of the voter or the proxy holder may be diverse, but the common equation is the value of the vote. A proxy holder looks for controlling return on investment — the voter for an advanced dividend for giving up the right to choosing the management. Proxy is sustained as long at it results in the company can continue to grow and yield return-on-investment to the proxy owner as well as serve a better dividend today than the dividend from the better governance as a result of a different choice. As far as the latter is concerned, it is self-fulfilling to prefer proxy. Dividend payments upfront result in the exclusion of future dividends for the voter group that has given up its right to a future dividend. Therefore the choice of upfront dividends seems always better than otherwise.

A nation elects its government for the dividends its citizens may receive from the management by the new "board". If the use of proxy serves to be more beneficial to the voters than the management by a government, it may well be the lesser evil to voting without receipts.

Transaction Trail

In a voting process a transaction trail would require each vote be identified with the voter, location and time. This trail would ensure that every vote can be tracked to the source. If there is a transaction trail, it becomes impossible to add or remove votes that do not come from a voter, a location and during a legitimate period.

Those against a transaction trail argue of its making the ballot free of secrecy. Those for the trail argue about the inability to ensure legitimate votes from illegitimate ones as those may be cast by any compromise of the polling process.

Whatever the merits of secrecy, it certainly fails to enthuse confidence about the voting process and in voter based democracy. What is the difference between the acts of a dictator and a secretly elected ruler? Whatever but a leap of faith can stand witness to the democratic election of the ruler?

Rabindranath Tagore dreamt of a land where the mind is without fear and the head held high — will a secret democracy ever lead us into this world where everyone can walk fearlessly and honourably with the choices they make about the way they may be ruled?

It is interesting that a secret Sunday confession does not rid the world of sinners. Would a Sunday of public celebration of virtues make the world a better place?

Auditability

Although voting is a blank cheque to trillions of rupees of spending, a license to control the civil liberty in a country, a framework that pushes thousands of decisions to every citizen it is the most unauditable process in a country. There is no way anyone can verify the claims of those in control of the voting process and certify them to be true and correct. There is no way that anyone can follow the transactions of voting and certify that a candidate did indeed get as many votes as counted from legitimate sources. There is no way anyone can certify that the vote cast by anyone actually ended up for the candidate for whom it was destined. There is no way anyone can certify that every voter counted at the polling booth was actually the one who was entitled to vote.

Arguably the process of audit requires a transaction trail. A publicly auditable process would require a public access to the trail. In an age of open-source it is surprising that we opt for closed-audit systems in the name of secrecy.

Ease of Voting

The most that has happened to ease elections is an Electronic Voting Machine. There is little simplification, transparency and security that is built into the system.

Why cannot elections happen at ATMs in banks across the country over a specified week in the year? Why can voters not visit the ATM to change their vote — or at least view it as many times as they like over the period of the election? Imagine the value of exchanging the receipt for money if that were possible!

Or imagine the mobile being the sign-in with a pin to vote over an election week, as many times as you wish? What an idea sirji? Why not vote not just for the representative but also for key bills brought before the legislative and parliamentary bodies? What use is technology if it cannot widen the base of voting?

Secrecy

They say secrecy is the difference between a marriage and an affair. Hold anything secret and even a RTI may not be able to get you justice. The hallmark of civilization is when dissenters can walk fearlessly in a world of pluralism. Are we that far away from a civilized society?

The men of character in every civilization rarely hid their true opinions behind secret ballot or diplomatic guile. No land of secret decisions ever yielded a world without fear. Certainly not one where you may hold your head high. Such a land cannot have free knowledge, there would be a price for every information.

To create a honest and trusting society we must cast secrecy of voting to history, teach everyone to be proud to stand to their choice and even welcome dissent.

Election reform can yield us the world Tagore dreamt about — it can leapfrog the world's biggest democracy to being the world's greatest nation. Let us embark on a journey to build our nation together. Let us celebrate the diversity of our votes!

References

(http:// www.techdirt.com/articles/20080304/134146430.shtml

(http://people.csail.mit.edu/rivest/Rivest-ElectronicVoting.pdfhttp:// uchicagolaw.typepad.com/faculty/2008/02/voting-machines.html)

(http://www.democraticunderground.com/discuss/duboard.php?az= view_all&address=104x833897)

(http://www.bmeacham.com/evote/EvotingUseCase_v2.htm)

(http://www.pbs.org/cringely/pulpit/2003/pulpit_20031204_000794.html)

(http://www.pbs.org/cringely/pulpit/2003/pulpit_20031211_000795.html)

(http://www.pbs.org/cringely/pulpit/2004/pulpit_20040311_000805.html)

(http://edition.cnn.com/2004/ALLPOLITICS/03/10/voting/)

(http://www.verifiedvotingfoundation.org/article.php?id=6422)

(http://www.votehere.com/old/audittraildre.php)

(http://www.techdirt.com/articles/20070820/113332.shtml)

(http://whatreallyhappened.com/WRHARTICLES/usa_vote_facts.html)

(http://government.wikia.com/wiki/Voting_Reforms:_Options_in_an_imperfect_world)

5. Letter to ECI Officials on Coded Data on the ECI Website

7 July 2009

Gentlemen

- Beginning 16th April 2009 we have obtained a list of candidate: for analysis of the elections from the CandidateAC.xls from you website at the Election Commission of India. Since this list wa being updated (as candidates were being added) we kep downloading the newer versions of the file.
- From the 6th of May through the 15th of May the candidate infoı mation was unavailable as it appeared in "coded form" along wit

"coded" candidate performance data (6th May: CandidateAC-2.xls, CandidateAC-3.xls, 7th May: CandidateAC-4.xls,11th May: CandidateAC-5.xls, 15th May: CandidateAC-6.xls).

- On the 6 May itself we alerted the NIC / ECI to the availability of this "coded" spreadsheet. It continued to be available till the 15th of May. We requested clarification about the coded nature of the files, but as yet, we do not have your clarification of the facts. In a democratic polity, silence results in speculation, which may give rise to disturbing interpretations, as seems to be taking place now.
- The information available on 16th May, CandidateAC-7.xls, till today does not yet have the votes polled data. This has further fuelled speculation. Belief in the inviolability of the vote is at the core of democracy, and any system of enumeration needs to ensure that such a belief is well-founded. It cannot be based purely on faith and trust in the myriad individuals carrying out the processes, but on a system that ensures transparency and accountability.
- On the 4th and 5th of July various sections of the Press reported Mr Saigal, former CS of Delhi, demonstrated the introduction of Trojan Horses into the EVM (http://news.rediff.com/report/2009/jul/04/was-election-2009-rigged.htm,http://www.dailytimes.com.pk/default.asp?page=2009\07\04\story_4-7-2009_pg7_4and http://www.indianexpress.com/story-print/484802/). Add to that the blogger Senthil Raja's (http://psenthilraja.wordpress.com/2010/08/29/omesh-saigals-letter-to-pm-on-evm-hacking/) scenarioof Trojan Horses, wireless chips in EVM and Excel spreadsheet are raising questions about the reliability of the election process, as carried out recently.
- The CEC has called for a healthy debate on EVMs. This is welcome, and we as citizens have put together various questions about the case against EVMs and need for technology reforms at the ECI at (http://government.wikia.com/wiki/Case_to_ban_EVM) as a part of this debate.

We request you to please clarify the coded spreadsheets that were downloadable from the ECI site. We would request that we be told why the results have not been uploaded on to the same spreadsheet.

We also request you to please ensure that the ECI correct and update the various questions raised about the election process in the various wiki pages listed here. The ECI has a heavy responsibility to ensure that that the peoples trust in democracy is alive and healthy, because of a foolproof system for recording the precious vote of each citizen who exercises her or his choice during the elections

With best wishes,
Sincerely,

Prof Madhav Nalapat and Dr. Anupam Saraph

(*Source:* http://government.wikia.com/wiki/Coded_data_on_ECI_ website)

6. Minutes Mailed to ECI

Gentlemen

On the 7th of August 2009, at the request of Kirit Somayia, Dr Anupam Saraph visited the ECI along with several technology experts. Security Expert Vijay Mukhi pointed out that the ECI should change its language that EVMs cannot be hacked as there is no technology that is hack proof. He also pointed out several holes in the EVM that can be used to compromise an EVM. Kirit Somayia highlighted the need to keep making improvements in the election process by seeking open and inclusive dialog with all stake-holders. He also highlighted the lack of audit of the votes or voters, as would exist in the finance profession. He asked the ECI to immediately switch to paper trail to EVMs.

Here is the summary of the points Dr. Anupam Saraph raised with the ECI:

1. Trust in EVMs: When people transact on an ATM and trust the machine in the wall with their hard earned money, the machine does NOT require any "observers", micro-observers", "agents of the bank", "agents of the Reserve Bank of India", "Representatives of the Account holder", etc. along with seals fixed on the machine by various persons, countersigned by others on specially printed paper from Nasik to build trust. Unfortunately, as indicated by the

ECI during the meeting itself, the EVM has to be viewed in its totality, including the administrative checks and balances and the various processes. These include a paraphernelia of observers, micro-observers, polling agents, returning officers, counting agents etc. as well as several seals on paper printed at the government press in Nasik to ensure and create the perception of trust. The transaction slip that the ATM generates, the ability to check the balance anytime on the ATM or on a counter in the bank — even update a "passbook" — creates trust. The EVMs, however, leave no such transaction trail and ability to build trust. They are purely faith based on the entire machinery and it is painful that the ECI is not giving adequate reasons to even build the faith in the machinery. The banking system also has a statutory Audit by a third party, not the manufacturer of the ATM or the bank. The EVM has no transaction trail, no audit and cannot be checked by anyone without the direction of the court. How many times had any audit been undertaken and where, by whom? Which of the "upgrade" features of EVMs were used on a regular basis and what were the results? Why instead was there no focus on simplifying the EVM to make it more trustable?

2. Consolidating databases: The election commission is required to track information on voters, constituencies, candidates, votes etc. This information is collected, stored and maintained in various databases of the ECI in multiple formats, multiple copies and multiple locations. There is no way to tell the authentic one. A query to one may generate a different answer from the other. There needs to be a broader open and inclusive *technology reform* agenda beyond the EVMs.
3. Tests and dummy data: The ECI must make public any tests, their schedule, the nature of such tests, the data used for such tests, the results obtained from such tests and the names of the persons and organizations responsible for such tests. Kirit Somayia asked the ECI to particularly comment on the queries raised by Professor Madhav Nalapat and Dr. Anupam Saraphabout the data available from the 6th of May.

ECI Responses

1. The ECI agreed that the simplification of the EVM was needed-the need for such an elaborate machinery should be done away with. They agreed to compile the list of audits undertaken, if any, and make them available. While conceding that none of the up-grade features had been used to generate reports, they said they were there in-case of direction by the court.
2. The ECI agreed that it had need to consolidate the databases and ensure that the system would be less error prone. They agreed to create a "technology reform agenda" beyond the EVMs.
3. The ECI said that tests are conducted on the "Genesys" software that transmits the results to the website. These tests are to ensure that the candidate name and results columns match. They also said all such tests are clearly labelled as tests on the website. They were unable to explain why the data available on the 6th of May through the 15th of May on the ECI website was not labelled test, was changing, was coded, did not display the candidate name and why the results were not uploaded on to the spreadsheet. They agreed that they would send a written communication about this serious issue.
4. The ECI conceded to the existence of holes, "Easter eggs" in the software and the absence of any process other than "black-box" testing to confirm the source code on EVMs and rationalized saying that the proprietary nature of the technology, the elaborate administrative procedure and the seals made sure that the EVM was unhackable and safe.
5. Even while arguing that the EVM was not a computer, but just a calculator, the ECI was closed to releasing the source or making the technology open-sourced. Their argument: open source will generate clones that compromise the process.

Actionable Points

1. An open and inclusive dialogue on process simplification to include transaction trail and independent auditability to be initiated by the ECI. The ECI should participate in the technology reform wiki already set up by the various stake-holders.

2. The ECI to provide a detailed response on the manner it conducts tests and specifically the questions raised due to the availability of the 2009 results data in coded form between the 6th and 15th of May.
3. The wiki community to list out case with examples of how open-source or closed-source technologies can create more trusted, highly secure and contemporary voting processes.
4. The ECI to move to a paper trail to the EVM for all elections beginning immediately.
5. The paper trail to be used as an audit record that must be counted independently at different locations by third parties during the counting process.

(Source: http://government.wikia.com/wiki/Minutes _mailed_to_ECI).

7. Researching the 2009 Election Data

The Problem

The startling discovery of results before voting by Nalapat and Saraph during the 2009 Lok Sabha Elections in India have sparked off a lot of questions and debate not just about the Indian Elections but about the whole idea of electronic voting. The implications of even a remote possibility of such a scenario are worse than Orwellian.

There are several large questions that need to be addressed by researchers — several researchers across the world have already taken up some of these.

These questions are clearly a clarion call for research in more countries than just India. This research would be a vast project with enormous legacy for the future of mankind and democracy across the world. The methodology will have to be open, inclusive and collaborative. It should be documented in an open and inclusive manner on a wiki such as this one.

(Source: http://government.wikia.com/wiki/Researching_the_2009_Election_Data).

8. Review the 2009 Lok Sabha Election Process: Promises and Reality

Elections were held in 5 phases across India. The last phase of polling was completed on the 13th of May 2009. The counting of votes was to begin on the 16th of May 2009.

Prior to the election the Election Commission had ruled that the election will be held in 5 phases with each phase dealing with voting in geographically discrete locations. Furthermore, to avoid any potential effect of the voting pattern in a given phase over that in subsequent phase(s), Exit Polls were formally disallowed and no interim counting of votes would be conducted or permissible prior to the completion of polls in all phases. Thus by virtue of the decisions of the Election Commission the final counting of the votes was to be undertaken and completed on the 16th of May 2009. Consequently Election Commission had specifically given the impression that it had formally disallowed any pre-emptive counting of votes including sampling either through Exit Polls or by downloading EVM data.

The data on the final votes polled would be expected to be uploaded / made available on the http://eci.nic.in/candidateinfo/frmcandidate.aspx on the 16th of May 2009. The nature of these data would concern names of the candidates, individual party affiliation, name of the constituency, the voting phase, votes polled by each candidate. It is only a matter of serendipity that, in order to obtain the information on the names of candidates their constituencies and party affiliations that on May 6th 2009 Prof. Madhav Nalapat and Dr. Anupam Saraph went to the site and must have been amazed to discover the results of the votes compiled for all five phases although the election / voting were yet to take place in phase 4 and 5. It thus appears that either this was mischief by some hacker or that some data was actually uploaded. The site was visited again on the 7th and11th with the same result. In conclusion, contrary to the rules set up by the election commission, not only was the voting data for the first three phases available but surprisingly data for the two subsequent phases (before actual polling took place) appeared.

Could this have been a mistake? Some software mix-up? Some sort of interference from interested parties? On the 11th they downloaded the data again to find that:

1. The same "votes polled" data was still available.
2. Barring a few candidates, the data was the same for most others.
3. The data on votes was available for 8023 candidates out of 8070 for 543 Lok Sabha Constituencies well before the completion of the election process.

It will be interesting to note the actual voting dates for different phases and the names of the constituencies, candidates and parties, the information for which the original exercise was undertaken by Prof. Madhav Nalapat and Dr. Anupam Saraph.

The extraordinary feature of this discovery concerns availability of data at a time when the events had yet to take place such as votes for elections and vote counts yet to be held prior to the date of their availability on the (http://eci.nic.in/candidateinfo/frmcandidate.aspx) website. To verify the validity of this information the concerned website was continuously monitored and enquiry made with the Election Commission about possible irregularity in the vote counting and revealing processes. Surprisingly, however, the "votes polled" data disappeared on the 15th and did not reappear as one would have expected on the 16th, or immediately thereafter, i.e., the date of formal declarations of the results by the Election Commission. Eventually ECI seems to have uploaded the final data on 3rd June 2009. It is at this point that the June 3rd data were compared to those appeared on 6th May, 7th and 11th May. This comparison clearly shows that the actual trends pre-empted for all phases were mostly the same. This raises a serious question as to how was it possible to predict / prempt the voting trends for phases 1 to 3 for which the voting had been completed but neither exit polls nor immediate counting were allowed / implied / undertaken / completed. It is even more surprising that the voting trends for the phase 4 and 5 for which the elections had yet not taken place pre-empted / published / allowed / implied / undertaken / completed were similar to those from the data published on June 3rd.

The sequence of these events preceded by the nature of rules and regulations set forth by the Election Commission as a priori for the conduct of the election process for Lok Sabha 2009, India, were not followed in practice and grossly violated in form of publication of voting data on the ECI website, completely contrary to the premise of sanctity presumably guaranteed by the Election Commission. Indeed it almost makes one feel that the final result of the election was electronically pre-planned. Is this possible? With all the promises made on the fool-proofedness of the security of the poll data, its storage as well as retrieval process, would it have been possible to prematurely access, download and manipulate the data contents on the EVMs? It is clear that EVMs need to be manually / electronically accessed to retrieve the data but it does not appear impossible to transmit to modify existing data. Furthermore the actual process of downloading contents from EVMs involves a "control unit" that retrieves the information / data from the "ballot unit" and reads the stored votes for manual compilation. While it is possible to manipulate data during manual compilation, this seems to be fraught with presence of too many individual operators involved in the final counting process. In contrast, however, if the control unit has a programme that reads of "votes polled" that were downloaded to it from an excel spreadsheet, not unlike those that were available in coded form between 6th May and 11th May the number of votes for each candidate could be manipulated.

In conclusion there is a strong possibility / probability that the election process was / could have been rigged such that specific group of candidates / political parties were favoured to garner majority votes irrespective of the actual votes cast by the electorate. This is not only possible in India but it is well known that a similar situation affected the vote counting process during the US Presidential Elections in 2004 in the State of Florida.

According to Brad who quotes this article by Atul A. the EVMs used in India can be readily rigged by a Computer Scientist. With so many ifs and buts, therefore, a time has come to undertake independent inquiries by the Supreme Court and CVC and two stay the results of the last election.

Devlem 14:57, 8 June 2009 (UTC)

(*Source:* http://government.wikia.com/wiki/Review_the_2009_Lok_Sabha _Election_Process:_Promises_and_Reality)

9. Results Before Voting?

The Analysis

The various versions of the files downloaded from ECI website by Nalapat-Saraph on 6th, 7th and 11th May and the data were merged together along with the final results found on ECI site on 2nd June.

1. The original excel spreadsheets have been maintained as Source Data.
2. Candidates in every constituency were ranked as 1, 2 and 3 on the basis of the votes seen in ECI excel sheets on 6th, 7th and 11th May.
3. Then the same candidates were ranked within each constituency based on the votes recorded on 2nd June spreadsheet by ECI.

Results

1. Out of 543 constituencies, we find 106 winning positions (rank 1) matched for all four dates,
2. 80 candidates matched for the rank 2 and
3. 59 for the rank 3.
4. Furthermore, in 14 constituencies ranks 1, 2 and 3 matched among all 4 data sets.
5. In 27 + 14 (41) constituencies ranks 1 and 2 matched among all data sets.
6. In 5 +14 (19) constituencies ranks 1 and 3 matched among all data sets and
7. In 7 + 14 (21) constituencies ranks 2 and 3 matched among all data sets.
   - 1. INC: AP-11; Raj-3;Aruna-1, Assa-2, Mah-3, Goa-1, Guj-3,Hary-3, Him-1, Karn-2, Ker-1, TN-2, MP-1, Oris-1, Punj-2, Del-1,Uttarkh-1, UP-5 [44]
   - 2. NCP: Mah-5, Megh-1 [6]
   - 3. BJP: Mah-1, Bih-1,Guj-1, Assa-1, Him-1, Karn-5, MP-3, Punj-1,WB-1, Chattis-3, Jhar-1, UP-3 [22]
   - 4. JD(U): Bih-3 [3]

- 5. INDEP: Bih-1, Zhar-1 [2]
- 6. AUDF- Assa-1
- 7. AGP: Assa-1
- 8. JKN: JK-1
- 9. CPM: Ker-1, WB-2 [3]
- 10. DMK: TN-2
- 11. AIDMK: TN-2
- 12. NagaPP: Naga-1
- 13. SAkalD: Pun-2
- 14. BSP-UP: UP-9 [9]
- 15. SP: UP-2 [2]
- 16. RLD: UP-1 [1]
- 17. SS: Mah-3 [3]
- 18. TrinaCg:WB-1

— Spmanalysis 09:07, 21 July 2009 (UTC)

(*Source:* http://government.wikia.com/wiki/Results_Before_Voting%3F)

10. EVM Issues

- EVMs have a closed source and a proprietary design- If the EVM is a mere calculator and completely secure, why the secrecy about its design and software, why not allow use of any EVMs that confirm to a standard? We do not restrict to using HP calculators and ban the use of any other calculator for number crunching.
- EVMs cannot work without elaborate supervised pre and post-poll process involving observers, agents and security paper seals. This is a huge risk and cost. Like a calculator that cannot work unless scientists, teachers and examiners certify that the calculator is secure and not fraudulent.
- There is no verification of software on the EVM — no checksum or debug programmes to confirm identity and version of software — besides black-box testing. What can distinguish an authentic EVM from an unauthentic one?
- There are no standards and procedures for data-storage, data-retrieval, archiving, data-transfer, data-verification. In fact the BEL and ECIL machines are not even compatible when it comes to obtaining, storing retrieving, archiving or transferring data.

What is the standard? Why are there no third party designs? Who are the OEMs? This is like NTSC and PAL- only the manufacturers benefit.

- There is a manual process for reading the votes — Why is there no print-out of the votes recorded on the machine with the machine id? Why can the entire data not be transferred to public website instantaneously? Why must the form 17C and form 20 be manually filled? Why can it not be printed by the EVM?
- There is no standard for maintaining a transaction trail and statutory independent audit by anyone who wishes to audit an EVM or entire constituencies. This is like allowing pass-books to be updated without entries in registers and without payment slips or cheque-book entries in the registers. This is like trusting the system because it runs, not because there is a mechanism to check for points of malfunction or misuse.
- There is no transaction slip to the voter. For the voter, the vote is untraceable once it is cast. This is like depositing money without a deposit slip. It is like a bank that has no pass-book updates or ways to check that the money is still in your account.

(*Source:* http:// government.wikia.com/wiki/EVM_Issues)

Results

1. Coded "results" were available on the ECI website in the versions of the spreadsheet CandidateAC.xls downloaded between the 6th and 11th of May. They contained "results" for all but 47 of the 8071 candidate. If EVMs were secure with DEO / district collectors, and elections were not even held in many constituencies, how was did the ECI have this data?
2. Was this data not in control of the ECI? Was their site hacked? Or was data from various EVMs uploaded in advance? Was this generated by someone in access of the website?
3. How can the ECI distinguish between real and dummy data?
4. If this data is generated as test / dummy data by "Genesys" software that collects and transfers data from districts to the ECI then:
   - Why did this happen during the poll process?
   - Why did the ECI not put up notice to the effect on its website?

- Why did it not react to the alert to this data sent to them on the 6th of May by NIC and Dr Anupam Saraph? Why is there no response to date? Why is there no clarification on this?
- If the purpose of the test is to match names with votes, why were the names coded to match the order in which they appear on the EVM?
- If it is just meant to tally the match, why was the data changing for at least some constituencies in this period?
- Why do 108 winners tally with winners as per this data?
- Why do the ranks of 662 candidates match the finally declared?
- In many cases multiple ranks in the same constituency match — this is a highly non-random event considering each of the "n" candidates in a constituency would have "1 / n" chance of making it to any position and "p" positions matching is a low probability chance with probability 1 / (n)**p.
- If previous years data is used to generate "dummy data", why are there only 108 matches? Also where does the data for those who did not contest previously come from?
- Why was this data "sanitized" on the 15th of May?
- Why were the final results never uploaded onto the spreadsheet?
- Why was the link to the spreadsheet removed on the 15th of July when the media asked the ECI questions about it?
- Why has the ECI not replied to the mails and [of the meeting with ECI] sent to them by Dr Anupam Saraph and Prof Madhav Nalapat?

5. Why does the voters and votes polled data reported by the ECI in different documents on its own website differ significantly?
6. The existence of this data also contravenes the Order passed by the Supreme Court on 19-01-2009, in writ petition (C) No. 207 of 2004th See ECI press release on the Supreme Court Order.

EC predicted on its spreadsheets on 6 May 2009 the Rank 1 (winning), Rank2 and Rank3 candidates (while poll was to close only on 13 May 2009). In a total of 108 constituencies, the number of votes polled by the winner. matched remarkably with the final declared results. Here are some samples of the results of EC "predictions" or pre-counting analysis. State Lok Rank 1 Rank 2 Rank 3 AP 42 11 6 4 Assam 14 5 5 2 Gujarat 26 4 5 1 Haryana 10 3 1 1 K'natak 28 8 8 6 MP 29 4 6 4 Maha'ra 48 12 9 9 Orissa 21 1 3 3 Punjab 13 5 3 1 R'sthan 25 3 4 4 T'nadu 39 6 2 1 UP 80 20 7 5 C'garh 11 3 4 2 J'khand 14 2 3 4 Pondi 1 0 0 1 U'khand 5 1 1

Coded "results" were available on the ECI website in the versions of the spreadsheet CandidateAC.xls They contained "results" for all but 47 of the 8071 candidates.

(*Source:*http://government.wikia.com/wiki/Results_before_voting)

7

Electronic Voting — Danger and Opportunity

Dr. J. Alex Halderman*

Prof. J. Alex Halderman started his presentation with an explanation of EVMs supplied by diebold Inc. in USA. Diebold Inc. is a security systems corporation and had supplied machines comparable, in computing processes, to the voting machines in India by ECI. He explains that his team demonstrated how the Diebold systems used in US elections could be tampered with. (*Editors' note*)

Diebold's History of Secrecy

- Diebold prevented states from allowing independent security audits — hid behind National Democratic Alliance's, trade secret law.
- Source code leaked in 2003, researchers at Johns Hopkins found major flaws, Diebold responded with vague legal threats, personal attacks, disinformation campaign.
- Internal emails leaked in 2003 reveal poor security practices by developers. Diebold tried to suppress sites with legal threats.
- Obtained legally from an anonymous private party, the software is 2002 version, but certified and used in actual elections.

* Professor of Computer Science, University of Michigan, USA

Direct Recording Electronics are Computers

Below we present the first complete, public, independent security audit of a DRE.

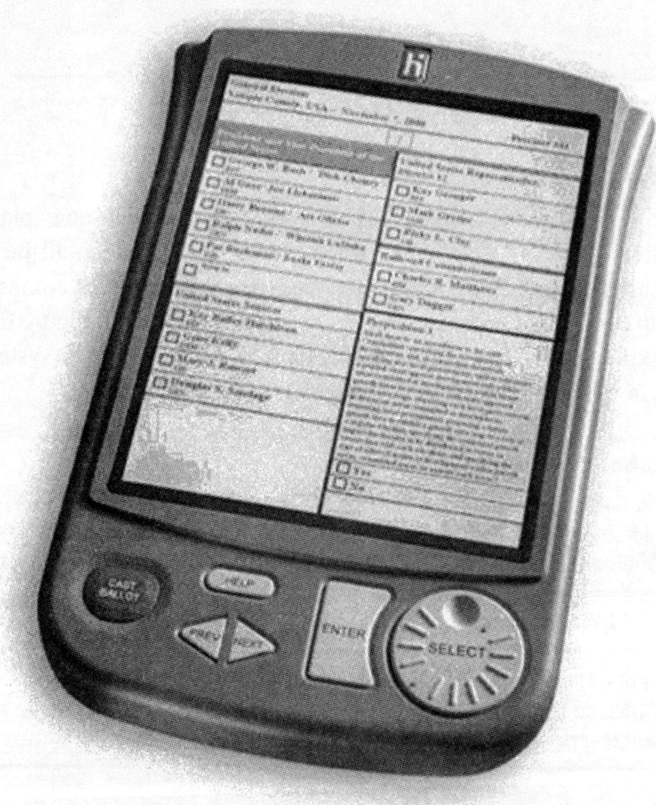

Research Goals

- Conduct *independent* security audit.
- Verify threats by building demonstration attacks.
- Figure out how to do better.

  Who wants to know?.

  Voters, candidates, election officials, policy makers, researchers.

SH3
CPU
32 MB
RAM
16 MB Flash
128 KB EPROM
Boot Jumper
2 PCMCIA Slots
Table

Our Findings

- Malicious software running on the machine can steal votes undetectably, altering all backups and logs [Feldman, Halderman & Felten 2007] Correct result: George **5**, Benedict **0**

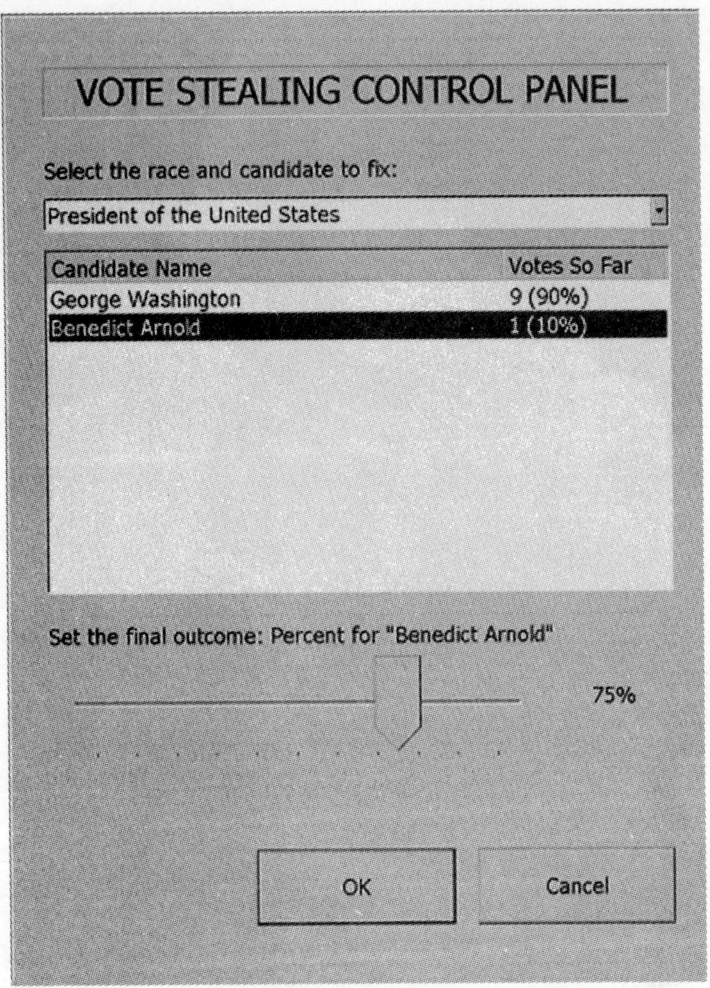

Vote Stealing Control Panel

Our Findings

- Malicious software running on the machine can steal votes undetectably, altering all backups and logs.
- Anyone with physical access to the machine or memory card can install malicious code in as little as one minute [Feldman, Halderman & Felten 2007].

The Key

Our Findings

- Malicious software running on the machine can steal votes undetectably, altering all backups and logs.
- Anyone with physical access to the machine or memory card can install malicious code in as little as one minute.
- Malicious code can spread automatically and silently from machine to machine in the form of a voting machine virus [Feldman, Halderman & Felten 2007].

Voting Machine Virus

Viral Spread

California "Top-to-Bottom" Study

Joe Calandrino Ari Feldman

Bill Zeller Alex Halderman Harlan Yu

Debra Bowen

Hart Sequoia Diebold

California "Top-to-Bottom" Results

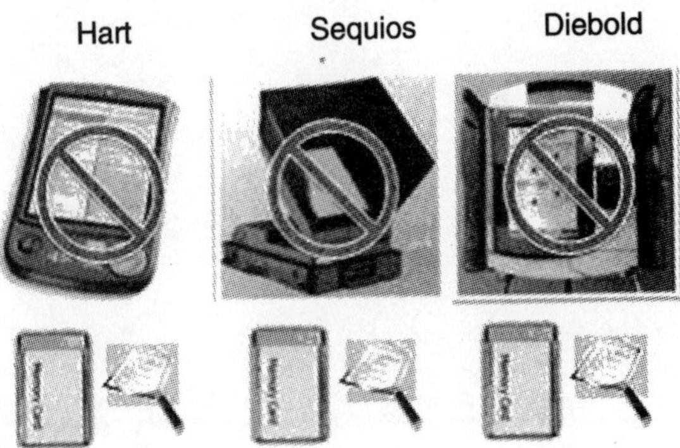

We can do better!

Electronic + Paper Records

Touch-screen (DRE) machine,

plus voter-verifiable paper trail

Hand-marked paper ballot,

+++machine-scanned immediately

Failure Modes

Paper Ballots Electronic Records
Physical tampering
"Retail" fraud
After the election

Cyber□tampering
"Wholesale" fraud
Before the election

Redundancy + Different failure modes = Greater security
But . . .Redundancy only helps if we use both records!

8

Are India's EVMs Reliable and Do They Meet Legal Requirements?

Ajay Jagga *

Part I

Democracy is defined as a government by the people; a form of government in which the supreme power is vested in the people and exercised directly by them or by their elected agents under a free electoral system. The fundamental basis of election integrity is transparency in elections. In transparent elections, all the processes of handling and counting ballots are completely open to public view. Nothing is hidden; nothing is secret — except, of course, each individual's voting choices.

Accordingly democratic government is elected by way of elections in India for which enough laws has been framed including Representation of People Act, 1951. Further, in order to outline the procedure of elections and support the R. P. Act 1951 the "Conduct of election rules, 1961" were framed. The most important and relevant form of elections is "Voting by Ballot". Now here the abovementioned Rules has defined so many things but the most relevant definitions are of "Ballot Box" and "Ballot Paper", as these two things are main instruments for conducting a fair, transparent and impartial elections. The purpose of law was to define that there should be a ballot paper and ballot box, so that the voter after entering polling room receives a ballot paper, mark his / her choice of candidate and then put that ballot paper in the sealed ballot box.

* Advocate, Punjab and Haryana High Court, Chandigarh

This procedure ensures that the voter make his choice and then ensure that his or her ballot has gone to the ballot box and will be considered and counted in favour of the candidate of his or her choice. For instant reference both the definition are given below;

Rule 30: Form of Ballot Papers:

1. Every ballot paper shall have a counterfoil attached thereto, and the said ballot paper and the counterfoil shall be in such form, and the particulars therein shall be in such language or languages, as the Election Commission may direct.
2. The names of the candidates shall be arranged on the ballot paper in the same order in which they appear in the list of contesting candidates.
3. If two or more candidates bear the same name, they shall be distinguished by the addition of their occupation or residence or in some other manner.

Rule 33: Preparation of Ballot Boxes for Poll.

1. Where a paper seal is used for securing a ballot box, the presiding officer shall affix his own signature on the paper seal and obtain thereon the signatures of such of the polling agents present as are desirous of affixing the same.
2. The presiding officer shall thereafter fix the paper seal so signed in the space meant therefore in the ballot box and shall then secure and seal the box in such manner that the slit for the insertion of ballot paper there into remains open.
3. The seals used for securing a ballot box shall be affixed in such manner that after the box has been closed it is not possible to open it without breaking the seals.
4. Where it is not necessary to use paper seals for securing the ballot boxes, the presiding officer shall secure and seal the ballot box in such manner that the slit for the insertion of ballot papers remains open and shall allow the polling agents present to affix, if they so desire, their seals.
5. Every ballot box used at a polling station shall bear labels, both inside and outside, marked with:

- The serial number, if any, and name of the constituency;
- The serial number and name of the polling station;
- The serial number of the ballot box (to be filled in at the end of the poll on the label outside the ballot box only); and
- The date of poll.

6. Immediately before the commencement of the poll, the presiding officer shall demonstrate to the polling agents and other persons present that the ballot box is empty and bears the labels referred to in sub-rule (5).
7. The ballot box shall then be closed, sealed and secured and placed in full view of the presiding officer and the polling agents.

After going through the above definitions and procedures, one can immediately come to know how important are these rules for fair elections and that's why the law makers had framed the Act and the rules, meant for fair, free and transparent elections.

The Electronic Voting Machines (EVMs) were adopted by India in 2004 elections to the Parliament with about 375 million electors had cast their ballots using electronic voting machines. In India the EVMs are designed and developed by Bharat Electronics Limited (BEL) and Electronics Corporation of India Limited (ECIL) (both Government owned). Both these systems are similar. These systems are developed according to the specifications of Election Commission of India. The EVMs System is a set of two devices running on 6V batteries. The Voting Unit is used by the Voter, and the other device, known or called as the Control Unit is operated by the Electoral Officer. Both the units are connected by a 5 meter cable. The Voting unit has a Blue Button for every candidate, the unit can hold 16 candidates, but up to 4 units can be chained, to accommodate 64 candidates. The Control Units has Three buttons on the surface, namely, one button to release a single vote, one button to see the total number of vote cast till now, and one button to close the election process. The result button is hidden and sealed, It cannot be pressed unless the Close button is already pressed.

Now in the system of Electronic Voting Machines, the question is how a voter will come to know two things, i.e.:

- His vote has been cast, and
- His vote has gone to the candidate of his choice.

Certainly in the present system of electronic voting in India, the voter can not come to know both the things, mentioned above. Whereas in the past or in ballot paper system the voter is sure of both the things. The Representation of People Act 1951 and Conduct of Election Rules 1961 are meant for ensuring both the things i.e. the vote has been cast and it has gone to the credit of the candidate of the voter's choice. Hence the present system of voting by electronic voting machines (EVMs) is not in tune with the election law of India and needs to be looked at with fresh ideas, which are legal.

According to the election law in India, three implied rights has been guaranteed to the voter, i.e.:

- The right to a cast a vote;
- The right to an equally weighted vote; and
- The right to have one's vote accurately counted.

Interestingly these rights are available to the voters throughout the world, where democracy prevails.

Apart from being legal hitches there are other concerns also which are as under:

1. Lack of a tangible record — A paper ballot, for example, is a tangible physical object which can be indelibly marked. Computer memory, however, can be easily altered leaving no trace of its original marking.
2. The possibility of fraud on a monumental scale: A single programmer can insert self-erasing code that can alter millions of ballots and the outcome of elections.
3. Insufficient standards, testing and certification: voting systems are typically certified to federal and / or state standards that are several years old and older standards often will have gaping flaws. Implementing new standards has been a slow, cumbersome and costly process. Certification is done by for-profit labo-

ratories accredited by the National Institute of Standards and Technology, but chosen and paid by the manufacturers.

4. Insufficient oversight: Various electronic voting companies were found to have employees who have previously been convicted of serious crimes, including felonies.

Election fraud may occur and go undetected in systems with indelible (e.g., paper) ballots, but it is, in principle, detectable, and flagrantly egregious behaviour can usually be limited through the courts and public pressure. If legal procedures are pursued or if an investigative team is dogged, fraud can be exposed and justice served. With electronic voting systems, however, fraud may be undetectable, and those who have been declared the losers are left with no recourse to verify results.

Voting by electronic machines (EVMs) was supposed to be the cure for ballot fiascos during elections, but in its present system / form it has only worsened the problem and these EVMs also do not meet the legal requirements set out by the relevant laws and rules there under. It also creates worries about the future of our democratic system.

The votes on the paper ballots or paper receipts of EVMs must be regarded as the definitive legal votes, taking precedence over electronic records or counts.

International Opinion Against EVMs

France

Campaigners have filed law suits to prevent the use to EVMs. They say the machines do not meet the legal requirements set out by the country's Constitutional Council

Seven electors from Issy-les-Moulineaux, on the outskirts of Paris, recently attended the Administrative Court in nearby Versailles, seeking an injunction preventing their city council from using the machines. They also filed complaints from 19 others, while campaigners in other cities petitioned their courts.

French elections are conducted via secret ballot. Traditionally, electors enter a polling booth and place a slip of paper printed with the name of their chosen candidate in an unmarked envelope. The next step is quite literally transparent: They then place the envelope in a transparent ballot box. This allows observers to ensure that the ballot box was empty at the start of the election, and for voters to ensure that their ballot has been received.

But electronic voting machines do not allow lay-observers to verify proceedings in the same way, and the voter has no way of knowing that their vote has been registered as they wish, the campaigners say — they must simply have faith in the programming of the machine.

Florida, USA

Malwitz: No voting machine is going to be perfect — and not just in Florida (Published in the *Home News Tribune* 11 / 30 / 00) Verified Voting Foundation of USA passed the following resolution:

> "Computerized voting equipment is inherently subject to programming error, equipment malfunction, and malicious tampering. It is therefore crucial that voting equipment provide a voter-verifiable audit trail, by which we mean a permanent record of each vote that can be checked for accuracy by the voter before the vote is submitted, and is difficult or impossible to alter after it has been checked. Many of the electronic voting machines being purchased do not satisfy this requirement. Voting machines should not be purchased or used unless they provide a voter-verifiable audit trail; when such machines are already in use, they should be replaced or modified to provide a voter-verifiable audit trail. Providing a voter-verifiable audit trail should be one of the essential requirements for certification of new voting systems."

Tennessee, USA

The Tennessee Voter Confidence Act requires replacement of paperless touch screen voting machines with optical ballot scanners by November 2010. Optical-scan voting systems read marked paper ballots and tally results, providing a tangible record of the voter's intent. They are now the most widely employed voting systems in the nation, used by 60 percent of voters in other states.

The act was adopted nearly unanimously by the Tennessee legislature — by both Democrats and Republicans — and in 2008 enthusiastically signed into law by Gov. Phil Bredesen. But implementation of the law has been ensnared in legalities and technicalities.

Tennessee's secretary of state and coordinator of elections have argued that the new law requires scanners be federally certified to 2005 standards, and because no machines have yet been certified to that standard, the law cannot be put into effect in time for 2010 elections.

That's why Common Cause Tennessee and other voters' rights advocates, in an effort to break the logjam, filed a lawsuit seeking clarification of the law's language. Nothing is more important than having verifiable ballots. There is no good reason for running the 2010 elections with systems that are vulnerable to error and don't allow a recount or an audit.

Errors with Paperless System

In a 5 November ruling, Chancellor Russell T. Perkins concluded that the voter confidence act does not require new ballot scanners to meet those 2005 standards but declined to issue an injunction forcing application of the law. Still, the court ruled that the secretary of state was "obligated to take prompt, effective steps to meet the statutory deadline" as long as their choice of standards "does not jeopardize meeting the legislative mandate to implement...on or before the November 2010 election."

Tennesseans need — and deserve — to have verifiable ballots in place for the 2010 election. Paperless systems are subject to unintended errors and possible hacking; hence votes might not be recorded as intended.

Without a paper ballot available for audit or contested election, there is no way to tell whether a voter's intent was accurately recorded.

New Jersey, USA

[Union County Clerk says voting machines are unreliable; encourages voting by mail. Posted on 22nd October 2008 at 8:20am by Bile.] Citing concerns over the vulnerability of New Jersey's electronic voting machines raised in a Princeton University professor's report, the top Union County election official is encouraging residents to vote by mail.

Union County Clerk Joanne Rajoppi today reminded voters that the Clerks Office will be open Saturday to hand out last minute absentee ballots before the November 4th, saying that she didn't feel confident that all votes would be counted accurately by the current stock of machines. She plans to redeploy her agency's staff to deal with the expected increased volume of paper ballots.

Rajoppi had asked the state to investigate tallying errors she found in the voting machines, manufactured by Sequoia, during the February presidential primary. No investigation took place, however.

"The state, despite urging by COA-NJ (the Constitutional Officers Association of NJ) and others, would not agree to an independent test but instead relied on the vendor, Sequoia who reported that poll workers were responsible for the errors which occurred not just in Union County but throughout the state," she said.

Superior Court Judge Linda Feinberg had requested that Princeton University computer science professor Andrew Appel compile a report on the status of New Jersey's voting machines. He and other researchers found several flaws in the machines and warned that they're easy to tamper with:

> "I believe the state, who hired their own consultant to review the Princeton report, should own up to problems with the machines. Perhaps the problems do not, as a NJ Division of Elections employee said, rise to the level of 'overturning an election,' however, voters deserve a transparent process and greater confidence in their voting machinery than is now provided. Despite the outstanding job done by county election officials across the state," said Rajoppi. "If there are problems in the design of the voting

machine, there is a problem. An alternative is of course to vote by mail."

Commission on Issue of Federal Election Refoms, USA

Statement of computer science Professor David Dill, founder of the voter advocacy group VerifiedVoting.org, before a commission headed by former Presidents Carter and Ford on the issue of federal election reform:

> "It is not sufficient that election results be accurate. The public must also know the results are accurate, which can only be achieved if conduct of the election is sufficiently transparent that candidates, the press, and the general public can satisfy themselves that no errors or cheating have occurred. Unfortunately, the advent of paperless electronic voting is moving us away from election transparency."

Bush v. Gore, 531 US 98, 105 (2000) (USA)

A well known case titled as Bush *vs* Gore shed new light on three core voting rights and how they relate to voting technology. These rights are:

1. The right to cast a ballot,
2. The right to an equally weighted vote, and
3. The right to have a vote counted.

Gray v. Sanders (USA)

The Supreme Court has recognized the fundamental right to an accurate count of one's vote, holding in *Gray v. Sanders* that "[e]very voter's vote is entitled to be counted once. It must be correctly counted and reported."

Help Americans Vote Act (HAVA), USA

HAVA's minimum requirements mandate that *all* voting systems must:

- Permit the voter to verify (in a private and independent manner) the votes selected by the voter before the ballot is cast and counted,

- Notify the voter of an over-vote prior to the ballot being cast,
- Provide the voter with the opportunity (in a private and independent manner) to change the ballot or correct any error before the ballot is cast,
- Produce a permanent paper record with a manual audit capacity for such system, and
- Provide the voter with an opportunity to change the ballot or correct any error before the permanent paper record is produced.

Netherlands

The government of Netherlands, in 2008, has also banned the electronic voting machines, on the pretext of eavesdropping. The nation is going back to paper voting.

Germany

On 3rd March 2009 the German Federal Constitutional Court decided that electronic voting used for the last one decade, including for the general elections, was not constitutional and thus the same is not to be used for the next elections in September 2009. The court also confirmed that the use of the electronic machines is against the normal elections and also pointed out that the deficiency in the equipments, being used for the elections.

The petition challenging the use of e-voting was filed by political scientist Joachim Wiesner and his son, physicist Ulrich Wiesner who alleged about the deficiency in the system of e-voting. It was also alleged that in the system the voter can not check the fate of his vote and as such it is not transparent. The petition also stated that since there is no system of paper receipts, the results could be manipulated

Risks

Erroneous Results

Computer-related errors occur with alarming frequency in elections. Last year there were reports of uncounted votes in Toronto and doubly counted votes in Virginia and in Durham, North Carolina. Even the US Congress had difficulties when 435 Representatives tallied 595 votes on a Strategic Defence Initiative measure. An election in Yonkers NY was reversed because of the presence of leftover test data that accumulated into the totals. Alabama and Georgia also reported irregularities. After a series of mishaps, Toronto has abandoned computerized elections altogether. Most of these cases were attributed to "human error" and not "computer error" (cf. the October 1990 Inside Risks column), and were presumably due to operators and not programmers; however, in the absence of dependable accountability, who can tell?

Fraud

If wrong results can occur accidentally, they can also happen intentionally. Rigging has been suspected in various elections, but lawsuits have been unsuccessful, particularly in the absence of incisive audit trails. In many other cases, fraud could easily have taken place. For many years in Michigan, manual system overrides were necessary to complete the processing of non computerized precincts, according to Lawrence Kestenbaum. The opportunities for rigging elections are manifold, including the installation of trapdoors and Trojan horses, child's play for vendors and knowledgeable election officials. Checks and balances are mostly placebos, and easily subverted. Incidentally, Ken Thompson's oft-cited Turing lecture, *Commun. ACM 27, 8*, (August 1984) 761-763, reminds us that tampering can occur even without any source-code changes; thus, code examination is not enough.

Viruses

Additionally, with computer viruses, internet worms, and malicious hackers in the news on a regular basis, there is concern that electronic voting machines are vulnerable to security breaches in which a malicious programmer could alter elections results.

Conclusion

Election fraud and miscounts have occurred throughout history, and they will continue to occur. Transparency is the only way to minimize them, but with electronic voting machines, transparency is eclipsed. Electronic processes that record and count the votes are not open to public scrutiny. With electronic voting, the most important and vulnerable election processes — storing and tallying the votes — are performed in secret, without public oversight. These processes were not developed by government officials charged with ensuring election integrity, but by anonymous software engineers, hired by vendors and not publicly accountable for the results of their work.

Internationally it has been observed that the state of electronic voting security is not good. Many of today's electronic voting machines have security problems. The ones at greatest risk are the paperless voting machines. These machines are vulnerable to attack: A single person with insider access and some technical knowledge could switch votes, perhaps undetected, and potentially swing an election. With this technology, we cannot be certain that our elections have not been corrupted.

A growing number of election integrity advocates are realizing that software technology has no place in the election systems of our country because of the inability to even detect mischief.

Accordingly the laws relating to elections, in India, are very clear and ensure transparency by ensuring to the voter that his or her vote has been cast and registered as per his or her wish. Whereas the method adopted by Election Commission of India i.e. voting by Electronic Voting Machines is not transparent at all and denies the fundamental right of voter to be sure that his vote and has been cast and registered as per his wish and also it violates the procedures as defined in Conduct of Election Rules 1961. So if election officials want to convince the voters that electronic voting machines can be trusted, they should be willing to make it transparent by allowing the paper receipt generated by the EVMs. The paper receipt will ensure both the things to the voter i.e. his vote has been cast and has been registered as per his or her wish. Accordingly in the elections, by way of EVMs, even the right to file an election petition, as provided under the Election law to challenge an election on various grounds such as fraud, improper counting etc, will be practically not available to a looser because the machines can not detect errors and make a fresh counting and will give the same results. Hence there is an urgent need to relook at the EVMs in its present shape in the interest of law, democracy and justice.

Part II

Voting through Electronic Voting Machines (EVMs) is undoubtedly an act of electronic transaction, which carries data in an electronic manner. Hence it is essential to go through the provisions of the law with regard to the electronic transactions, in order to find out whether EVMs in India, in its present form, meet the legal requirements. Accordingly, three Acts i.e. Representation of People Act 1951, Information and Technology Act 2000 (India) and Indian Evidence Act, 1872 were examined to find out whether the EVMs in India, in its present form i.e. without any e-receipt, meet the legal requirements and it has been found that e-receipt is almost mandatory. This receipt can / should be similar to the receipt generated by the ATM machines and Credit Card Machines, so as to ensure that data has been sent / received as per the wish of the voter / elector.

Representation of People Act 1951, India

This is an Act to provide for the conduct of elections of the Houses of Parliament and to the House or Houses of the Legislature of each State, the qualifications and disqualifications for membership of those Houses, the corrupt practices and other offences at or in connection with such elections and the decision of doubts and disputes arising out of or in connection with such elections. The relevant legal provision is as under:

> Section 61A. Voting machines at elections.— Notwithstanding anything contained in this Act or the rules made there under, the giving and recording of votes by voting machines in such manner as may be prescribed, may be adopted in such constituency or constituencies as the Election Commission may, having regard to the circumstances of each case, specify. *Explanation.*— For the purpose of this section, "voting machine" means any machine or

apparatus whether operated electronically or otherwise used for giving or recording of votes and any reference to a ballot box or ballot paper in this Act or the rules made there under shall, save as otherwise provided, be construed as including a reference to such voting machine wherever such voting machine is used at any election.

Information and Technology Act 2000, India

This is an Act to provide legal recognition for transactions carried out by means of electronic data interchange and other means of electronic communication, commonly referred to as "electronic commerce", which involve the use of alternatives to paper-based methods of communication and storage of information, to facilitate electronic filing of documents with the Government agencies and further to amend the Indian Penal Code, the Indian Evidence Act, 1872, the Bankers' Books Evidence Act, 1891 and the Reserve Bank of India Act, 1934 and for matters connected therewith or incidental thereto. The provisions which are relevant and applicable in the case of electronic voting are as under:

Section 2 (r)

"Electronic form" with reference to information means any information generated, sent, received or stored in media, magnetic, optical, computer memory, micro film, computer generated micro fiche or similar device;

Section 2 (t)

"Electronic record" means data, record or data generated, image or sound stored, received or sent in an electronic form or micro film or computer generated micro fiche;

Section 7. Retention of Electronic Records

(1) Where any law provides that documents, records or information shall be retained for any specific period, then, that requirement shall be deemed to have been satisfied if such documents, records or information are retained in the electronic form, if-

(a) The information contained therein remains accessible so as to be usable for a subsequent reference;
(b) The electronic record is retained in the format in which it was originally generated, sent or received or in a format which can be demonstrated to represent accurately the information originally generated, sent or received;
(c) The details which will facilitate the identification of the origin, destination, date and time of despatch or receipt of such electronic record are available in the electronic record:

Provided that this clause does not apply to any information which is automatically generated solely for the purpose of enabling an electronic record to be despatched or received.

(2) Nothing in this section shall apply to any law that expressly provides for the retention of documents, records or information in the form of electronic records.

Section 11. Attribution of Electronic Records

An electronic record shall be attributed to the originator:

(a) If it was sent by the originator himself;
(b) By a person who had the authority to act on behalf of the originator in respect of that electronic record;
or
(c) By an information system programmed by or on behalf of the originator to operate automatically.

Section 12. Acknowledgment of Receipt

(1) Where the originator has not agreed with the addressee that the acknowledgment of receipt of electronic record be given in a particular form or by a particular method, an acknowledgment may be given by:

(a) Any communication by the addressee, automated or otherwise;
or

(b) Any conduct of the addressee, sufficient to indicate to the originator that the electronic record has been received.

(2) Where the originator has stipulated that the electronic record shall be binding only on receipt of an acknowledgment of such electronic record by him, then unless acknowledgment has been so received, the electronic record shall be deemed to have been never sent by the originator.

(3) Where the originator has not stipulated that the electronic record shall be binding only on receipt of such acknowledgment, and the acknowledgment has not been received by the originator within the time specified or agreed or, if no time has been specified or agreed to within a reasonable time, then the originator may give notice to the addressee stating that no acknowledgment has been received by him and specifying a reasonable time by which the acknowledgment must be received by him and if no acknowledgment is received within the aforesaid time limit he may after giving notice to the addressee, treat the electronic record as though it has never been sent.

Section 92. Amendment of Act 1 of 1872

The Indian Evidence Act, 1872 shall be amended in the manner specified in the Second Schedule to this Act.

Amendments to the Indian Evidence Act, 1872
(1 of 1872)

1. In Section 3,-

(a) In the definition of "Evidence", for the words "all documents produced for the inspection of the Court", the words "all documents including electronic records produced for the inspection of the Court" shall be substituted;

According to the above said provisions of law it is clear that the voting by EVMs are equal to Ballot Box & Ballot Paper, voting by EVMs is an electronic form, the data sent and received is an electronic record and the electronic record is to be retained in the format in which it was originally generated, sent or received or in a format which can be demonstrated to represent accurately the information originally generated, sent or received. It also stipulates that, if the originator has not agreed with the addressee that the acknowledgment of receipt of electronic record be given in a particular form or by a particular method, an acknowledgment be given by the acknowledgment of receipt of electronic record be given, to the originator in a particular form or by a particular method, an acknowledgment may be given by any communication by the addressee, automated or otherwise. The law is not limited to this only but it also confirms and clarifies that under the Indian Evidence Act, 1872 now evidence means not only record but electronic record and hence an acknowledgment be given to the elector / voter, in compliance with the laws. The voting by way of EVMs, without the e-receipt or paper receipt is violation of the Representation of People Act 1951, Conduct of Elections Rules 1961, Information & Technology Act 2000 and the Indian Evidence Act, 1872 and above all the against the democracy.

Notes

1. EVMs and Law of India

Electronic voting machines (EVMs) were first adopted by India in 2004 elections to the Parliament with about 375 million electors had cast their ballots using electronic voting machines. In India the EVMs are designed & developed by Bharat Electronics Limited (BEL) and Electronics Corporation of India Limited (ECIL) (both Government owned). Both these systems are similar. These systems are developed according to the specifications of Election Commission of India.

Every one has been guaranteed the following constitutional rights:

- The right to a cast a vote;
- The right to an equally weighted vote; and
- The right to have one's vote accurately counted

As per section 61-A, of the Representation of Peoples Act 1951

EVM = Ballot Box + Ballot Paper

(Inserted by Act 1 of 1989, s. 11 (w.e.f. 15-3-1989).

As per Section 2 (r) of the Information and Technology Act 2000 transaction on EVM, i.e. voting is an electronic form

As per Section 2 (t) of the Information and Technology Act 2000 the data sent and received is an electronic record and

As per Section 7 (b) of the Information and Technology Act 2000 the electronic record is to be retained in the format in which it was originally generated, sent or received OR in a format which can be demonstrated to represent accurately the information originally generated, sent or received.

As per Section 12 (1) (a) of the Information and Technology Act 2000, if the originator has not agreed with the addressee that the acknowledgment of receipt of electronic record be given in a particular form or by a particular method, an acknowledgment be given by any communication by the addressee, automated or otherwise. This has been done in order to ensure that the data has been sent and received, as per the wish of the originator.

The law is not limited to this only but it also confirms and clarifies that under the Indian Evidence Act, 1872 now evidence means not only record but electronic record and hence an acknowledgment be given to the elector / voter, in compliance with the laws.

In view of the above mentioned provisions of law the voting by way of EVMs, without the e-receipt or paper receipt appears to be not in tune with the Representation of People Act 1951, Conduct of Elections Rules 1961, Information & Technology Act 2000 and the Indian Evidence Act, 1872 and above all the against the democracy. Moreover when a voter votes according to his or her wish on EVM, the result is that he hears a beep and a flash of light but what has happened to data which he has sent, is not known. In similar transactions like ATMs or Credit Cards the paper receipt is the evidence of the electronic transaction.

Testimony of David L. Dill (Professor of Computer Science, Stanford University) before the Commission on Federal Election Reform (Carter-Baker Commission), on 18 April 2005 hearing, at American University, Washington D. C.

> "The real job of an election is not to convince the winners that they won, but to convince the losers that they lost. So, it is not sufficient that election results be accurate; the public must know that the results are accurate. That can only be achieved by making election processes as transparent as possible. Voters have no means to confirm that the machines have recorded their votes correctly, nor will they have any assurance that their votes won't be changed later."

Hence in my opinion, based on relevant laws, the EVMs without e-receipt or paper receipt or voter verifiable trail are not fully trust worthy, as per prevalent laws and needs to be given a fresh look in order to make the election process completely transparent. At present, the voter only comes across a beep and a flash of light, but what has happened in the machine or to the data which he or she has sent, is not known. This receipt can be similar to that of ATM receipt, which is issued even for a 100 /- rupees transaction, to provide evidence to the particular electronic transaction. The receipts generated by the EVMs can be then, put into the sealed box kept over there and remain with Election Commission of India, so that in case of audit or disputes, the box can be opened, counting can be done and the results can be compared with the EVMs.

2. "EVMs Illegally Being Used for a Decade"*

The electronic voting machines (EVMs) are being used in violation of the Information Technology Act 2000, a research paper has revealed.

Author of the research paper, advocate Ajay Jagga, told *The Times of India*, on Sunday that as per IT Act, 2000, a verifiable audit trail has to be provided in case of any electronic record, which is now admissible as evidence as per Evidence Act but in case of electronic voting, the voter does not get any receipt with regard to his voting.

---

* (Sanjay Sarma, TNN, 22 February 2010, 03.44 a.m. IST, Chandigarh)

The research paper recently attracted the attention of experts when a conference on "EVMs: How trustworthy?" in Chennai passed a unanimous resolution on 13 February asking Jagga to approach the Election Commission of India (ECI) for bringing the electronic voting procedure in tune with IT Act, 2000.

Jagga said he would soon approach ECI seeking formation of legal committee to remove the illegality or will knock the doors of court.

The lawyer said, "Unless the voter gets a receipt like the one we get in ATM or after the use of debit or credit cards, all electronic transactions including a vote, are illegal." What is the evidence that the vote cast has really been recorded and that it has been recorded in the manner the voter intended, he asked.

For the purpose and to protect the secrecy of ballot, all such receipts, after the voter has checked his transaction, should be put in a box which should remain with ECI to be produced as evidence in case of a dispute, he said. The government amended the relevant laws in 1989 to equate EVM with ballot and ballot box to facilitate transition from ballot paper to EVM but the IT Act 2000 created a new complication that has to be immediately resolved in the interest of fairness of things, Jagga pointed out.

The lawyer also proved that the machine can be tampered with which has been accepted by the government itself in its letter to withdraw patent applications filed by Electronics Corporation of India and Bharat Electronics Ltd, makers of the machine. The PSUs withdrew their patent applications on the ground that the machine may not be tamper-proof, he said, adding that America and Germany had to return to ballot paper after their machines were found wanting.

(*Source:* http://timesofindia.indiatimes.com/city/chandigarh/EVMs-illegally-being-used-for-a-decade/articleshow/5601297.cms)

Linked on USA Today 23 Feb. 2010 (http://content.usatoday.com/topics/article/Places,+Geography/Countries/India/05zF4kBeFJ47y/1).

3. Intellectual Property Does Not Exist with ECI, ECIL or BEL

Chief Election Commissioner has often claimed that public sector units make India's EVMs whose intellectual property rests with ECIL / BEL.

This is a classic instance of *suppressio veri, suggestio falsi.*

Private sector companies some of whom operate as Alliance partners of foreign-based companies (like Renesas / Microchip) are also involved in the making of / offering EVMs, EVM Components and EVM related services. The burning of the programmes in micro controllers of EVMs is performed abroad by the foreign companies. ECI has to explain how this vital process in the making of Indian EVMs, is supervised and authenticated by the Indian manufacturers / suppliers of EVMs, EVM components and Services.

Election Commission of India has claimed to have made new EVMs with new features such as date-time stamp, "Authentication Unit" for the manufacturers to verify that EVM being used in the election is the same that they have supplied to the Election Commission.

Simply, the election process in the sovereign democratic republic of Bharat, appears to have been compromised by making information available to a private company in Bengaluru.

The justification provided for this authentication patent application:

> "Tamper-proofing is not sufficient for embedded computing platform security as it solves only half of the problem and replication can defeat all sophisticated measures of tamper-proofing. A replicated platform means look-alike and functionally equivalent model of original device . . . ."

This is clear admission by ECI that tamper-proofing claimed in an embedded computing platform (Computing !!!) can be defeated by replication. HEXATRIK, e.g. can make an exact replica of India's EVM.

What are the legal constraints referred to by SecureSpin and what amounts were spent by ECI or ECIL or BEL or all of them, for the reportedly aborted authentication process. And, the current status of the authentication process should be explained by ECI, for a tamperable EVM system with the possibility of multiple trojans.

4. SecureSpin Engaged and Disengaged for Using "Authentication Unit" of EVMs*

Since they claim expertise in locating trojans, it is surprising that Election Commission of India (ECI) did not pursue with the initiative reported in 2006 to engage SecureSpin to authenticate EVMs through the "Authentication Unit" provided in the improved design EVMs (which are claimed to include date-time stamp).

About SecureSpin's E-Voting innovations:

E-Voting Innovations

This important link when clicked leads to this statement.

SecureSpin has innovated standards in platform security and its patent-pending distributed root of trust security model has generated lot of interest internationally and is under active consideration.

"Request for Information" by vendors requires prior-submission of NDA electronically at info@securespin.net. Due to legal constraints details can not be provided in public domain.

(http:// securespin.net/evoting.htm).

One wonders what the legal constraints are. ECI has to explain.

Advancement in computation and communication technologies has changed the way mainkind in living their lives. Some of the top trends in computation and communication is integration of computation and communication, Packetized radio, IP enabled embedded devices, network architecture transitioning to NGN, seam less mobility, etc.

While all this is taking place, it's also throwing different kind of challenges and problems which needs to be tackled. Some of the problems are like making IP of global network technologies, seamless mobility, QoS, security, etc.

---

* (Information about SecureSpin Systems: #1060, 7th A Main, 3rd Blk, Koramangala, BLR- 34. Phone: +91-80-41313731 Fax: +91-80-41313732).

Securespin is a start-up with a vision to solve part of the problem that is security. Though security was all the way there for last 10-15 years, but meaning of the security has changed a lot during this change . . . . It's not all about IPSec, SSL, Firewall, etc.

SecureSpin has targeted two niche area of security, which we at secureSpin believe that without which protection of asset, privacy is not possible. Two areas which secureSpin has identified are — platform security and deep packet inspection technologies. SecureSpin holds IP in this area.

We envision to use these IPs as a horizontal IP as well as can be used in fully vertical product.

Area of application can be GPS, Voting machine, communication platform, network appliance, Vehicle security, etc.

Deep Packet Inspection Technology is required to secure the productivity layer of NGN. As network is transitioning to all IP and PSTN network is getting replaced by IP data network it also implies that IP data network should be PSTN GRADE from security and reliability perspective. Typical downtime for carrier class PSTN network is 59 minutes that is 2 hrs in 40 years. With increasing threat of Virus, torjan, worms IP network is prone to much higher downtime than the one above. Even existing lifecycle for solution to fix virus, torjan and worms are not good enough to meet this stringent requirement. To be as reliable as PSTN IP network needs to be self reacting to the threat posed by Virus, Worm and Trojans.*

Details of the patent pending with WIPO for E-Voting Platform are presented below. **

WO 2007148258 20071227 Indian Provisional Patent Application Number 1055 / CHE / 2006 filed with Indian Patent Office on 21 June, 2006 and Indian Complete Patent Application Number 1055 / CHE / 2006 filed with Indian Patent Office on 29 January, 2007 and titled "Integrity Checking and Reporting Model for Hardware Rooted Trust Enabled E- voting Platform"

---

* http:// securespin.net/solutions.htm

** http:// www.wipo.int/pctdb/en/wo.jsp?WO=2007148258

International Filing Date: 12.06.2007

International Application Status Report

Received at International Bureau: 23 July 2007 (23.07.2007)

Information valid as of: 20 September 2008 (20.09.2008)

Report generated on: 18.03.2010

(10) Publication number: WO2007 / 148258

(43) Publication date: 27 December 2007 (27.12.2007)

(26) Publication language: English (EN)

(21) Application Number: PCT / IB2007 / 052219

(22) Filing Date: 12 June 2007 (12.06.2007)

(25) Filing language: English (EN)

(31) Priority number(s): (31) Priority date(s): (31) Priority status:

1055 / CHE / 2006 (IN) 21 June 2006 (21.06.2006) Priority document received (in compliance with PCT Rule 17.1)1055 / CHE / 2006 (IN) 29 January 2007 (29.01.2007)

(51) International Patent Classification: G07C 13 / 00 (2006.01); G06F 21 / 00 (2006.01)

(71) Applicant(s): ANAND, Ashish [IN / IN]; No.1060 7th A Main, 3rd Block, Koramangala Bangalore 560095 (IN) (for all designated states)

(72) Inventor(s): ANAND, Ashish; No.1060 7th A Main, 3rd Block, Koramangala Bangalore 560095 (IN) (74) Agent(s): V.N, Sabitha; M / s WHITE FOREST LAW OFFICES No.118, B-wing, Carlton Towers, 1 Airport Road Bangalore 560008 (IN)

(54) Title (EN): INTEGRITY CHECKING AND REPORTING MODEL FOR HARDWARE ROOTED TRUST ENABLED EVOTING PLATFORM

(54) Title (FR): VÉRIFICATION DE L'INTÉGRITÉ ET MODÈLE DE REPORTING POUR PLATE-FORME MATÉRIELLE

DE VOTE ÉLECTRONIQUE DE CONFIANCE ROUTÉE

(57) Abstract:

Tamper-proofing is not sufficient for embedded computing platform security as it solves only half of the problem and replication can defeat all sophisticated measures of tamper-proofing. A replicated platform means look-alike and functionally equivalent model of original device. This invention uses hardware rooted trust in a novel way to guarantee platform security without hardware upgrade and re-certification. Tangible assurance about integrity of platform is essential to secure maximum public trust using an external attestation and certification unit (020). Attestation and certification unit (020) along with platform (021) is provisioned with security credentials using a provisioning server (018 & 019) shown as core root-of-trust at platform-vendor premises in a auditable and verifiable manner, beyond any disputes or litigations. This invention is based on distributed root-of trust security model (as shown in Diagram 11) wherein both attestation unit (020) and platform (021) is on same trust hierarchy and hence can be used in many horizontal applications which are otherwise complex from legal, public-trust aspects and onus of anything going wrong is mostly one-sided. This also provides a maximum security against insider threats from inside of vendor premises.

(81) Designated States: AE, AG, AL, AM, AT, AU, AZ, BA, BB, BG, BH, BR, BW, BY, BZ, CA, CH, CN, CO, CR, CU, CZ, DE, DK, DM, DO, DZ, EC, EE, EG, ES, FI, GB, GD, GE, GH, GM, GT, HN, HR, HU, ID, IL, IN, IS, JP, KE, KG, KM, KN, KP, KR, KZ, LA, LC, LK, LR, LS, LT, LU, LY, MA, MD, ME, MG, MK, MN, MW, MX, MY, MZ, NA, NG, NI, NO, NZ, OM, PG, PH, PL, PT, RO, RS, RU, SC, SD, SE, SG, SK, SL, SM, SV, SY, TJ, TM, TN, TR, TT, TZ, UA, UG, US, UZ, VC, VN, ZA, ZM, ZW European Patent Office (EPO) : AT, BE, BG, CH, CY, CZ, DE, DK, EE, ES, FI, FR, GB, GR, HU, IE, IS, IT, LT, LU, LV, MC, MT, NL, PL, PT, RO, SE, SI, SK, TR African Intellectual Property Organization (OAPI) : BF, BJ, CF, CG, CI, CM, GA, GN, GQ, GW, ML, MR, NE, SN, TD, TG African Regional Intellectual Property Organization (ARIPO) : BW, GH, GM, KE, LS, MW, MZ, NA, SD, SL, SZ, TZ, UG, ZM, ZW

Eurasian Patent Organization (EAPO) : AM, AZ, BY, KG, KZ, MD, RU, TJ, TM Declarations:

Declaration made as to the identity of the inventor (PCT Rules 4.17(i) and 51bis.1(a)(i))

Declaration of inventorship (Rules 4.17(iv) and 51bis.1(a)(iv)) for the purposes of the designation of the United States of America (http://www.wipo.int/pctdb/iasr?IA=IB2007052219&LANGUAGE=EN&ID=0&VOL=0&DOC=0&WO=07/148258&WEEK=null&TYPE=&DOC_TYPE=IASR&PAGE=1).

World Intellectual Property Organisation (WIPO) rejected patent applications of ECIL / BEL in 2006

BEL's patent application filed on 24 Oct. 2002

Withdrawn on 13 April 2006

ECIL's patent application filed on 21 Nov. 2002

Withdrawn on 19 April 2006

Both applications had claimed non-tamperability of EVMs.

The rejection by World Intellectual Property Organization (WIPO) of the patent applications and consequent withdrawal prima facie disprove the claims made by ECI through ECIL / BEL and hence, Election Commission of India's claims of non-tamperability stands rejected by the highest technical review process, that of WIPO.

ECI is specifically mentioned in the patent applications and hence becomes a party to the patent application and rejection.

Citizen voters are taken for a ride vitiating the public nature of the election in a democratic republic. Why should the voting, counting processes be electronic secrecy devices? EVMs are unconstitutional because the voter does NOT understand how voting, counting are done hush-hush.

Shouldn't vote recording and counting be done in public, consistent with the definition of a democratic republic?

There are two types of EVMs. One with date-time stamp (introduced for 2009 polls by ECI) and another WITHOUT such stamping feature. According to ECI website, the processor chip is imported from Japan.

5. "Improved EVMs to Make Voting Tamper-Proof in this Election"*

The Electronic Voting Machine (EVM) has just got smarter. It not only does the obvious — record your vote — but also notes the exact time you cast it. The new and improved machines will also give hourly updates of balloting.

Amol Newaskar, general manager of Bharat Electronics Limited (BEL), Bangalore, which is one of the two public sector companies manufacturing EVMs for the Election Commission, said the machines which have been supplied for the April-May elections have more improvised features than the older ones.

"BEL has been manufacturing EVMs for a long time and since 2000 we have supplied 650,000 EVMs. However, the ones manufactured from 2007 onwards — which will be used in the April-May general elections — have improvised features like in-built clocks which record the exact time a ballot is cast," Newaskar told IANS on phone from Bangalore.

"Not just that, the EVM also records the exact time when the whole balloting process starts and when the last vote is being cast. It gives an hourly update of the number of votes cast, and if there is any unusual trend in the process, it can be easily detected. Thus the whole process becomes tamper-proof," he added.

For instance, if there is a heavy rush in polling at a particular hour, the officials can be on alert or if a voter thinks that his vote is being tampered with, the exact time when he cast his vote can be retrieved.

The Election Commission, according to Newaskar, placed an order for 102,000 EVMs to BEL for the 2009 general elections — all of which have been supplied by January.

Besides BEL, the other company authorised by the Election Commission to manufacture EVMs is the Hyderabad-based Electronics Corporation of India Limited (ECIL). Both the companies supply an almost equal number of EVMs.

---

* [Azera Rahman, 30th March 2009 — 12:48 pm IST by IANS, New Delhi].

According to K.S. Rajasekhara Rao, chairman of ECIL, they have supplied 78,000 machines with the improvised features to the Election Commission.

"We have to supply another 3,000 EVMs by March 31," Rao said.

Explaining some of the new features of the machine, Newaskar said: "The new EVMs are also more user-friendly. Earlier most of the instructions on the machine were printed in short form which was not easily understood, but now more images are used instead," he said.

For the benefit of the visually impaired, the EVMs also have Braille markings on them.

"So that a visually impaired person does not have any trouble in casting his or her vote, Braille markings have been made close to the serial number of the candidates. Since 2007, we have manufactured 250,000 such EVMs with Braille markings," Newaskar said.

The new EVMs, he added, also have a better battery life. If a machine is not used for 10 minutes, it goes on sleep mode and shows in its indicator if the charge is low. Data however is not lost in either case.

Each EVM costs about Rs.9,800, inclusive of taxes. An estimated 1.36 million electronic voting machines will be used in 828,000 polling booths across this vast country.

The Indian government has also supplied 500 EVMs to Nepal and is in talks with Namibia which wants 500,000 units.

(Azera Rahman can be contacted at azera.p@ians.in)

6. More About "Improved" EVMs to Make Voting Tamper-Proof*

In reality, the microchips are delivered by Microchip USA and Renesas Japan local agents to ECIL and BEL from Microchip, USA and Renesas, Japan as masked microchips (to ECIL), or one-time

* http://www.thaindian.com/newsportal/politics/improved-evms-to-make-voting-tamper-proof-in-this-election_100173031.html#ixzz0-guT2LbRR.

programmable read only memory (OTP-ROM) microchips (to BEL).

The following is the status of the patent pending according to the World Intellectual Property Organization website:

EVM India, BEL's application of 2002 for patent. (http:// www.sumobrain.com/patents/wipo/Electronic-voting-machine-evm /WO2002084607.html).

(http:// www.wipo.int/pctdb/en/wo.jsp?WO=2002084607).

Report generated on: 14.02.2010 (http://www.wipo.int/pctdb/ia sr?IA=IN2002000043&LANGUAGE=EN&ID=0&VOL=0&DOC= 0&WO=02/084607&WEEK=null&TYPE=&DOC_TYPE=IASR& PAGE=1) Intl. Application status report.

(http://www.wipo.int/pctdb/en/wads.jsp?IA=IN2002000043&LA NGUAGE=EN&ID=09006361800979b0&VOL=17&DOC=006533 &WO=02/084607&WEEK=43/2002&TYPE=A1&DOC_TYPE=P AMPH&PAGE=1) Drawings

Read on . . . (http://sites.google.com/site/hindunew/electronic-voting-machines).

EVMs use chips of questionable integrity and since the patent applications for EVMs stand rejected by World Intellectual Property Organization.

This is apart from the issue of transparency to ensure the public nature of the election process from balloting to counting to announcement of results.

Non-tamperability of EVMs has NOT been proved in WIPO, though the patent application made the claim of non-tamperability. Patent applications have been withdrawn after 3½ years of patent process and deliberations.

Election Commission of India should be asked by Her Excellency the President and Govt. of India to withdraw the EVMs forthwith and ECI should NOT be permitted to use them in any future election. This measure will be to safeguard the transparency of the most important process of the Democratic Republic, public nature of the election process.

BEL's patent application filed on 24 October 2002; withdrawn on 13 April 2006

ECIL's patent application filed on 21 November 2002; withdrawn on 19 April 2006

The withdrawal after 3½ years of patent deliberation process shows that the claims made of non-tamperability of EVMs have NOT been proven to the satisfaction of WIPO (World Intellectual Property Organisation)

Both applications had specifically claimed non-tamperability of EVMs.

The rejection by World Intellectual Property Organization (WIPO) of the patent applications and consequent withdrawal prima facie disprove the claims made by ECI through ECIL / BEL and hence, Election Commission of India's claims of non-tamperability stands rejected by the highest technical review process, that of WIPO.

ECI is specifically mentioned in the patent applications and hence becomes a party to the patent application and rejection.

Microchip USA and Renesas Japan have local agents who supply to ECIL and BEL imported chips from Microchip, USA and Renesas, Japan.

These are supplied as masked microchips (to ECIL) or One time programmable read only memory (OTP-ROM) microchips (to BEL).

ECIL and BEL have no way of knowing what the embedded programmes are, in the chips from USA and Japan.

These are the chips which are used in EVMs by ECI. There is no way of knowing what unknown programmes have been included in the chips which are used in the EVMs.

Local agents of Renesas Japan and Microchip USA may have supplied chips with trojan horses.

All the EVMs have to be audited thoroughly.

Private sector firm importing chips from Microchip and Renesas USA / Japan is engaged in EVMs; Navin Chawla was lying to the court stating that only ECIL / BEL public sector units are involved.

He also lied to the court about intellectual property and did not disclose that WIPO has rejected ECIL / BEL / ECI claims of non-tamperability of India EVMs

HEXATRIK to Make EVMs

Here is a project 2008 of HEXATRIK to make EVMs.

Source code is available.* Also documentation as to how to burn it in the EEPROM (Electrically Erasable Programmable Read Only Memory) / controller chip. This is a project very similar to the EVM in India. Note that they talk about the Ballot Unit, Control Unit and Cable. The exact Architecture like EC's EVMs. If this is the same how can ECIL / BEL claim any Patent / IP? Sounds very bizzare.

What is the likelihood that chips imported from Microchip / Renesis and delivered through HEXATRIK included HEXATRIK programme instead of ECIL / BEL programmes?

What is the likelihood that these chips with burnt-in programmes were used in four states with new design EVMs including time-date stamp feature (among 6 features)?

What is the possibility that these were the trojans used in select constituencies of UP, Chattisgarh, West Bengal and Arunachal Pradesh?

It is clearly an instance of *suggestio falsi* and *suppressio veri* when EC states that ECIL / BEL make the machines. They make the machines with private-globalMNC collaboration. Any number of Trojans can sneak in.**

It will be instructive to see if there is any cached information on past years' tenders awarded and the successful contractors supplying components for EVMs.

Some info. on the source of the source code etc.

Note that this HEXATRIK is located in ECIL Postal address. ECIL stands for Electronic Corporation of India Ltd. HEXATRIK is apparently the lead collaborator for making chips used in EVMs. ECI is not correct when it claims the EVMs are made by ECIL and BEL (*indulging in suggestio falsi* and *suppressio veri*) since private suppliers are involved in supplying electronic components of the EVMs to ECIL / BEL.

---

* http//www.8051projects.net/downloads205.html

** http:// www.ecil.co.in/tenders/archieve-tenders.html
http:// tender.bel.co.in/Default_Unit.htm?Unit=BANGALORE

HEXATRIK is closely associated with Microchip and Renesas.

See the nature of alliance with Renesas at the URL which is the homepage, global site, of the MNC: Renesas, Japan (http://secure-alliance.renesas.com/sg/searchPartner.partner?action=profile&userid=3125) HEXATRIK Claims to be a 3rd party alliance partner of Renesas.

There is a disclaimer on this page: "Please Note: Renesas is not affiliated with the Company profiled on this page, and cannot guarantee the accuracy of the information displayed above. For questions regarding the information provided on this page, please contact the company directly."

Why should a private company be making EVMs if ECI had declared that only ECIL / BEL as public sector units were the suppliers of EVMs

It should be a matter of serious concern that a private company (owned by whom?) called HEXATRIK which is an alliance partner of Renesas and Microchip (Global MNCs supplying embedded systems) was manufacturing its own EVM (control unit + balloting unit) under its own project title — not unlike the EVMs used by ECI.

Was this a response to any tender with ECIL or BEL? There is clearly only potential buyer of EVMs in India: ECI (which spent Rs. 90 crores during 2009 to get the new EVMs with six improved features).

The EVM of HEXATRIK is comparable to the failed patent applications' design of ECIL / BEL.

The following news items note that 180,000 new types of EVMs were used in four states during 2009 polls: UP, West Bengal, Chattisgarh and Arunachal Pradesh. Why were these new types only used in these states? Why were inferior design machines (without date-time stamp) used in other states? ECI has to answer these questions.

If HEXATRIK was involved in supplying the burnt-in controllers (also called embedded systems in electronic parlance, obtained from Renesas / Microchip), there is a clear conflict of interest: were the chips imported by HEXATRIK to be used in the Election Commission's EVMs or to be used in HEXATRIK EVMs?*

(*Source:* 20 March 2009, *Hindu Business Line*)

7. BEL Looks Beyond Government for EVM Biz**

The company, which has pioneered the manufacture of EVMs in India, presently supplies 50 per cent of the requirements of Election Commission whenever they come out with an order.

The strategic business unit for export manufacturing of BEL is presently exploring opportunities both in India and abroad for EVMs. It recently supplied 18,000 EVMs to the Gujarat government, 2,000 units to the Tamil Nadu government for municipal and local body elections.

Apart from the Central government and state government bodies, the company is now in the process of supplying EVMs to the corporate sector, a company official said.

The average cost of an electronic voting machine made by BEL is about Rs 10,000. Apart from BEL, the Hyderabad-based Electronics Corporation of India Limited (ECIL) also manufactures EVMs in the country.

For the current year, the Election Commission has placed an order for producing 78,000 units with the ECIL. Whereas, BEL will supply 102,000 units this year.

"We need to take permission from the election commission to supply to the corporate sector. We are exploring the option presently," he said.

He said BEL is also expecting another order from Gujarat for their local body elections. In order to meet the growing requirements from various government bodies, the company recently

---

* http://america.renesas.com/products/tools/partner_information/child_folder/a lliance_partner_listing_global.jsp;jsessionid=6E1350910F23040A8CB4204 87 A 1 DB387.02

** [Mahesh Kulkarni, Chennai / Bangalore, 2 October 2008, 0:18 IST Bharat Electronics Ltd (BEL)] modernised its mass manufacturing facility for EVMs at an investment of Rs 8 crore in Bangalore.

The SBU, which derives nearly 80 per cent of its business from the sale of EVMs is now all set to tap the growing segment of contract manufacturing from the global companies. The unit is presently in talks with several companies in the US and UK for providing RFID-based (Radio Frequency Identification) solutions.

"We have held preliminary discussions with a few companies in this connection and we are yet to firm up any order," the official said. BEL hopes to finalise the deal in the next six months, he added.

The company has already signed MoUs with some foreign companies who are very active in avionics like Boeing, Northrop Grummen and Lockheed Martin and some Israeli companies. BEL expects to bag some orders from these companies by end of the present financial year.

"These companies have already come and audited our quality, manufacturing, business process systems and certified us as their vendors for their requirements. With this type of upgradation of our infrastructure, we are confident that by this financial year end we will get quite a few good orders as part of the offset business," BEL chairman and managing director, V V R Sastry told *Business Standard*.

BEL is likely to end the present financial year with an order book position of Rs 10,000 crore. As of April 2008, it had an order book of Rs 9,000 crore and expects to get more orders during the course of the year. It is targeting a turnover of Rs 4,800 crore this year, a growth of around 18 per cent over last fiscal.

(*Source:* http://www.thehindubusinessline.com/2009/03/20/stories/2009032050540400.htm)

8. Letter of V.V. Rao* to the Former Chief Election Commissioner, N. Gopalaswamy (28 November 2009)

Respected Shri Gopalaswami,

It was a pleasure to see you at the convention on electoral reforms last week in New Delhi. The comments made by you reflected the ground realities quite well. I feel proud to say that, with all your co-operation in the recent elections in A.P. the election watch iniative in association with several CSOs (supported by former CEC Lingdo, K. J. Rao and I. V. Subba Rao) could control 100% flow of illegal liquor, and about rupees forty crores of cash was caught while the money is getting distributed and it is the first of its kind in the country. And achievement is appreciated by everyone in this state.

Today, the biggest challenge before us is to get the attention of the policy makers (politicians or the parties) in this country to realize the importance of the electoral reforms. As you know, political parties have a limited perspective and also have vested interest, which is the root cause for all these problems. They should be supported by experts and the organisations working on different electoral reforms. Simultaneously, the Election Commission should also have a separate expert group consisting of retired election commissioners, experienced officials who worked for the EC and people from different fields including the civil society activists who have the abreast with the latest developments in the country and elsewhere in the world to suggest suitable alternatives.

We heard from the Election Commissioner, Shri S. Y. Quraishi saying in the meeting on 21 November that some "previous" solutions to the problems have given rise to "new" problems. He specifically referred to the issue of property defacement as per the code of conduct which has become a tool for the media to exploit the politicians and parties, leading to the unethical practice of "paid articles". Similarly, the expenditure limit set for the candidates is of

---

* Convener, Ennikala Nigha Vedika, (Election Watch, Andhra Pradesh)

no use, as politicians are resorting to new illegal methods to spend money to influence voters.

Similar thing is happening in the case of Electronic Voting Machines (EVMs). EVMs have replaced the ballot paper and this was aimed at reducing the time of counting and man power and other malpractices like rigging during the elections. But today, after twenty years of its introduction the EC is unable to answer the basic questions relating to EVMs convincingly: whether they are tamperable and if not, do they have a verification mechanism for these EVMs? Are they accountable? And are they transparent? Why the expert committee recommendations constituted by EC itself have not been met? If at all EC is confident about foolproof EVMs, why they are not responding to their applicants. Why the manufacturers of EVMs are giving notices to threaten the petitioners in the PIL to say unconditional apologies for raising droughts on EVMs which they are claiming to interfere with the patent rights? Why the source code for the EVMs is with the manufacturer? If the ownership of EVMs is with manufacturers, then who has control over the elections?

Throughout the world, particularly in Europe and the United States, this is a concern at this point of time. Supreme Court of Germany had held that the use of EVMs is unconstitutional as the public nature of elections is not ensured by the EVMs.

If every thing is fine why a retried IAS officer, Shri Omesh Saigal, who is very much associated with the conduct of elections in Delhi has asked for an enquiry into the EVMs and which was backed by the leader of the opposition, Shri L. K. Advani. When we are insisting on verifiability of vote with a paper trail, there is a negative response from the EC. While the Election Commission is not in a position to give simple answers to an election watch activist in this country how can one have trust in this institution?

In spite of the Supreme Court of India directions to clarify the doubts of the petitioners, EC failed to answer the questions raised two months ago, and in spite of letters written by at least a dozen political parties to organize an all party meeting on the subject, prominent among are them former central minister Subramanian

Swamy, former CMs, Chandra Babu Naidu, Jailalita, Lalluprasad Yadav, Chaotala, Political Party Presidents includes Prakash Karat, Brdan, etc, while the Election Commission has shown no response to concerns being expressed. Why is it not in a position to answer questions raised on the legal aspects, on the technical aspects and on the processes? Even after pointing out the violation of human rights like secrecy of vote is lost in EVMs, why EC is reluctant to respond. The "right to know" whether the vote cast by a voter has gone to the candidate he / she is interested in is a part of basic right and that is denied by the EVMs.

It was at the insistence of the expert committee from EC, our technical experts have even decided to show the tamperability of EVMs on 3rd of September, but it was stopped in between, when they opened the EVMs to show the tamper ability in front of the cameras arranged by the EC and in the presence of several prominent people which includes senior advocates of the Supreme Court, politicians and technical experts. And we asked for the video CDs and they have not responded to it.

How is that CEC repeatedly giving false press statements claiming that the EVMs cannot be tampered when they have not allowed us to tamper the ECI-EVMs? Neither they have respect to the verdict of the Supreme Court nor to any one concerned in this country. The high constitutional body in this country should exhibit an open mind, show more honourable intentions and be willing to accept suggestions for improvement. This is all what we are concerned about.

It is my humble request to you, to use your good offices for the public cause on electoral reforms in this country; I hope you can share some of your valuable experiences so as to contribute to the society.

9

Electronic and Internet Voting

International Experience and What India May Do

Dr. T. H. Chowdary*

[Except the first paragraph, which is introductory and points to ultimate acceptance of electronic and Internet voting in the information age, and the last paragraph in which I suggest how e-voting can be made more trustworthy, all others paras are a survey of issues, opinions and actions (of governments) concerning electronic and Internet voting. I had gone through about twenty papers published in USA, France, and UK all available on the Internet and searched by Google. There are full quotes from the papers studied. As these are many, they are not individually acknowledged.]

Electronic Voting Seems Inevitable in the Information Age

Electronics and I.T are pervasively intruding into every aspect of life of individuals, families, society and the nation. In an average home, the number of electronic devices and I.T- embedded appliances are ever on the increase. They range from cell phones, fax machines, PCs, TV sets, DTH reception devices, microwaves, Air conditioners, refrigerators, surveillance camera systems, medicare;

* Fellow, Tata Consultancy Services

devices inserted in the human body (e.g. pacemakers), hearing aids, insulin injectors, and programmed voice for intake of medicine. When we are thus in the sea of electronics, software and Internet, it is natural that governments as well as companies use electronics voting systems. When we are having electronic banking, e-shopping, and e-mailing how can we shy away from electronic balloting? Boards of Directors and Share Holders are also using the Internet and telecommunications for holding meetings as well as voting on resolutions. From the mid- 1970s onwards, developed countries especially America to start with, have been initiating measures for electronic-voting.

There is however a great difference between electronic voting for electing people's representatives who make laws for the nation, state and for individuals on the one hand and using e-devices and Internet for all other purposes on the other hand. This is especially so when the margins between the winner and the loser are coming down, as for e.g.: in the election of Bush -II as the President of the USA in year 2000, in Florida out of 5mln votes, Bush won only with over 500 votes. And that decided who should be the president of the US. In India, with the disappearance of the dominance of a single party and several regional parties coming to power in states and forming coalition governments at the Centre, winning and loosing make a tremendous difference to the candidates, parties and the nation. That is why the integrity of voting and the dependability of counting especially when the voting is transported over a network are very important.

Evolution of Voting

Voting progressed from paper ballots, mechanical leaver machines, punch cards, mark sense (optical scan) cards, direct reading electronic (DRE) devices and finally, to Internet by anybody from any where at any time.

DRE voting machines used in USA on a very large scale are made by Premier Elections Solutions (formerly Diebold Election

Systems). These are now used in all Brazilian elections and plebiscites. World wide electronic voting devices manufacturers are:

- AccuPoll.
- Advanced Voting Solutions, formerly Shoup Voting Machine Co.
- A VANTE international Technology Inc.
- Bharat Electronics Limited (India).
- Dominion Voting Systems Corporation (Canada).
- Electronic Corporation of India Ltd.
- ES&S (USA).
- Hart InterCivic (USA).
- Micro Vote.
- Nedap (Netherlands).
- Premier Election Solutions (formerly Diebold Election System) (USA).
- Sequoia Voting Systems (USA).
- Smartmatic.
- UniLect.
- VOTEX / TM Tecnologies Electiosn Inc (Canada).

Corporations and other organisations are using Internet voting to elect offices and Board Members and for other proxy elections. Internet voting systems are used privately in many modern nations and publicly in the United States, the UK, Ireland, Switzerland and Estonia. In Switzerland citizens get passwords to access the ballot through the postal service. Estonia in the European Union has a nearly all complete e-voting system. This is made possible because most Estonians carry a national identity card equipped with a computer readable microchip and it is these cards, which they use to get access to the online ballot.

Development of voting machines: Leaver voting machine 1892; optical scanner 1962; punch card 1964; EVMs 1974 (American voting began in the late 1700s; the secret ballot originated in Australia in 1888.

Problem with EVMs

The fundamental problem with electronic voting is that it depends upon the reliability of Software. A Professor Rubin says, that he is less concerned about external hacking or tampering than about Software going wrong, or the risk of malicious actions from within voting- machine manufacturers. He added that he would not claim that any manufacturer is corrupt but thinks it is foolish to use systems that depend on them (manufacturers) not being corrupt.

The complaints are about machine glitches, unrecorded votes and "flipped votes" allocated to the wrong candidate". 13% of votes failed to register any choice at all in the closely fought US Congressional race between Republican Vern Buchanan and Democrat Christine Genning on 8 November 2006. Buchanan was officially declared the winner by 369 votes. The conclusion was painfully clear: one set of problem had been traded for another.

In the US, Florida, New Mexico, Iowa and some other States have now rejected electronic voting and gone back to paper ballots that are marked by hand by filling in a blank oval and scanned by machine.

Hardware

Inadequately secured hardware can be subject to physical tampering. Foreign hardware could be inserted into the machine or between the user and the central mechanism of the machine itself, using a man -in the -middle attack technique, and thus even sealing DRE machines cannot make them fraud-proof.

Software

Security experts demand that the source code of voting machines should be publicly available for inspection. They have also suggested that voting machine Software should be the free software licence as is done in Australia.

Critics of DRE system concede that no voting system is perfect but insist that electronic voting is uniquely susceptible to failure with catastrophic, system -wide consequences.

Defrauding a paper ballot is labour- intensive whereas for an ingenious hacker, to mount an attack on electronic systems is easy, "the cost of throw out an election is dirt cheap".

Paul DeGregorio former Chairman of the US Election Assistance Commission (EAC) (set up in the Year 2002) said, "I would argue that we can trust this technology, and it is no less safe than paper ballots or the optical system". He even proposed voting via Internet.

Measures to Make e-Voting Less Objectionable

Cryptographic Verification

One feature to mitigate the occurrence of incorrectly recorded votes is to allow a voter to prove how they voted with some form of electronic receipt signed by the voting authority using digital signatures.

Transparency

In the year 2009 the Federal Constitutional Court of Germany ruled that when using voting machines the verification of the result must be possible by the citizen reliably and without any specialist knowledge of the subject. The DRE Nedup-computers used till then did not fulfil that requirement. The decision did not ban electronic voting as such but required all essential steps in elections to be subject to public examinability.

Audit Trails and Auditing

Researchers at the National Institute of Standards and Technology (NIST) which is entrusted by the US government to evolve standards for EVMs and e-balloting observed that the DRE architecture is unable to provide for independent audits of its electronic records and so makes it a poor choice for environment in which detecting errors and fraud is important.

Voter Verified Paper Audit Trail (VVPAT)

This concept was proposed in October 2000 in the US for auditability. It suggested that the voting machines print a paper ballot or other paper facsimile that can usually be verified by the voter before being entered into a secured location.

Voters use a touch screen to make their selections, and the machine prints a paper ballot that has all the choices that they made. If the software on that system fails, they wouldn't get a printed ballot that they could approve. The voter then takes the printed ballot and puts it into a scanner. The scanner tallies the ballots.

After the election, you pick a bunch of scanners randomly and audit them. You compare the totals. In any stage of the process, a flaw in the software will prevent you from proceeding. Now compare that to an existing direct recording electronic touch-screen machine. The voter comes in and marks his or her choices, and they are stored on a magnetic card on the inside of the machine, and at the end of the day, the voting officials get the card, and it has all the tallies.

Nevada State in the USA was the first to successfully implement in the year 2004, a DRE voting system that printed an electronic record. The $9.3 mln voting system was provided by Sequoia Voting Systems. This replaced the punch card voting systems.

A Few Documented Electronic Voting Problems

On October 30, 2006 the Dutch Minister of Interior withdrew the license of 1187 voting machines from the manufacturer Sdu NV Capitals, about 10% of the total number to be used because it was proved by the General Intelligence and Security Service that one could evesdrop on voting from up to 40 meters using Van Eck phreaking.

During voting in Miami, Hollywood and Forte Lauderdale, Florida in October 2006 three votes intended to be recorded for the Democratic candidate were displayed as cast for the Republican candidate Election officials attributed it to calibration errors in the touch - screen of the voting system.

Cuyahoga County Ohio

The Diebold computer service froze and stopped counting votes; then the printers jammed. So the paper copies could not be retrieved for many votes and there was no way to be sure of the accuracy of the votes, when the votes were counted.

Waldenburg, Arkansas: The touch -screen computer tallied zero votes for one mayoral candidates who confirmed that he certainly voted for himself and therefore there should be a minimum of one vote! This is a case of disappearing votes on touch -screen machines.

Humboldt County, California: A security flaw erased 197 votes from the computer data base.

In the March 2008 primary elections in Ohio, poll workers found that votes were sporadically lost during the transfer of data from individual voting machine memory cards to the central system. The manufacturer, Diebold claimed that the data loss resulted from a Software clash with an anti-virus programme on the central system. The company acknowledged to the Ohio Secretary of State that it found an internal software bug that could cause votes to be dropped when data from two memory cards were being read at the same time. Premier devised a Software patch that repaired the glitch.

In the US currently the certification process for machines impinges on the question of Software disclosure. Both critics and advocates of DRE systems generally argue that the manufacturing company should make public the software they use, which would give them greater incentive to resolve security issues.

Faulty technology and security issues were documented in Aug 2001 in the Brennan Centre at New York University Law School to report that more than 60 examples of e-voting machine failure in 26 states in the year 2004 and 2006.

In the US more than 90% of votes are caste are counted electronically.

Civil Society Intervention

In December 2005 the US Election Assistance Commission (EAC)adopted the 2005 Voluntary Voting System Guidelines, which increase security requirements for voting. The guidelines became effective December 2007 replacing the 2002 voting system standards (VSS) developed by the Federal Election Commission.

The Open Voting Consortium of the US demanded that to restore voter confidence, all electronic voting systems must be completely available to public scrutiny. It also proposed that Election Mark-up Language (EML) standard developed by Oasis, Corporation and now under consideration of the ISO (International Standards Organisation) be used in all DRE / EVM systems.

Legislation

The Help America Vote Act (HAVA) was passed in the year 2002 in which one of the requirement is that EVMs must produce a paper audit trial for every vote.

The Help America Act of 2002 directed NIST to work with the US Election Assistance Commission to create voluntary standards for receiving federal certification from the EAC. The current guide lines are known as VVSG 2005. The latest draft guidelines are called VVSG Next Iteration (VVSG-NI). They address hardware, usability, and security issues.

There have been more election laws and regulations promulgated in the US during the past seven (7) years than in the previous 200 years of American history.

HAVA created a Federal Agency, the US Election Assistance Commission (EAC) to provide national focus on election administration and provided $ 3 bln in Federal Funds to improve the voting systems. It is a four -member body of 2 Democrats and 2 Republicans appointed by the President and confirmed by the US Senate.

The biggest challenge for all election officials is the training of poll workers and voters on the new voting technologies (the US had a shortage of 1.3mln trained poll workers in the year 2006. USA has only 180 mln voters on the rolls whereas India has over 650 mln).

In many States in the USA the election law generally states that the paper records, not the electronic data, constitute the legal ballot.

The National Institute of Standards and Technology (which was specifically tasked to study and oversee the development and production of EVMs in the USA) identified a breakthrough property in an e-voting machine, which is the idea of making it software independent. That means a Software failure does not have any possible impact on the accuracy and integrity of the election. -P111

NIST laid down one transparent set of tests to improve government and voter confidence, while also giving manufacturers an improved understanding of how to ensure that their systems comply with Federal Standards.

Internet Voting is Our Future

All professionals and leading intellectuals and enlightened policy - makers talk of e- democracy, comparing it to the historic participatory Democracy in Athens (Greece) where instead of representative democracy as we have now, of all citizens participated in assemblies debating and deciding issues.

About 6 mln US citizens live out side the country and all want to vote. They are allowed to vote via the Internet. India has about 20 mln off- shore living citizens. There is now talk of dual citizenship even. If all of them are to vote, it can only be through Internet as postal ballots are delayed cumbersome and may not be availed of by many.

Estonia, Netherlands, Switzerland and England now allow citizens to cast ballots via the Internet. From even public libraries using hundreds of laptop computers placed in several locations throughout the area.

The winner of the 2004 US Presidential election got 62 mln votes. This is less than the 73 mln votes cast in 4 hrs in the USA's most popular television show- American Idol -P 29

EVM Situation across Nations

The Netherlands embraced electronic voting in the 1970s before hacker culture was widespread. But in the light of recent concerns and widespread hacking (even the Pentagon was hacked), the country decided to return to paper balloting.

Brazil introduced electronic voting beginning in 1996 and now has a fully electronic system. In the initial years as many as 7% of the voters trying the new system were unable to record their choices electronically, but that figure fell to less than 0.2 % by the year 2000 and the country remains committed to its voting technology. The success was due to extensive education of voters and the polling staff.

The paper audit trail system could failed in the May 2006 primary elections in Ohio. Printers jammed, ran out of paper or over printing. The same was the experience in Navada in year 2004.

Australia used online voting_in the year 2007 for its troops serving in Iraq and Afghanistan, raising participation by the military from 20% to 75%.

Philippines and Romania introduced Internet voting in the year 2009.

Beirne, Executive Director of the Election Technology Council Trade Association told a TV audience that that "electronic voting could allow for broader -scale tampering". But he said, " there has always been a risk with every type of voting system. If insiders for local election office want to fix an election, they don't have to hack a system to do that."

The US has got 170,000 Polling stations. Rosemary Rodriguez who chairs the US Election Assistance Commission, said in the year 2008, that the EAC hopes to start certifying e-voting systems against a set of functionality, accessibility and security requirements by the year 2009. The EAC launched its certification programme in early 2007 and six e-voting vendors applying for certification.

Maryland Tennessee and Colorado have adopted paper backups in the last Presidential elections.

Ireland embarked on e-voting system in the year 2006 that would dispense with "stupid old pencils", as the then -Prime Minister, Bertie Ahern put it, in favour of fancy touch screen voting machines. Three years and Euros 51 mln later, in April 2009 the government scrapped the entire initiative. But what doomed the effort was a lack of trust ; the electorate just did not like that machines would record their votes as mere electronic blips, with no tangible record.

One doesn't have to be a conspiracy theorist or a Luddite to understand the fallibility of electronic voting machines. As most PC users by now know, computers have bugs, and can be hacked. We take on this security risk in banking, shopping and e-mailing, but the ballot box must be perfectly sealed. At least that's what European voters seem to be saying. Electronic voting machines do not meet this standard.

A backlash against e-voting is brewing all over the continent (of Europe). After almost two years of deliberations, Germany's Supreme Court ruled in March that e-voting was unconstitutional because the average citizen could not be expected to understand the exact steps involved in the recording and tallying of votes. Political scientist Joachim Wiesner and his son Ulrich, a physicist, filed the initial lawsuit and have been instrumental in raising public awareness of the insecurity of electronic voting. In an interview with the German magazine Der Spiegel, the younger Wiesner said, with some justification, that the Dutch Nedap machines used in Germany are even less secure than mobile phones. The Dutch public-interest group Wij Vertrouwen Stemcomputers Niet (We Do Not Trust Voting Machines) produces a video showing how quickly the Nedap machines could be hacked without votes or election officials being aware (the answer: five minutes). After the clip was broadcast on national television in October 2006, the Netherlands banned all electronic voting machines.

Numerous electronic-voting inconsistencies in developing countries, where governments are often all too eager to manipulate votes, have only added to the controversy. After Hugo Chavez won the 2004 election in Venezuela, it came out that the government owned 28 percent of Bizta, the company that manufactured the voting machines.

Why are the machines so vulnerable? Each voting machine from the time it is developed and installed to when the votes are recorded and the data transferred to a central repository for tallying — involves different people gaining access to the machines, often installing new software. It wouldn't be hard for, say, an election official to plant a "Trojan" programme on one or many voting machines that would ensure one outcome or another, even before voters arrived at the stations.

What the Election Commission and Government Should Do

In the light of the extensive experiences of different countries as surveyed in the previous paragraphs and as an engineer and a professional, my recommendations for India would be:

- A lot of informed opinion must be generated in bodies which can be given a semi legal status to continuously get all the facts of things giving wrong in electronic voting, in all the elections, in all the States at different levels like Mandals, Zilla Parishads and Co-operative societies etc.
- The Election Commission may have an Advisory Committee drawn from national political parties which in consultation with technical experts (hardware and software) must draft specifications for the EVMs and put in place a Certification Program (the UK had a Type Approvals Board for telephones in the 1980s when telephones and PBXS made by several companies were allowed to be attached to the network of the British Telecom. India's Telecom Engineering Center (TEC) has a Type Approvals mechanism). This will encourage different companies to come with better and yet better and more secure and tamper -proof EVMs.
- The Indian Bureau of Standards (IBS) may have as special unit which shall work closely with hardware and software companies in India to draw specifications for the hardware and software in EVM and the interconnections between these EVMs for aggregating the ballots. It must also put in place a certification process for the vendors.
- The vendors must deposit the source code of the machines they make with the IBS. And any professional body which wants to test the integrity of the software and hardware, must be given access under oath of secrecy, and its findings must be published.
- Voter verified Paper-audit trail machinery must be added to every EVM.
- Millions of polling officials must be trained in the proper use of EVMs and to render first aid when EVMs are malfunctioning.

- There must be a Help Line from every polling booth for receipt of information about malfunctioning of EVMs either from the poling officials or from the public and these must be immediately attended.
- Brazil the only country where the electronic voting system is very enthusiastically and without any doubt being operated, must be studied by our Election Commission, by the IBS and by a Committee of Members of Parliament assisted by their chosen domain experts. Another country which could be studied is Estonia which is also enthusiastically implementing even Internet voting.
- A study of the evolution and experience of the e-voting in US may be undertaken by a group of experts chosen by different political parties (say, those who have got in any State more than 15% of the votes caste).
- The e-voting machines supplied to the Election Commission are made by two central PSUs, the ECIL and the Bharat Electronics. Their ownership by the government gives rise to questions about their integrity (In Venezuela where the State government is owning 28% of the equity in the EVM manufacturing company, there is a grave doubt about the authenticity of the EV system.

10

Failure of ECIL and BEL to Obtain International Patent for Indian EVMs

Intellectual Property Does Not Exist with ECI, ECIL or BEL

This is a documentation of claims for the same invention by two entities: ECIL / BEL. It has to be explained how two entities could claim that they have invented the same phenomenon — Indian EVM.

In response to information sought under the RTI Act, ECIL (Nalini Ravikaran, Chief Public Information Officer, ECIL) responded, *inter alia*, as follows (Ref. ECIL CC RTI 2009-082 9 March 2010): "However, as we were initiating the process, marketing department reviewed the scenario noted that the demand was lukewarm and advised us not to process further so as to minimize patent related expenditure." The process was initiated in 2002 by filing an application with WIPO on 21 Jan. 2002. The patent application was withdrawn in 2006 (See details below)

In view of the withdrawal of patent applications made to WIPO both by ECIL / BEL, it is unclear what types of EVMs are being deployed for elections in India.

It is a matter of serious concern if unverified, untested and unvalidated EVMs are being used for the elections. There are also indications that private parties including foreign electronic component makers are involved in the manufacturing and supply of the EVMs to Election Commission of India.

Non-tamperability of EVMs has NOT been proved in WIPO, though the patent application made the claim of non-tamperability.

Patent applications have been withdrawn after 3-1 / 2 years of patent process and deliberations.

It is amazing that both ECIL and BEL should have sought to obtain patents for comparable "inventions" of computer network instruments called EVMs. How could both have claimed intellectual property right for the comparable designs of EVMs?

Election Commission of India should be asked by Her Excellency the President and Govt. of India to withdraw the EVMs forthwith and ECI should NOT be permitted to use them in any future election. This measure will be to safeguard the transparency of the most important process of the Democratic Republic, public nature of the election process.

BEL's patent application filed on 24 October 2002 ;withdrawn on 13 April 2006

ECIL's patent application filed on 21 November 2002;withdrawn on 19 April 2006

The withdrawal after 3½ years of patent deliberation process shows that the claims made of non-tamperability of EVMs have NOT been proven to the satisfaction of WIPO (World Intellectual Property Organisation)

Both applications had specifically claimed non-tamperability of EVMs.

The rejection by World Intellectual Property Organization (WIPO) of the patent applications and consequent withdrawal prima facie disprove the claims made by ECI through ECIL / BEL and hence, Election Commission of India's claims of non-tamperability stands rejected by the highest technical review process, that of WIPO.

ECI is specifically mentioned in the patent applications and hence becomes a party to the patent application and rejection.

Microchip USA and Renesas Japan have local agents who supply to ECIL and BEL imported chips from Microchip, USA and Renesas, Japan.

These are supplied as masked microchips (to ECIL) or One time programmable read only memory (OTP-ROM) microchips (to BEL).

ECIL and BEL have no way of knowing what the embedded programmes are, in the chips from USA and Japan.

These are the chips which are used in EVMs by ECI. There is no way of knowing what unknown programmes have been included in the chips which are used in the EVMs.

Local agents of Renesas Japan and Microchip USA may have supplied chips with trojan horses.

All the EVMs have to be audited thoroughly.

Now that the strate-transition diagram and flow have been described in the Patent application, it would be easy to reverse engineer the description and point out the flaws and possibilities for trojan horses in the EVMs in use in India.

The following is the status of the patent (Patent application WITHDRAWN) according to the World Intellectual Property Organization website:

EVM India, BEL's application of 2002 for patent. (http://www.sumobrain.com/patents/wipo/Electronic-voting-machine-evm/WO 2002084607.html)

(http:// www.wipo.int/pctdb/en/wo.jsp?WO=2002084607).

EVM India Computer Description by ECIL in WIPO Patent Documents

[Report generated on: 14.02.2010] (http://www.wipo.int/pctdb/iasr?IA=IN2002000043&LANGUAGE=EN&ID=0&VOL=0&DOC=0&WO=02/084607&WEEK=null&TYPE=&DOC_TYPE=IASR&PAGE=1) Intl. Application status report

(http://www.wipo.int/pctdb/en/wads.jsp?IA=IN2002000043&LANGUAGE=EN&ID=09006361800979b0&VOL=17&DOC=006533&WO=02/084607&WEEK=43/2002&TYPE=A1&DOC_TYPE=PAMPH&PAGE=1) Drawings

World Intellectual Property Organization website

The patent application was made on behalf of ECIL by an official of the Instruments and Systems Division of EECIL Alamelu Vaidyanathan seems to be the Patent Attorney from Bangalore.

This invention relates to an Electronic Voting Machine . . . .The model, proposed to be patented, is developed based on the cumulative experience gained by the company during the past two decades of involvement with the process of modernizing the election process under the direct supervision and guidance of Election Commission of India.

(WO / 2002 / 093503) ELECTRONIC VOTING MACHINE

Source

(http://www.wipo.int/pctdb/en/wo.jsp?IA=IN2002000011&DISPLAY=DESC)

Latest biblio data:

International Application No.:

PCT / IN2002 / 000011

Publication Date: 21.11.2002

*International Filing Date: 21.01.2002

Chapter 2 Demand Filed: 02.12.2002

Intl. Patent Classification:

G07C 13 / 00 (2006.01)

Applicants

ELECTRONICS CORPORATON OF INDIA LIMITED, A GOVERNMENT OF INDIA ENTERPRISE [IN / IN]; At ECIL (PO), Hyderabad 500 062, Andhra Pradesh (IN) (All Except US).

GADDE, Raya Koteswara Rao [IN / IN]; (IN) (US Only).

http://www.wipo.int/pctdb/en/wo.jsp?IA=IN2002000011&DISPLAY=STATUS

Status: Withdrawn: 19.04.2006

(http://www.wipo.int/pctdb/en/wo.jsp?IA=IN2002000011&DISPLAY=NATIONAL)

(72) Inventor(s):

GADDE, Raya Koteswara Rao; Instruments and Systems Division Electronics Corporation of India Limited At Flat No. 601, Vishnu Classic, Madhura Nagar Hyderabad 500 038 Andhra Pradesh (IN)

(74) Agent(s): ALAMELU, Vaidyanathan; 451, 2nd Cross, 3rd Block, 3rd Stage Basaveshwaranagar Bangalore 560 079 Karnataka

(IN) [Same person who applied for the patent for Bharat Electronics (BEL)]

Pub. No.: WO / 2002 / 084607 International Application No.: PCT / IN2002 / 000043

Publication Date: 24.10.2002 International Filing Date: 13.03.2002

Chapter 2 Demand Filed: 18.09.2002

IPC: G07C 13 / 00 (2006.01)

Applicants

BHARAT ELECTRONICS LIMITED [IN / IN]; At Trade Center, 116 / 2, Race Course Road, Bangalore 560 001, Karnataka (IN) (All Except US).

RAJAGOPALAN, Jagannathan [IN / IN]; (IN) (US Only).

Inventor: RAJAGOPALAN, Jagannathan; (IN).

Agent: ALAMELU, Vaidyanathan; 451, 2nd Cross, 3rd Block, 3rd Stage, Basaveshwaranagar, Bangalore 560 079, Karnataka (IN).

Patent application was ON BEHALF of BEL. Status: Withdrawn: 13.04.2006

ECIL withdrew its application on 19.04.2006

(http://www.wipo.int/pctdb/en/fetch.jsp?SEARCH_IA=IN2002000043&DBSELECT=PCT&ABIMAGE=24102002/IN0200043_24102002_gz_en.x4&C=10&TOTAL=1&IDB=0&TYPE_FIELD=256&SERVER_TYPE=19-10&ELEMENT_SET=B&START=1&QUERY=(WO/2002084607)+&SORT=41275304-KEY&RESULT=1&DISP=25&FORM=SEP-0/HITNUM,B-ENG,DP,MC,AN,PA,ABSUM-ENG&IDOC=680493&IA=IN2002000043&LANG=ENG&DISPLAY=NATIONAL).

World Intellectual Property Organization website

The patent application was made on behalf of ECIL by an official of the Instruments and Systems Division of EECIL Alamelu Vaidyanathan seems to be the Patent Attorney from Bangalore.

This invention relates to an Electronic Voting Machine . . . .The model, proposed to be patented, is developed based on the cumulative experience gained by the company during the past two decades of involvement with the process of modernizing the election process under the direct supervision and guidance of Election Commission of India.

(WO / 2002 / 093503) Electronic Voting Machine

Source

(http://www.wipo.int/pctdb/en/wo.jsp?IA=IN2002000011&DISPLAY=DESC).

Latest biblio data:

Pub. No.:WO / 2002 / 093503

International Application No.:PCT / IN2002 / 000011

Publication Date:21.11.2002

International Filing Date:21.01.2002

Chapter 2 Demand Filed: 02.12.2002

Intl. Patent Classification:G07C 13 / 00 (2006.01)

Applicants: ELECTRONICS CORPORATON OF INDIA LIMITED, A GOVERNMENT OF INDIA ENTERPRISE [IN / IN]; At ECIL (PO), Hyderabad 500 062, Andhra Pradesh (IN) (All Except US).

GADDE, Raya Koteswara Rao [IN / IN]; (IN) (US Only).

(http://www.wipo.int/pctdb/en/wo.jsp?IA=IN2002000011&DISPLAY=STATUS).

Status: Withdrawn: 19.04.2006

(http://www.wipo.int/pctdb/en/wo.jsp?IA=IN2002000011&DISPLAY=NATIONAL).

Comment by an IT Expert (16 February 2010)

I'm reading what appears to be the application:

(http://www.wipo.int/pctdb/en/wadList.jsp?IA=IN2002000043&LANGUAGE=EN&ID=0900).

6361800979b0&VOL=17&DOC=006533&WO=02/084607&WEEK=43/2002&TYPE=A1&DOC_TYPE=PA.

It's not clear that the patent has been issued yet. Do you have the text of the issued patent?

The first thing that strikes me is that the preamble reads like bad Advertising copy — proof by adjective — so I'm already skeptical.

First question: how "tamper-proof" is the candidate list, really?

What prevents malicious users from pressing the "clear" button and erasing all votes? (Looks like some seals — do these really work?)

What prevents a malicious user from limiting the number of candidates to, say, three, even though there are eight?

What prevents someone from putting a key press interceptor between the ballot unit and the control unit?

(This seems like a fairly obvious attack: the ballot units seem to be little more than passive switch matrixes.)

What algorithm does the microntroller use to check the data integrity of the EEPROM (page 14, line 14)?

What sort of encryption is actually used in the microcontroller? (Page 14, line 18)

(Crypto people don't believe any code or algorithm that's not made public — they assume the people are hiding something and are afraid it would break if it got out)

Can the programme contents of the microcontroller be read?

It suggests sealing the unit with thread and wax; can't wax be melted?

Does it really adhere well to the unit?

There are some mechanisms for sealing the buttons like "clear" (page 22).

Was this actually done?

It seems like there's a really good chance someone will incorrectly transcribe count information on the voting machine when adding up the total votes.

In summary, the way this patent is written, I don't believe much of it. It sounds like someone's trying to sell me something rather than convince me it works from a technical standpoint.

EVM India Computer Description, Patent Application in 2002 by BEL, Bangalore

EVM India, BEL's application of 2002 for patent. http://www.sumobrain.com/patents/wipo/Electronic-voting-machine-evm/WO2002084607.html

(http://www.wipo.int/pctdb/en/wo.jsp?WO=2002084607)

Report generated on: 14.02.2010 (http://www.wipo.int/pctdb/iasr?IA=IN2002000043&LANGUAGE=EN&ID=0&VOL=0&DOC=0&WO=02/084607&WEEK=null&TYPE=&DOC_TYPE=IASR&PAGE=1 Intl). Application status report.

(http://www.wipo.int/pctdb/en/wads.jsp?IA=IN2002000043&LANGUAGE=EN&ID=09006361800979b0&VOL=17&DOC=006533&WO=02/084607&WEEK=43/2002&TYPE=A1&DOC_TYPE=PAMPH&PAGE=1) Drawings.

(http://www.wipo.int/pctdb/en/wads.jsp?IA=IN2002000043&LANGUAGE=EN&ID=09006361800979b0&VOL=17&DOC=006533&WO=02/084607&WEEK=43/2002&TYPE=A1&DOC_TYPE=PAMPH&PAGE=1) Figure 18.

Title:

Electronic Voting Machine (EVM)

Abstract

The ballot unit (BU) which contains sixteen candidate buttons and indicator lamps for each candidate button is interconnected to control unit (CU) through a five-meter-length twenty-five core flat jacketed cable. The control unit (CU), initially set for a particular number of contesting candidates, activates the ballot unit (BU). The voting continues until all the voters cast their votes. On completion of voting, operating the close button (28) closes the control unit (CU), machine power switched off, and control unit (CU) is packed into carrying case and taken into the counting centres for the counting of votes. The result of the election is displayed on the display screen (12) upon pressing of a result button (29, 30) in the control unit (CU). The recorded votes cast against each candidate are displayed sequentially in the display screen (12) with a buzzer beep sound. The voting data is retained in the memory even if power is switched off. The machine can be used for conducting simultaneous elections using the auxiliary control unit (ACU) along with the main control unit (CU). The entire machine is operated by a 7.5V battery and allows the selection of a maximum of sixty-four contesting candidates. Compartments are provided in the machine constructed according to the invention with interlocking and thread sealing features, the machine thus being tamper proof, error free and easy to operate. The voting data recorded once are retained in the memory until it is erased by operating a clear button (31). The entire machine is constructed in injection moulded plastic for mass manufacture and fabricated of light weight. The machine is convenient to use and portable.

Inventors

Rajagopalan, Jagannathan (353 11th Cross, 14th Main J.P. Nagar, II Phase, Bangalore 8 Karnataka, 560 07, IN)
Publication Date: October 24, 2002
Filing Date: March 13, 2002
Export Citation:

Assignee

BHARAT ELECTRONICS LIMITED (At Trade Center, 116 / 2 Race Course Road, Bangalore 1 Karnataka, 560 00, IN)
Rajagopalan, Jagannathan (353 11th Cross, 14th Main J.P. Nagar, II Phase, Bangalore 8 Karnataka, 560 07, IN)
International Classes:G07C13 / 00
Attorney, Agent or Firm: Alamelu, Vaidyanathan (451 2nd Cross, 3rd Block 3rd Stage, Basaveshwaranaga, Bangalore 9 Karnataka, 560 07, IN)

Claims

1. An Apparatus for conducting elections for Parliament, State Assembly, Municipal and other local bodies on the majority voting scheme as per constitution of India on secret ballot and one voter one vote principle comprising. a) A control unit having an OTP Micro controller (One time programmable) to col-

lect, record and store, count and display, a non volatile data memory being interfaced serially to the Microcontroller, the said memory stores the data during voting process, the various control signals are generated through the shift register, a power monitoring circuit to generate the reset to the Microcontroller, a seven segment drive decoder to generate display data, a ballot unit interface along with the necessary connector, all being housed in a housing, the top portion of the control unit being divided in to four sections i.e., (i) A display section consisting of two lamps ON to indicate that the machine is ready for use and BUSY to indicate that the voter can record his vote, and the display panelsone of 2 digits and the other of four digits to display the number of candidates, total number of votes polled, individual votes for each candidate and the errors, if any, (ii) Candidate set section divided into two parts, one having "Candidate Set Button" to set the number of contesting candidates, the other part for carrying the power pack, two doors, one to cover the candidate set button individually and the other which covers the entire section, (iii) Result section divided into two parts, one having the close button to close the polling operations, the other part divided into three sub sections wherein result I and Result II buttons and clear buttons are housed, the result buttons are used to display the results and clear button is used to clear the previous voting records, two separate doors, one to lock the result button sub sections and another to cover the entire section and (iv) Ballot section wherein "ballot button" to permit the voter to cast a vote and total buttons to show the total number of votes polled are housed, and (b) a ballot unit having a base which encloses a printed circuit board and a cover thereof, a connector box for inter connecting cables to the control unit, sixteen push button voting switches (one switch for each contesting candidates), an indicator lamp which glows when the voter is permitted to vote, a slide switch to indicate the ballot unit number.

2. Apparatus as claimed in claim 1, wherein multilevel thread sealing provision is made to protect against any possible tampering.
3. Apparatus as claimed in claim 1, wherein the control unit and ballot unit are made by injection moulded plastic parts, fastenerless heat sealing assembly technique, which provides consistent quality for mass production at economical cost.
4. Apparatus as claimed in claim 1, wherein said base comprises of rectangular moulded base providing locating latches, guides for inserting PCB, self tapping bosses to fix PCB, heat sealing pipes to seal door II and III, cut-out for accommodating rear door and pips with depression for fixing serial number plate.
5. Apparatus as claimed in claim 1, including cover, rectangular moulded part contains compartments for ballot, total, close, result I, result II, cand. set and clear buttons, a cavity to accommodate doors II, door III & door IV, a compartment for power pack, windows for ON, Serial number, Votes and busy indication, protrusion to hold the rear door, counter bore to fix cover to base at the four locations with self tapping screws.
6. Apparatus as claimed in claim 1, wherein said door I is a moulded cover including cut-outs to reach result keys form cover, latches to open from inside, lugs for thread sealing to the cover.
7. Apparatus as claimed in claim 1, wherein said door II is a cover hinged to base and enclosing the close, results and clear button, slots for latching to base, and slant surface with hole to thread seal to the base.
8. Apparatus as claimed in claim 1 including door III comprising moulded panel hinged to base enclosing cand. set switch, power pack compartments, slot for latching to base, and slant surface with hole to thread seal to the base.
9. Apparatus as claimed in claim 1 including door IV, comprising moulded cover hinged to the main cover and enclosing cand. set swich and lugs for thread sealing to the cover.

10. Apparatus as claimed in claim 1, wherein a panel enclosing the out going connector compartment, rotates and opens out for interconnection, latch and thread sealing lugs on both sides.
11. Apparatus as claimed in claim 1, including spacers for sandwich mounting of PCB between base and cover.
12. Apparatus as claimed in claim 1, including the construction of recessed switch knob to ensure deliberate pressing by voter to record the votes.
13. Apparatus as claimed in claim 1, wherein said base is a rectangular moulded panel with self tapping holes to fix PCB, provision for fixing stand, compartment for connector interconnecting and sealing pipes to fix serial number plate.
14. Apparatus as claimed in claim 1, wherein said base is a rectangular moulded panel with self tapping holes to fix PCB, provision for fixing stand, Compartment for connector interconnecting and sealing pipes to fix serial number plate.
15. Apparatus as claimed in claim 1 including cover, rectangular moulded panel with oblong cut-outs to operate switch knob to register the vote, stepped slot to fit cover ballot sheet, slots to hold right and left flops at extreme corners and pips for fixing hinges at the bottom side.
16. Apparatus as claimed in claim 1 including PCB cover, rectangular panel enclosing the PCB and providing holes for inserting sixteen sets of switch and close knobs.
17. Apparatus as claimed in claim 1, including cover ballot sheet, transparent cover for inserting paper containing name, serial number and election symbol of contesting candidates, fixed to cover with round latch for easy rotation.
18. Apparatus as claimed in claim 1, including switch knob and closing knob constructed in that form to operate one at a time in the oblong opening, the construction of movement of one knob brings other knob into position.
19. Apparatus as claimed in claim 1, including flap right and left enclosing latch of main cover and provided with thread sealing

slots to cover and base to protect against possible tampering by the voters.

20. Apparatus as claimed in claim 1, including door connector box, moulded cover enclosing rear compartment to protect cascading connector and cable.
21. Apparatus as defined in claim 1, including the signal integrity established between Microcontroller, Data memory and ballot unit so that these three will work in unified manner.
22. Apparatus as claimed in claim 1, including the construction of Battery pack in moulded case with polarised plug, which is unique and fool proof that different battery cannot be used along with low battery indication means to facilitate replacement of battery at any stage of polling process and the process can be continued without any loss of voting data.
23. Apparatus as claimed in claim 1, including the powering scheme of ballot units from the control unit, which gives a unique nature of signal integrity (Scanning process) for the machine, high current drivers used to drive the ballot unit to cater to the twenty meter distance between the polling officer and voting compartment and the slide switch setting in ballot unit makes it unique and cannot be interchanged during poll.
24. Apparatus as claimed in claim 1, including the method Micro-Controller (OTP) used to store the firmware, which cannot be changed or modified once fused, the non volatile data memory (EEPROM) is tightly coupled to the microcontroller through unique protocol to store the data during the voting process, and every time the microcontroller checks the check sum of the data memory (EEPROM) to establish link to proceed with the voting process, in case of mismatch the machine displays Er message, which eliminates the tampering the micro controller of EEPROM by replacement of external components.
25. Apparatus as claimed in claim 1, including the scheme of data memory written in encrypted form and has been split into two banks and the ballot counting is stored in both banks, at every instance of a change in the data memory, the data is stored in

two different ways and both are verified to check the correctness of the operation and the data can be decrypted only by the firmware in the micro controller, hence it is not possible to corrupt firmware of data by any known means.

26. Apparatus as claimed defined in claim 1, including the implementation of effective redundancy scheme with two independent non-volatile memory devices (EEPROM) to store the data, effectively four banks are used to store data and at every operation all the four banks are checked and at least two banks should contain the correct data as per the firmware's expectations and if data are not found in at least any of the two banks then a fatal error is declared and the whole unit is unusable at this state.
27. Apparatus as defined in claim 1, including the printing of stored data memory through a printer interface module at any number of times in the life of the machine unless deliberately erased by operating the clear button. This emulates the manual ballot paper method as per the constitutional requirements.
28. Apparatus as defined in claim 1, including the unidirectional operational sequence of Machine in which a) Contesting candidate setting cannot be changed unless the result is seen once, b) Votes cannot be cast on the machine unless it is in the cleared condition (Previous voting data erased), c) Votes cannot be added to the machine once it is closed (by pressing the close button), d) Result cannot be seen unless the machine is closed, e) The machine cannot be cleared unless the result is seen at least once and the clearing operation requires the ballot unit inter connection, which eliminates accidental erasing.
29. Apparatus as defined in claim 1 including the regulation of voting in which the machine accepts maximum of 5 votes per minute and this feature discourages rigging and booth capturing.

Description

This Invention relates to an Electronic Voting Machine (EVM) PREAMBLE The prior art is known as manual ballot paper voting method in which every voter is provided with a ballot paper containing serial number, names of the contesting candidates, their election symbol and space to record votes. The recording of vote is done by putting "X" mark using rubber stamp in the space provided against the candidate in the ballot paper. After recording vote, the voters deposit the ballot paper in a sealed metallic box (Ballot box). On completion of voting, the ballot papers are taken to the counting centres. The seals of ballot box is opened in the presence of candidates / agents and the votes are counted manually by identifying "X" stamp mark against the candidate. The candidate who secured highest number of votes is declared winner as per the constitution of India.

The shortcomings of the prior art (manual ballot paper voting method) are:

1. Involves printing of huge volume of ballot paper.
2. Storage and distribution of ballot paper requires large manpower and security.
3. Accounting and issue of ballot paper is a tedious work and error prone.
4. Manual counting of votes requires large manpower, time and prone to human error.
5. Re-counting is time consuming and costly.
6. Segregation of invalid votes is cumbersome and leads to disputes flights, among candidates.
7. Manual voting is prone to mal-practices, booth capturing-not tamper proof.

Due to the ever increasing population and frequency of elections, there is a definite need to bring out improvement over manual ballot paper voting method, which is:

1. Fool proof, trouble free and cost effective.
2. To conduct election, paper less and count the votes automatically, so that the result can be declared immediately.
3. To eliminate the invalid votes so that the dispute of segregation of invalid votes eliminated.

4. Reduce the overall election expenditure, to the government (The election expenditure is increasing due to the frequent elections).
5. Reduce drastically the volume of Ballot paper printing from the current requirement of more then 70 million papers for manual voting for one general election (Papers less system). The Electronic Voting Machine (EVM) of the present invention is provided with all the \ above needed improvements over the manual ballot paper voting method which are explained in the succeeding paragraphs.

Summary of the Invention

The present invention relates to an Electronic Voting Machine (EVM) consisting of Control Unit (CU) and Ballot Unit (BU) for conduct of elections in place of conventional manual ballot paper voting method. The invention totally replaces the existing manual method by the use of apparatus constructed in accordance to the invention and operational requirements as per the constitution of India for fool proof, error free and cost saving way to conduct elections for electing members of state assembly, parliament and other municipal bodies based on majority voting scheme. The apparatus of the invention is convenient, simple to operate and portable. Another important feature of this machine is the facia construction of the control unit and ballot unit, which is as per the constitutional requirement of India. Use of this machine eliminates invalid voters, cumbersome procedure and disputes in segregation of invalid votes as in manual ballot voting scheme. By the use of EVM, the labour can be minimized at poling centres as well as counting centres. The feature of the machine are illustrated below.

The Electronic voting machine of the present invention consists of two units, i. e. a balloting unit which the voter operates to exercise his / her franchise and a control unit which controls the polling process. It is operated by the Presiding Officer or the First Polling Officer.

The Control Unit (CU) constructed in accordance with a invention is built around a Micro — Controller [One time Programmable (OTIR)]. The control unit is divided into four sections, i. e. a. display section, b. candidate set section, c. result section and d. ballot section. The said sections, are provided with seven control buttons namely cand. set, ballot, close, result I, result B, total and clear buttons. Light emitting diode (LED) indicates ON and BUSY condition of the machine. Six digits of seven segment LED is provided for the display of result and error messages. Operation of cand. set switch sets the number of contesting candidate in control unit. Ballot switch operation energizes the ballot unit, receives and records one vote in control unit. Close button operation ends the voting process, The machine records the total number of votes polled and votes against each contesting candidate during the polling. On the operation of Result switch, the vote recorded against every contesting candidate is displayed sequentially. Clear operation erases all previous voting data stored in the machine. Print of recorded voting data is obtained through a printer interface unit.

The Ballot Unit (BU) constructed in accordance with the invention has sixteen (16) push button voting switches and indicator lamps. The voting buttons are provided in a recessed oblong cut-out in the cover so that the buttons are deliberately pressed by the voters for recording of votes and not by accidental pressing. The top cover has a transparent cover for inserting ballot paper to display the names of contesting candidates, their serial number and election symbol. This cover can be sealed inside the panel by thread seal to protect the ballot paper against any tampering. Green LED lamp is provided for indicating the energized condition of the machine to the Voter. Five meter flat cable provides interconnection to the control unit to receive the signal. Slide Switch is used to indicate the ballot unit number, which is set depending on the number of contesting candidates. The rear compartment receives the interconnecting cable of the cascading ballot unit when the machine is used for more than sixteen contesting candidates.

The machine is constructed using injection moulded plastic parts, which provides consistent quality, high volume output for mass production. Fastnerless assembly of plastic components used in the construction of machine to achieve consistent quality and cost effective product. The voting machine designed with injection moulded carrying cases for movement / transportation to any location for usage. The machine constructed to operate with 7.5V battery power source. It can be deployed in places where no electrical power is available. Machine construction with multilevel interlocking panels / section makes it fool proof, easy to use by common man.

http://www.sumobrain.com/patents/wipo/Electronic-voting-machine-evm/WO2002084607.html

Details of the design of EVMs explained by ECL in their patent document available at:

http://www.wipo.int/pctdb/en/wo.jsp?IA=IN2002000011&DISPLAY=DESC

Biblio Data: (WO / 2002 / 093503) Electronic Voting Machine

This invention relates to an Electronic Voting Machine.

Background Voting systems adopted throughout the world typically use either Paper Ballots or mechanical counters. The disadvantages of these systems are

(i) The paper ballots can become physically damaged or altered.
(ii) Inadvertent error of placing the markings in the place not actually intender for.
(iii) Sizable expenses involved in printing the ballot papers.

Electronic Voting Machines are preferable because all the above disadvantages could be eliminated and also further security checks can be included to avoid rigging, booth capturing, etc.

Summary of the Invention Electronic Voting Machine, henceforth referred to, as EVM in this document, is an electronic machine / gadget developed specifically for use in the conduct of election to elected bodies based on secret ballot and "one voter one vote" principle.

This machine can be used for conduct of election to elected bodies like Parliament / Senate / House of Delegates, State / Country Legislatures, local bodies like municipalities, panchayats, industrial trade unions, etc.

This gadget has been developed after a detailed study of the election procedures and related statutory laws in the country and conditions prevalent in the country as well as the average literacy levels of the population.

The model, proposed to be patented, is developed based on the cumulative experience gained by the company during the past two decades of involvement with the process of modernizing the election process under the direct supervision and guidance of Election Commission of India. The experience gained during the deployment of the earlier version of the machines in the various elections for Parliament, State Assemblies as well as in local election of the trade unions has been gainfully utilized for incorporating innovative ideas and procedures to offer a superior machine.

Accordingly it is an object of the present invention to provide a simple Electronic Voting Machine, which is easy to handle, accurate and also cost effective.

It is still further object of the present invention to provide an improved Electronic Voting Machine, which instils confidence in the Voting public as to the accuracy and relative difficulty in tampering with the system.

It is yet further an object of the present invention to provide an improved Electronic Voting Machine, which is easy to store, easy to set-up and easy to operate.

Additional objects, advantages and novel features of this invention shall be set forth in the following description:

Disclosure of the Invention EVM is a very simple machine requiring minimal training on the part of election officials, contesting candidates and their agents and the voting public.

It is an electronic instrument based on a micro controller designed to collect, record and store, count and display the voting data. The voter has to simply press a button to vote in favour of a candidate of his / her choice. The votes polled for each candidate of his / her choice are duly recorded in memory module. The votes polled for each candidate can be displayed immediately after the poll by the press of a button. The machine incorporates several unique mechanical, electrical and software security features to ensure and protect the integrity of the voting data. The machine retains many of the time-tested features and operational sequences of the conventional ballot paper method to enable quick adaptability.

Electronic Voting machine is a gadget developed specifically for use in conduct of elections to elected bodies based on secret ballot and "One Voter per post per Vote" principle. Electronic Voting Machine comprises of Control Unit, Ballot Unit and Interconnecting Cable.

Control Unit

Control Unit is designed around a micro-controller. This is designed to collect, record, store, count and display the votes when called for. The machine incorporates several unique features to ensure and protect the integrity of the voting data. Top portion of the control unit consists of 4 sections, i. e. Display Section, Cand Set Section, Result Section and Ballot Section. In these sections, the following switches are provided to control the operation. A toggle switch is provided to turn-on / off the control unit and the "On" lamp glows when the machine is switched on. When Polling Official presses the ballot button, the busy lamp glows RED. When the voter casts his vote, the busy lamp goes off There is also a detachable display unit, which has two display panels — a two-digit display panel on the left side and a four-digit display panel on the right side.

Cand. set button is used for setting the number of contesting candidates. Clear button is required to be pressed before the start of the pole for clearing the machine from the previous data. Ballot button has to be pressed for enabling a voter to record his vote.

Total button when pressed will show the total number of votes recorded till then. Once close button is pressed no further voting is possible. This button is to be pressed at the close of poll. When EVM is used for simultaneous poll, i.e. Lok Sabha and Assembly poll, both result-1 and result-2 buttons are to be used. When the machine is used for single poll only result 1 button is used.

Ballot Unit

Ballot Unit has a green LED, which glows when the voter is permitted to vote and goes off, after the voter casts his vote. Candidate lamp is provided for each candidate. This glows momentarily when the voter presses the corresponding vote button. The glowing indicates that a vote in favour of that candidate has been recorded in the memory. A four- position slide switch is provided to set the position number of the ballot units. A compartment is also provided to securely house the ballot paper up to 16 candidates and the arrangement for sealing the ballot paper housing.

Interconnecting Cable

The said units are interconnected through this cable and housed in a multi part moulded plastic cabinets and the electrical power for operating the units is derived from power pack located in control unit in a polling booth. The Control Unit is kept under the control of presiding election officials (presiding officer / polling officer) in such a way that the displays are visible to candidates' agents also. The ballot unit is kept in a separate enclosure to enable the voter to exercise his / her franchise secretly. The machine is designed to operate in Single Post Single Vote (SPSV) mode or Double Post Single Vote (DPSV) mode on the principle of one vote per post per voter. Double Post Single Vote mode enables the use of these machines for conducting simultaneous elections to National Parliament and State Legislatures etc., as mentioned earlier.

Advantages of the Present Invention

Eliminates printing of voter wise individual ballot papers. Requires only as many ballot papers as the number of polling booths in a Constituency. Retains the use of booth wise ballot paper with serial numbers, names and election symbols of the candidates. Provides for secured placement of the ballot paper under a transparent cover.

- No scope for invalid votes.
- Ensures full integrity of voting data.
- Enables conduct of elections at a very short notice.
- Enables declaration for results on the same day.
- Provides for the printing of voter wise voting data in case of election disputes for legal verification.
- Enables collection of voting data at the voters doorstep through mobile polling stations.

Enables remote interfacing with computers through a modem for quick declaration of election results. Option to display hourly voting data for statistical analysis.

Sealing the Candidate Set Section

Close the Candidate Set Section. Pass a thread through the two holes provided on the left side and seal with the seal of the Returning Officer. While sealing take care that direct flame does not come in contact with the Control Unit and molten wax does not fall on any part of the Control Unit.

Put back the Ballot Unit and the Control Unit in their respective carrying cases. They are ready for transportation to the Polling Station.

On the day of Election, the presiding Office shall make the following preparations: The Ballot Unit sill be checked to see if the Ballot Paper is properly fixed in place and that the two seals are intact.

In the Control Unit, the presiding officer will check if the Candidate Set Section is intact and then connect the Ballot Unit to the Control Unit by plugging the connector of the interconnecting cable, put the "Power" switch to "ON" position and then close the bottom compartment. Then open the "Result" Section in the Control Unit and press the "Clear" button to set all counts to "ZERO". It takes about fourteen seconds and the buzzer is "ON" during the clearing process.

On completion of the clearing process, the display panel will start displaying that all counts are set to "ZERO" sequentially (i. e. one by one, the display panel will show the total number of candidates, total votes polled and number of votes for each candidate). If need be the presiding officer will conduct a "MOCK POLL" in the presence of some polling agents and others.

During the actual poll, the "Result Section" should be sealed. Using special security paper serially numbered. This paper seal has to be firmly fixed in the inner cover frame of the Result Section. A thin cardboard padding may be provided. The seal should be so fixed that its green surface is seen through the apertures from the outer side. Here is also a provision for making a thread seal on the left side of the inner door. After this, the outer cover of the Result Section has to be pressed for closing this section.

Procedure During Poll

The Poll shall commence at the hour fixed for such commencement Press the "Total" button and ensure that the total votes polled is zero. After all procedural requirements relating to identification of voter, application of indelible ink on his forefinger and obtaining his signature / thumb impression in the Register of Voters have been completed with regard to the first voter, the voter concerned has to be allowed for recording his vote.

For that purpose, press the "Ballot" button on Ballot Section of the Control Unit which would make the Ballot Unit ready for recording of the vote by that voter as has been explained herein above. Repeat that procedure every time the next voter is to be allowed to record his vote. It should be ensured that only one voter goes inside the voting compartment to vote. Special care should be taken to ensure that a voter goes in that compartment in the same order in which his Name is entered in the "Register of Voters". Also ensure that the Ballot button is pressed only when the earlier voter has come out of the voting compartment. At any time, if the total number of votes polled has to be ascertained, "Total" button should be pressed. The Display panel will then show the total number of votes polled by that time. Please remember that the "Total" button is to be pressed only when the "Busy" lamp is OFF.

After the close of the poll, the close button will be pressed. When this button is pressed the display panel will show the total number of candidates and the total number of votes polled during the day.

On the day of counting, after making the necessary checks, the Result button I in the Control Unit pressed to start the Result computation process. On completion of the result computation process, the total number of candidates, the total number of votes and the total number of votes for each candidate will be displayed in the "Display Panel" sequentially.

Uniqueness of the Invention — Control UNRR

The software for setting the number of contesting candidates works in a unique way and provides a simple and ancient method to set the machine to the number of contesting candidates.

The "display on demand" provision in the control unit greatly reduces the power requirements for the machine and at the same time provides adequate time for the viewer to take note of the displayed data.

The software, which detects the presence of ballot units, works in a unique way. When the ballot key is pressed and is a valid key, the software periodically checks for the presence of the ballot unit and gives a clear audio-visual indication (Link Error'LE) regarding the error condition if the ballot unit is disconnected.

The provision in software for reading back the vote data as soon as it is written in the memory provides a unique way of continuously checking the memory retention as well as functioning and leads to "so far so good" type of working. Error at any time during the poll is immediately detected and further polling is stopped. The votes recorded till then are secure and the result of the poll thus far conducted can be seen at the time of counting. Poll can be continued with a new machine.

The software for the detection of pressed error condition works in a unique way to detect the jammed buttons on the ballot unit. Under this error condition, the control unit display PE' (Pressed Error).

The method of recording the votes in the non-volatile memory inside the control unit helps in reducing the numbers of write cycles per cell in the memory thereby greatly increasing the usability of the machine. In fact, during every poll, any specific location in the non-volatile memory is written, on an average ten (10) times. With a non-volatile memory, with about a million write cycle durability, this machine can be used for at least one hundred thousand elections (one Lakh) election before the memory needs a replacement. The provision to include an error-checking bit with the recording of each vote inside the memory greatly enhances the reliability of the recorded data.

The provision to record the vote cast by a voter in "QUADRUPLICATE" inside the control unit helps in computing and displaying the result of the poll in a more reliable fashion. This feature also provides for adequate redundancy of data storage.

The unique software in the control unit, which computes the result of the poll, performs up to 10 compare and validation checks before the vote is assigned to a candidate.

The unique software inside the control unit provides for a sequence looking for the control buttons-ballot, close, result 1 / result 2, clear and Cand Set in such a way that

(i) Contesting candidate setting cannot be changed unless the machine is in the condition.
(ii) Votes cannot be cast on the machine unless it is in the cleared condition.
(iii) Votes cannot be added to the machine once it is closed (by pressing the close button).
(iv) Result cannot be seen unless the machine is closed (by pressing the close button)
(v) The machine cannot be cleared (by pressing the clear button) unless the result is seen at least once if there are non zero votes recorded on the machine.

The unique software inside the Control unit provides for regulating the voting on the machine. This is achieved by ensuring that a maximum of only 5 votes per minute can be cast on the machine. This is especially useful to discourage rigging during poll.

The interlocking feature built into the software in the control unit, which requires the connection of ballot unit for the clear operation to commence, prevents accidental erasure of voting data.

The gray code conversion of the binary scan codes by the control unit when scanning the ballot units reduces the frequency of signals on the cable connecting the ballot unit with the control unit This helps in reducing the susceptibility of the machine to induced electromagnetic interface.

The control unit has the unique feature of retaining the voting data without the need for applying any power.

The control unit can retain, securely, the voting data without any power connection for up to 10 years.

The control unit can be switched off safely at any stage of operation and still continue to work satisfactorily after reapplying the power.

Using a gadget called "Auxiliary Display Unit (ADU)" which is connected to in parallel to the display board and the result data can be conveniently displayed even if the internal display digits / segments in digits on the control unit have failed.

The provision for connecting a gadget called "Totalizer" to the MCU connector of the Control unit and its subsequent detection by the CU when Result buttons. are operated, help in mixing of votes and prevent the results of individual polling stations from being displayed.

The machine provides unique provision for conducting "Simultaneous poll". This feature enables one control unit along with a mini-control unit to conduct polls simultaneously to two posts-like Member of Parliament and Member of State Legislative Assembly.

Ballot Unit

The mechanical blocking tabs provided in the ballot unit to block the unused candidate buttons with colour identical to that of the body of the ballot unit removes any confusion in the minds of the voter regarding the actual candidate buttons in use. This also prevents votes being cast on buttons not in use.

The software in the control unit for scanning the candidate keys in the ballot unit works in a unique way such that only the buttons of those candidates who are in poll are scanned. Rest of the buttons as well as boxes, if connected, is ignored.

No invalid vote can be cast on the voting machine.

The hardware daisy chaining provision implemented in the ballot unit prevents wrong connection of the ballot units when more than one ballot unit is used (As in the case where the number of contesting candidates is more than 16). The control unit always detects any error in the sequential connection of the ballot units at the appropriate time and an error message is flashed and further operation stopped. This prevents wrongly registering the votes on the machine.

The locking pins, provided under the transparent ballot paper screen on the Ballot unit, prevent the movement of the ballot paper placed under the screen.

No part inside the machine, which requires periodic reconditioning or replacement.

The machine has unique feature of providing for up to 64 candidates on both the polls when used for simultaneous poll.

The cabinet designs for both the control unit and the ballot unit provide for adequate interlocking of the required functions / keys.

The carrying cases provided separately for the control unit and the ballot units provide for easy transport of the machines and also enable them to be carried over rugged terrain without causing any damage to the units.

Claims

1. An Electronic Voting Machine specifically to conduct elections based on secret ballot and "one voter per post per vote" principle, which comprises of:

   (i) A control unit having an unique Micro controller embedded with a set of instructions to collect the votes, record and store, count and display the same when called for, the said micro controller being connected to a memory module for storing the vote cast, a display interface along with a display printed circuit board to display the necessary information as and when called for, a Buzzer interface with two buzzers to give aural indications, a ballot unit interface along with the necessary connector, all being housed in a housing, the outer top portion of the control unit is being divided into four sections, i.e. (a) display section where a detachable seven segment having a two digit display for the number of contesting candidates along with their serial number, a four digit display for displaying the number of votes; an indicator to indicate that the voting machine is "ON"; another indicator which glows when the ballot button is pressed to enable voter to record vote and turns off when the vote is recorded; (b) candidate Set section wherein the control switch "candidate set button" to set the number of contesting candidates in conjunction with corresponding ballot unit (s) and a compartment for power pack are located; a separate cover for the candidate set button and a separate door for locking the entire section being provided; (c) Result Section wherein "Close button" to close the polling operation is located on one side and the other side having a separate cover is provided with a control switch" clear button" to clear all the previously recorded voting data and set all the counts to zero; and control switches "result buttons" i.e. "RESULT I AND RESULT II" to display the results sequentially; a door being provided to lock the entire section; (d) Ballot section wherein the control switches "Ballot button" to permit the voter to cast a vote ;"Total button" to display the number of contesting candidates and the total number of votes polled for each post during polling ; a control switch" Toggle switch" to turn on / off battery power to control unit along with two connectors are being provided on the rear side thereof;

(ii) A ballot unit having a housing wherein an "EPM" having a set of instructions embedded therein is housed along with a green LED which glows when the voter is permitted to vote and goes off after the voter cast his / her vote ; candidates lamp, one for each candidate which glows momentarily when the corresponding vote button is pressed by the voter indicating the record of a vote in favour of that candidate, 16 vote buttons and 16 masking tabs, one for each candidate that records the voters franchise, a slide switch to set the position number of the ballot units, the housing being covered by a door wherein provisions have been made to receive the visual indications and a compartment to securely house a copy of the ballot paper for up to 16 candidates, and

(iii) The said units being inter connected by cable and housed in a multi part moulded plastic cabinet and the electrical power for operating the said units being derived from a battery kept in the control unit.

2. An Electronic Voting Machine as claimed in claim 1, wherein a mini control unit is connected to the control unit in case of simultaneous polls.
3. An Electronic Voting Machine as claimed in claim 1 or 2, wherein the micro controller of the control unit has means which detects the presence of ballot units and gives a clear audio-visual indication (Link Error LE) regarding the error condition if the unit is disconnected.
4. An Electronic Voting Machine as claimed in claim 1, 2 or 3, wherein means for detecting the jammed buttons on the ballot unit is provided in the control unit with the display of "PE" (Pressed Error).
5. An Electronic Voting Machine as claimed in any one of claims 1 to 4, wherein a non-volatile memory inside the control unit helps in reducing the number of write cycles per cell in the memory thereby greatly increasing the usability of the machine.
6. An Electronic Voting Machine as claimed in claim 4, wherein the memory module has two memory banks and each bank having two memory locations along with an error checking bit with the recording of each vote inside the memory.
7. An Electronic Voting Machine as claimed in 6, wherein the vote cast by a voter is recorded in "Quadruplicate".
8. An Electronic Voting Machine as claimed in any one of claims 1 to 7, wherein an unique firmware is provided in the control unit to compute the result of the poll, perform up to 10 compare and validation checks before the vote is assigned to a candidate.
9. An Electronic Voting Machine as claimed in any one of claims 1 to 8, wherein an interlocking means is built in the firmware which requires the connection of ballot unit for the clear operation to commence, prevents accidental erasure of voting data.
10. An Electronic Voting Machine as claimed in any one of claims 1 to 9, wherein the control unit has the provision to retain the voting data without the need for applying any power.
11. An Electronic Voting Machine as claimed in any one of claims 1 to 10, wherein the control unit can retain, securely, the voting data without any power connection for up to 10 years.

12. An Electronic Voting Machine as claimed in any one of claims 1 to 11, wherein the control unit is provided with means to output the display data related signals on the connector of the Ballot Unit and Mini Control Unit, which helps in displaying the result data properly even if the internal display digits on the control units have failed.
13. An Electronic Voting Machine as claimed in any one of claims 1 to 12, wherein an "Auxiliary Display Unit (ADU)" is connected in parallel to the display board enabling the result data to be displayed conveniently even if the internal display digits / segments in digits on the control units have failed.
14. An Electronic Voting Machine as claimed in any one of claims 1 to 13, wherein a "Totalizer" is connected to the Mini Control Unit connector of the control unit to help in mixing of votes and prevent the results of the individual polling stations from being displayed.
15. An Electronic Voting Machine as claimed in any one of claims 1 to 14, wherein mechanical blocking tabs are provided in the ballot unit to block the unused candidates buttons with colour identical to that of the body of the ballot unit.
16. An Electronic Voting Machine as claimed in any one of claims 1 to 15, wherein means are provided in the micro controller for scanning the candidate keys in the ballot unit, which works in a unique way such that only the buttons of those candidates who are in poll are scanned.
17. An Electronic Voting Machine as claimed in any one of claims 1 to 16, wherein the ballot unit has daisy chaining provision to prevent wrong connection of the ballot units when more than one ballot unit is used.
18. An Electronic Voting Machine as claimed in any one of claims 1 to 17, wherein locking pins are provided under the ballot paper screen on the ballot unit, to prevent movement of the ballot paper placed under the screen.
19. An Electronic Voting Machine as claimed in any one of claims 1 to 18, wherein means are provided such that the ballot unit can be used for up to 64 candidates on both the polls when used for simultaneous poll.

20. An Electronic Voting Machine as claimed in any one of claims 1 to 19, wherein interlocking means are provided to lock the required control switches.
21. An Electronic Voting Machine substantially as herein before described and illustrated in the accompanying drawings.

National Phase: (WO / 2002 / 093503) Electronic Voting Machine

Available information on National Phase entries (more information)

Status: Withdrawn: 19.04.2006

Documents

International Application Status

The International Application Status Report shows the latest available status information and bibliographic data on record at the International Bureau. It is generated on request and contains:

Published International Application Date 21.11.2002

Initial Publication with ISR (A1 47 / 2002)

Related Documents on file at the International Bureau (more information) Date Title

08.01.2004

21.11.2002 IN 379 / MAS / 2001 11.05.2001 (Pr. Doc.)

Bharat Electronics Limited application details with World Intellectual Property Organization Source: http://www.wipo.int/pctdb /en/wo.jsp?WO=2002084607

Pub. No.: WO / 2002 / 084607 International Application No.: PCT / IN2002 / 000043

Publication Date:24.10.2002 International Filing Date:13.03.2 002

Chapter 2 Demand Filed: 18.09.2002

IPC:G07C 13 / 00 (2006.01)

Applicants: BHARAT ELECTRONICS LIMITED [IN / IN]; At Trade Center, 116 / 2, Race Course Road, Bangalore 560 001, Karnataka (IN) (All Except US).

RAJAGOPALAN, Jagannathan [IN / IN]; (IN) (US Only).

Inventor:RAJAGOPALAN, Jagannathan; (IN).

Agent:ALAMELU, Vaidyanathan; 451, 2nd Cross, 3rd Block, 3rd Stage, Basaveshwaranagar, Bangalore 560 079, Karnataka (IN)

Designated States: AE, AG, AL, AM, AT, AU, AZ, BA, BB, BG, BR, BY, BZ, CA, CH, CN, CO, CR, CU, CZ, DE, DK, DM, DZ, EC, EE, ES, FI, GB, GD, GE, GH, GM, HR, HU, ID, IL, IN, IS, JP, KE, KG, KP, KR, KZ, LC, LK, LR, LS, LT, LU, LV, MA, MD, MG, MK, MN, MW, MX, MZ, NO, NZ, OM, PH, PL, PT, RO, RU, SD, SE, SG, SI, SK, SL, TJ, TM, TN, TR, TT, TZ, UA, UG, US, UZ, VN, YU, ZA, ZM, ZW.

African Regional Intellectual Property Org. (ARIPO) (GH, GM, KE, LS, MW, MZ, SD, SL, SZ, TZ, UG, ZM, ZW)

Eurasian Patent Organization (EAPO) (AM, AZ, BY, KG, KZ, MD, RU, TJ, TM)

European Patent Office (EPO) (AT, BE, CH, CY, DE, DK, ES, FI, FR, GB, GR, IE, IT, LU, MC, NL, PT, SE, TR)

African Intellectual Property Organization (OAPI) (BF, BJ, CF, CG, CI, CM, GA, GN, GQ, GW, ML, MR, NE, SN, TD, TG).

Publication Language: English (EN)

Filing Language: English (EN)*

[Endnote: Details of a project (including source code) by a Private Sector Company in India to make EVMs is available on the website:

Source: http://www.8051projects.net/downloads205.html. World, World of Microcontrollers.]

---

* http://www.wipo.int/pctdb/images/PCT-IMAGES/24102002/IN0200043_24102002_gz_en.x4.jpg (Image of control unit of EVM)

11

Resolution of International Conference on Electronic Voting Machines*

At the International Conference on EVMs, the participants consider in detail the current international practice and law relating to the deployment of EVMs, the evidence on and the scope for their tamperability and the safeguards that are necessary to ensure that the deployment of EVMs, does not, in any manner, compromise the central requirements of transparency and accountability to the voter, at each and every stage of the election process.

In the interest of the electoral process remaining free and fair, transparent and accountable to the voter, the participants unanimously resolved that the EVMs should provide for a voter verifiable paper trail, and if not feasible then we should return to the paper ballot system.

The participants further resolved that, without such an auditable paper trail, the two essential requirements, namely transparency and accountability to the voter and the related requirement of verifiability of the validity of the votes cast by the voters envisaged under sections 100 and 101 of the Representation of People Act, 1951 will stand and seriously compromised as well as infringing Sections 11 to 14 of the Information Technology Act (2000) and the Indian Evidence Act (1872).

---

* Centre For National Renaissance Conference on Electronic Voting Machines (EVMs) — Savera Hotel, Chennai, 13 February 2010. Convenor: Dr. Subramanian Swamy.

Swamy for Expert Panel on Secure EVMs*

Janata Party president Subramanian Swamy has demanded that an independent expert committee be appointed to find out how electronic voting machines could be safeguarded securely.

Talking to journalists after an international conference on Electronic Voting Machines: How Trustworthy? convened by the Centre for National Renaissance, New Delhi, he said several countries had banned the use of EVMs. The international consensus was that EVMs were a danger to democracy as they were not trustworthy. The Election Commission had not demonstrated that EVMs could never be rigged. If the Commission wanted to continue their use, it should give a printed receipt to every voter just as people used to get in automated teller machines after cash withdrawal. This receipt was a requirement under the Information Technology Act of 2000, which the Commission was "adamantly and obstinately" refusing to comply with.

He said renowned computer experts were ready to demonstrate that EVMs could be rigged, and stressed the need for an in-built safeguard.

* Special correspondent, *The Hindu*, 13 February 2010.

International experts who participated are:

1. Dr. Rop Gonggrijp, Netherlands, Computer hacker, successful Entrepreneur who is instrumental in banning of EVMs in Netherlands due to security reasons, in spite of huge investments made by Netherlands in EVMs.
2. Dr. Till Jaeger, Germany Attorney who argued the landmark German Supreme Court Judgement that effectively banned EVMs in German Elections.
3. Professor David Dill, USA (via Video Conference), University of Stanford, pioneer for reformation of usage of EVMs in US elections that resulted in 21 states in US either ban EVMs or require paper trail and additional 18 states require paper trail in state or local jurisdictions. Founder of Verified Voting Foundation. In 2004, Dr. Dill received the Electronic Frontier Foundation's "Pioneer Award" for spearheading and nurturing

the popular movement for integrity and transparency in modern elections."

4. Dr. Alex Halderman, USA, Computer Science Professor, University of Michigan, noted expert of Electronic Voting Security who demonstrated first voting machine virus, lead team of Scientists from Princeton and Berkeley for "Top to Bottom" review of California EVMs.

12

Independent Experts Raise Serious Questions

Letter of Professor David Dill* to Navin Chawla, Chief Election Commissioner

Only Secure Method is Voting by Ballot-Paper

I am writing this letter at the request of Satya Dosapati from the Save Indian Democracy Organization with regard to the ongoing debate on the usage of EVMs in India. I am an American computer science professor who has spent significant time over the last six years on policy issues in electronic voting. During that time, I have founded two organizations, testified before the US Senate, and appeared in several nationally distributed news shows and documentaries. I would like to share with you some facts and conclusions I have come to during that work.

An important function of elections is to establish the legitimacy of the elected officials in the eyes of the public. Skeptical, untrusting observers should be able to see that election results are correct. It is not sufficient for election results to be accurate; the public must know that the results are accurate. Civil society is damaged if elections are not credible, even when fraud cannot be demonstrated. In traditional elections, paper ballots contribute to election credibility because voters can ensure that their votes have been properly recorded (when they write them on the ballot), and poll workers and observers at the polling place can ensure that ballots are not

* Professor of Computer Science, Stanford University, dill@cs.stanford.edu. This letter is dated 3 February 2010

changed, added or removed after being deposited in the ballot box. In contrast, purely electronic voting machines do not allow voters to verify that their votes have been accurately recorded, and do not allow observers to witness that the ballots have not been tampered with. Electronic voting machines provide no evidence during or after the election to convince a skeptic that the election results are accurate.

It is not clear that this situation would be acceptable even if electronic voting machines could be guaranteed to be accurate and honest. But such assurances are well beyond the current state of computer technology. It is not practical to design fully error-free and reliable computing equipment. More importantly, it is not feasible to prevent malicious changes to the machines' hardware or software. Computers are especially vulnerable to malicious changes by insiders such as designers, programmers, manufacturers, maintenance technicians, etc. Indeed, it is not known how to build trustworthy paperless electronic voting systems even using extreme security measures. Of course, these problems are magnified enormously when the design of the machines is held secret from independent reviewers.

I understand that the argument has been raised in India that the EVMs are safe because they are not connected to a network. All of the concerns I raise apply to non-networked machines, since voting machines in the US are also never connected to the Internet. For example, a manufacturer or technician can maliciously change the software or hardware on a machine whether it is connected to a network or not.

With current technology, the only trustworthy voting methods are those that allow individual voters to verify that their votes have been properly recorded on a paper ballot. In the United States, most voting systems rely on paper ballots that are filled out directly by the voters, and counted either by hand or by machine. If the votes are counted by machine, it is necessary to audit the performance of the machines by choosing groups of ballots at random and counting them by hand.

In 2003, I authored the "Resolution on Electronic Voting," which has been endorsed by thousands of computer professionals including many of the world's most respected computer scientists. It states: "Computerized voting equipment is inherently subject to programming error, equipment malfunction, and malicious tampering." It is time to recognize the reality that there is no basis for public trust in paperless electronic voting equipment.

I would be happy to discuss this topic with you further, including technical issues, referring you to individuals with various kinds of expertise who know, or sharing more detailed experiences with electronic voting issues in the United States. We can converse by telephone, email, or you would be welcome to visit me at Stanford if you are in the United States. I look forward to hearing from you.

Sincerely,
David L. Dill

Letter of US Professors and IT Experts to Chief Election Commissioner of India (CEC)

Note from the Editors

The editors thank the guardians of democracy from all parts of the globe, and participants of the international conference held in Chennai, in particular, who have supported the cause of Center for National Renaisssance, to save democracy in India.

The accompanying letter, is one evidence of such support from an expert Panel discussion held in Washington DC on August 9, 2010. It was sent on 12 August, 2010 to Dr. S.Y. Quraishi, Chief Election Commissioner of India, after the panel discussions in Washington DC participated in, among others, by Alok Shukla, Deputy Election Commissioner of Election Commission of India (ECI) and Indiresan, Head of ECI technical committee on EVMs.

This remarkable document signed by 28 US academics and IT experts, and the startling facts disclosed for the first time, in this book, should awaken the citizens of India to the risks posed to Indian democracy by the continued use of tamperable, non-transparent, non-verifiable, insecure Indian EVMs.

Indian democracy is a millennium-old institution and should not be allowed to be sullied by insecure, tamperable, unconstitutional systems like Indian EVMs.

This book would have served its purpose if it creates awareness among the citizens on this fundamental issue of voters' control over and voter verifiability of every step of the election process. Adult suffrage (election process) is a basic feature of the Constitution which the people have given to themselves constituting the Republic of India.

That eternal vigilance is the price of liberty is a universal adage. Indian citizens cherish the democratic heritage, will keep the flame of liberty shining bright for present and future generations. We are confident that citizens of India *believe in liberty, and are willing to fight for it.*

Wardman Park Hotel, Washington, D.C.
12 August 2010

Dr. S.Y. Quraishi, Chief Election Commissioner
Election Commission of India
Nirvachan Sadan
Ashoka Road, New Delhi-110001

Dear Dr. Quraishi,

We, the undersigned participants in the 2010 Electronic Voting Technology Workshop / Workshop on Trustworthy Elections (EVT / WOTE), had the privilege to attend a panel discussion on the state of India's electronic voting machines (EVMs). We greatly appreciate the participation of Dr. Alok Shukla, Deputy Election Commissioner, and Prof. P. V. Indiresan, Chairman of the Expert Committee, who were joined by G. V. L. Narasimha Rao of VeTA* and Prof. J. Alex Halderman of the University of Michigan. We were fascinated to learn about the complexities and challenges of conducting elections in the world's largest democracy, and about the Election Commission's accomplishments in this regard. However, as experts in electronic voting technology and computer security, we have significant concerns about the security, verifiability, and transparency of India's EVMs.

Although India's EVMs have a simple design that avoids many of the problems found in other direct-recording electronic (DRE) voting machines, they are still vulnerable to a wide range of attacks. New classes of attacks have been discovered since the time the EVMs were introduced that render many of their security assumptions obsolete. Therefore, we conclude, after listening to the arguments of the panellists, that India's EVMs do not today provide

* *Note:* VeTA: Citizens for Verifiability, Transparency, and Accountability in Elections

security, verifiability, or transparency adequate for confidence in election results.

We urge the Election Commission to explore other forms of voting that are suitable to the Indian context and that do provide adequate transparency, verifiability, and security. Other democracies have adopted and then abandoned DRE voting as science's understanding of election security has progressed. Our research community has been involved in this process around the world, and you are welcome to draw on our collective experience and expertise as you see fit.

Sincerely,

(All affiliations are listed for identification only.)

Dr. Ben Adida
Harvard University

Dr. Josh Benaloh
Microsoft Research

Prof. Matt Blaze
University of Pennsylvania

Prof. Mike Byrne
Rice University

Joseph A. Calandrino
Princeton University

Ariel J. Feldman
Princeton University

Russell A. Fink
University of Maryland, Baltimore County

Rick Carback
University of Maryland, Baltimore County

Stephen Checkoway
University of California, San Diego

Bill Cheswick
AT&T Shannon Labs

Prof. David Dill
Stanford University

Jeremy Epstein
Senior Computer Scientist, SRI International

Prof. Ronald L. Rivest
Massachusetts Institute of Technology

Prof. Hovav Shacham
University of California, San Diego

Prof. Ian Goldberg
University of
Waterloo

Dr. Joseph Lorenzo Hall
University of California,
Berkeley / Princeton University

Prof. Candice Hoke
Cleveland State University

Harri Hursti
CTO, Clear Ballot Group

Bo Lipari
Founder, New Yorkers for
Verified Voting

Neal McBurnett
Election Audits

Dr. Peter G. Neumann
Principal Scientist, SRI International
Computer Science Laboratory

Prof. Alan T. Sherman
University of Maryland,
Baltimore County

Prof. Philip B. Stark
University of California,
Berkeley

Dr. Vanessa Teague
University of Melbourne

Prof. Poorvi L. Vora
George Washington
University

Prof. Dan Wallach
Rice University

Director, ACCURATE*

Kai Wang
University of California,
San Diego

Luther Weeks
CTVotersCount.org

* ACCURATE (A Center for Correct, Usable, Reliable, Auditable, and Transparent Elections) is a multi-institution voting research center funded by the National Science Foundation (NSF).

Letter of Omesh Saigal to Prime Minister*

N-130B Panchshila Park
New Delhi 110017
27 August 2010

My Dear Prime Minister,

It is reported in today's papers that government suspects a "foreign hand" in the tampering of an allegedly stolen EVM by three foreign professors and have ordered an enquiry by RAW and IB. This is good but my request is these agencies should also be asked to enquire into the role of two of its own agencies (BEL and ECIL), who got the "program code", which really controls the functioning of the machine, written onto the chips, in USA by foreign private companies! The fact of the program having been written on these chips abroad has, reluctantly though, been admitted by both BEL and the ECIL in replies to my RTI queries. Since both these companies are also engaged in making highly sensitive defence equipment, the fact that chips are programmed in foreign countries does not augur well for the country's external security as well.

That these machines are tamperable there is no doubt and no one knows this better than your Minister of State who is also Minister in charge of both these agencies. He was a Director in a NOIDA company which designed an EVM with which the IIT Delhi alumni association conducts its election and because of doubts on such machines it has provision for a paper trail as an important safeguard against tampering.

I took up the issue of possible tampering of EVMs with the former CEC on 30 June, 2009 and I was invited vide their letter of 16 July, 2009 for a hearing and to conduct a mock poll, which was

---

* The letter was released to the media by Mr. Omesh Saigal, IAS (Retd), Ex-Chief Secretary, Delhi and Ex-Secretary to Government of India.

already done before several former Secretaries to the Government of India. In this meeting, even a member of the EC's advisory council conceded that an audit of these machines, especially of the foreign programmed chip, was a must to ensure its reliability and non-tamperable. This audit will also help to restore the credibility of the elections conducted since the introduction of the electronic machine.

A bucket of water needs only one leak to empty; the Flow Chart (*See* Annexure 13.1) discloses several leaks. This examines dispassionately each one of the safeguards introduced by the EC, as disclosed in its various manuals, statements and websites.

With respectful regards,

Omesh Saigal

Annexure 12.1

Flow Chart

Activity	*Examination of present position / safeguards*	*Are these adequate?*
1. Transparency as a concept in the election management has always been there, not just in India but in all democratic countries.	The Constitution of India calls for India to be a sovereign socialist secular democratic republic. The German Federal Constitutional Court recently held that 'the fundamental decisions of constitutional law in favour of democracy… prescribes that all essential steps of an election are subjected to the possibility of public scrutiny….' It says that this results from the 'principle of public nature of elections'. In the returning officers manual, ECI mandates that 'the election management should be transparent…'.	It is clear that 'possibility of public scrutiny' and the 'principle of public nature of elections' should guide every action connected with the management of the election process. This is the same as when the ECI talks of 'transparency' visiting all actions connected with the management of elections. The question of adequacy has to be judged in this slight.
2. By Act 1 of 1989 (w.e.f. 15-3-1989). Parliament amends the representation of the People Act,1951 to enable use of voting machines.	Section 61a provides that 'the giving and recording of votes by voting machines, in such manner as may be prescribed, may be adopted in such constituency or constituencies as the	Two points are clear here: one, that voting machines are not necessarily electronic voting machines and two, the legislative mandate is for constituency-wise use of such machines and

Contd. . .

Activity	*Examination of present position / safeguards*	*Are these adequate?*
	Election Commission may, having regard to the circumstances of each case, specify.' It is further explained that '"voting machine" means any machine or apparatus whether operated electronically or otherwise used for giving or recording of votes.'	not their use in all constituencies. It is a moot point if the decision of the ECI to use EVMs in all constituencies in 2009 will stand judicial scrutiny.
3. Decision of ECI to have electronic voting machines.	It is not clear if ECI examined other voting machines or apparatus, other than the electronic version, before going in for EVMs. We do know that EVM was first tried in a constituency in 1992. The present EVM merely records and totals the votes polled because of software loaded onto it. Because of high possibility of tampering in such systems, a whole lot of cumbersome and expensive safeguards have to be introduced. a mechanical machine would have been less cumbersome and less amenable to tampering. And far cheaper.	Disturbing possibilities: one, EVMs favoured because of prejudices of the scientific adviser of ECI. two, pressure from commercial interests who were experimenting with EVMs at that time. it is a known fact that a student of the Sr Adviser to the ECI was the director of a commercial concern which was at that time in the forefront of EVM development. Another director in this company, by the way, is now an important Minister in the Central Government.
4. Electronic Corporation of India and Bharat Electronics Ltd.	Just having a government owned company to design these machines is not	Section 28a of the RP Act provides for the returning officer, presiding officer, etc.,

Contd. . .

Activity	*Examination of present position / safeguards*	*Are these adequate?*
appointed advisers and manufacturers of the EVMs.	an adequate safeguard against malpractices and tampering. The minister's control on the staff of these companies makes their role even more dubious especially when even during election there is no provision of placing them under the control of ECI while at the same time the maintenance and upkeep of these machines may have to be given to them.	to be deemed to be on deputation to Election Commission but there is no similar provision for the staff of the public sector undertakings. in fact, apart from government servants on duty, none is allowed in the booths or counting centres.
5. Source code to be prepared by BEL / ECIL engineers.	It would have been better if the agency that prepares the source code is different from one that also manufactures the machine.	Since these are commercial undertakings, the sanctity of the source code can be held ransom to their commercial interests. Moreover, they being under the control of ministers cannot be trusted in election matters unless there is adequate control of the ECI.
6. Source code sent to quality assurance group (for BEL).	Not an independent check because QAG is part of BEL only.	
7. EVM evaluated and cleared by the technical expert group of the ECI and sent back to BEL.	It is not clear if ECI approval was taken. Under 19a functions of ECI can 'be performed also by a Deputy Election Commissioner	A more meaningful approval of the evm would have been for a Dy Election Commissioner with IT qualifications to be

Contd. . .

Activity	*Examination of present position / safeguards*	*Are these adequate?*
	or by the Secretary to the Election Commission' and none else. Technical expert group has no such authority. It is also not clear if the 'source code' was also cleared by this group or if this group has anyone who is competent enough in it.	appointed and empowered in this behalf. Or another agency of the government, like NIC, to have been involved.
8. Software frozen.	Not clear what happens now and where the 'frozen' software is kept for reference checking later. It is clear that it is not with the ECI.	Not keeping the frozen software exclusively with the ECI is a major security breach. Having it with commercial organizations, which can hold it ransom for commercial interests, is also not desirable. This point is amply proved when they rake recourse to these interests in denying information to the public under the RTI Act.
9. Source code converted to Object code by BEL engineers (ECIL presumably does the same; in the meeting in ECI, it was described as hex code by them).	A major step since it is at this stage that the code that is written in language that is intelligible to us gets converted to machine language. The code is now in a form that it can be fused onto the chip/micro-processor.	A very important breach of security is that the object code/hex code was not sent back to the ECI or its advisory technical expert group at this stage. It may not be difficult for a corrupt BEL / ECIL engineer to add a 'trojan' software at this stage. Second stage approval of the

Contd. . .

Activity	*Examination of present position / safeguards*	*Are these adequate?*
		ECI would have prevented this from happening.
10. M/s Microchip USA and Renasas, Japan selected by BEL and ECIL respectively for the microcontroller chip.	It is not clear at all why foreign companies were selected for this task and whether any security clearance was taken for them. A Task Force of the Defence Science Board of the USA (February 2005) suggested that "...shift.... to foreign manufacture endangers the security of classified embedded in chip designs; additionally, it opens the possibility that 'trojan horses' and other unauthorized design inclusions may appear in unclassified integrated circuits... ."	It is noteworthy here that the chip is the heart of the electronic machine and any tampering at this stage can effect the entire functioning of the machine. It is noteworthy that tampering is really altering the code or adding a virus (trojan), which will give the control of the machine to the one who has tampered. He can now activate the trojan as when he likes; and in whichever election he chooses without any danger of detection.
11. The object code conveyed to them in USA / Japan.	Even if these foreign companies had to be selected why the chip could not have been imported and the object code fused under the supervision of India engineers and under the guidance and control of the technical group of the ECI.	There must be some method by which the object code must have been conveyed to the company in USA / Japan. Whichever method is employed, it increases the chances of foul play of tampering with the object code.
12. Object code fused into chip during manufacturing	This would essentially make it a masked chip. This is the most dangerous decision	It is not that experts advising the ECI are unaware of this possibility. In para 4.3

Contd. . .

Activity	*Examination of present position / safeguards*	*Are these adequate?*
process.	taken by the concerned persons; it essentially makes it a masked chip, making it impossible to detect any manipulation that may have been done at the time of the manufacture. If a 'trojan' program is added at this stage, there will be no way to detect it. Since the 'trojan' can be activated in many possible ways, including through a wireless device, it gives the one tampering an open and safe way of rigging the poll in whichever way he likes without any possibility of being caught.	of his report of 2006, Prof Indiresan states that the program is 'permanently fused and hence cannot be read'. In para 4.7 he recognizes that the 'EVM is an embedded and factory masked'. This makes these machines absolutely impossible to be 'subjected to the possibility of public scrutiny, thus failing an essential test of transparency. That the program once fused cannot be read by anyone including the manufacturer is admitted by BEL in its website. It says: 'program codes once written and fused in this OTPROM (One Time Programmable Read Only Memory) cannot be read back or altered by anyone including the manufacturer'.
13. The chip is sent back for being fixed onto the Printed Circuit Board of the EVM.	Raises many questions, especially about the possibility of the chips being replaced while being shipped or at the time of clearing or by the clearing agents and so on. None have been	Needless to say if the masked chips are replaced with others made by the same manufacturer or similar product with tampered software, the chances of detection are almost

Contd. . .

Activity	*Examination of present position / safeguards*	*Are these adequate?*
	satisfactorily answered.	nil.
14. ECIL / BEL claim that they have elaborate electronic methods to check the software fused onto these masked chips.	The task force of the US Defense Department has this to say about this checking: "Trust cannot be added to integrated circuits after fabrication; electrical testing and reverse engineering cannot be relied upon to detect undesired alterations in military integrated circuits."	It is clear that the trustworthiness of these chips and the subsequent EVMs in whose PCBs there will be solder, has been seriously jeopardized. Apart from the fact that these EVMs and the chips inside cannot be 'subjected to public scrutiny' there is this further point that they are not 'trustworthy'. This is exactly what the German Federal Court too recognized when they said in their judgement holding use of EVMs in elections unconstitutional: "...programming errors in the software or deliberate electoral fraud committed by manipulating the software of EVMs can be recognised only with difficulty".
15. Orders placed on suppliers for material for the Printed Circuit Board of the EVMs.	The refusal of both BEL and ECIL to disclose details of these suppliers raises deep suspicion and points out to total lack of transparency as far as matters concerning PCB are concerned.	There needs to be public scrutiny of the companies who have supplied parts for the most important part of the EVM, i.e. the PCB. Non disclosure of the details makes that impossible. It is not clear that this

Contd...

Activity	*Examination of present position / safeguards*	*Are these adequate?*
		information has even been made available to the ECI.
16. Manufacture of the EVM with the PCB.	Again the same lack of transparency and secrecy by the two companies. It is obvious from their website that some important information which can be used later to detect tampering lies in the factory where these machines were manufactured. It is not clear how this information has been preserved in the factories and with what level of security. One thing is clear: that this is not with the ECI.	The following facts are in the factory: 1. Unique serial numbers captured on the PCB 2. Manufacturer's ID Number 3. Details of the soldering device with which the micro-controller IC and non-Volatile memory are soldered onto PCB. These facts are essential for a public audit but are being kept back not only from public but also from the ECI. The records are claimed to be in the factory but even the names and addresses of the factories are being kept back from the public in the name of 'commercial interests'. Whether they are properly secured in the factories is a moot point.
17. Quality Assurance Certificate is issued and machines are ready for delivery.	This is only a 'functionability' certificate and does not (obviously cannot) certify that the program in the chip is the same as was approved by the	If there is a 'trojan' in the software, the functionality certificate will not detect it because the 'trojan' only becomes active when the person who

Contd. . .

Activity	*Examination of present position / safeguards*	*Are these adequate?*
	ECI technical committee.	has put it in so desires.
18. Delivery is made to States and District Election Authorities.	Not being in the picture till now, since all earlier negotiations took place at the level of the ECI, State and District Authorities have to accept it on the basis of the functionality certificate supplied by the two companies. They can perform a 'mock poll' to check the functionality and that they must have done.	This cannot be taken as an independent check as would be required by the principle of 'public scrutiny' nor as a safeguard against any manipulation that may have taken place with the software. Mock poll cannot by itself check the software. Functionality checks alone cannot detect tampering in the software as stated earlier.
19. Stored in sealed rooms.	Adequate precautions are prescribed to prevent any tampering at the time of storage but cannot account for deficiencies and tampering that may already have taken place.	Useful to prevent any one in the State and District to tamper the machine in any way but trojans already there in the software cannot be detected.
20. Pre-election check (5% mock poll). Political parties invited.	This check is made by engineers of the ECIL / BEL. In a national election hundreds of engineers would be needed for this job since the EVMs lie scattered all over the country. It is apparent that this job is outsourced to private companies and/or to temporary staff recruited	It is not clear why the same companies who supplied the EVMs are called for this check. Companies other than these two or even engineers directly under the control of the ECI (drawn from various technical departments of the government) could

Contd. . .

Activity	*Examination of present position / safeguards*	*Are these adequate?*
	for the purpose. The antecedents of this staff are not verified as is routinely done for all government servants at the time of their recruitment.	ensure an independent check. They could do this on the basis of manuals already provided by the manufacturers. Since the crucial record which is there for checking tampering (unique serial numbers, manufacturer's ID and details of the special soldering device used) are known to them, they can easily tamper the machines without any fear of detection. It is clear that about 6 lakh machines were got manufactured after 2006; these are called the 'new machines'. ECI needs to explain why all these machines were sent to opposition ruled States and these were not distributed randomly. Randomisation could at least have allayed public fears of possible manipulation in these machines as opposed to the earlier ones.
21. 1st level randomization, mock poll, political parties invited.	Since the EVMs are in sealed rooms, the tampering could only have been done at the time of the manufacture or at the time of pre-	It is not understood why BEL / ECIL engineers (or the ones to whom the work has been outsourced) are present at this time. If

Contd. . .

Activity	*Examination of present position / safeguards*	*Are these adequate?*
	election check. Randomization would at best be a preventive for someone who is trying to selectively tamper EVMs for some booths and/or constituencies.	they have been privy to any tampering earlier, their presence here would only help them prevent detection.
22. 2nd level randomization and mock poll in presence of candidates.	This is touted as one of the best safety devices adopted by the ECI to ensure EVMs non-tamperability. It is only at this stage that the order in which the candidates will appear will come onto the ballet unit; if anyone at an earlier stage is trying to help some particular candidate, he cannot do it because he will not know his position on the ballot unit. Randomization here is a further safeguard introduced by the ECI.	This will help only if someone has been able to replace the PCB or change the chip in some machines at or after the pre-election stage. This will not prevent tamperability of the EVM if a trojan is already sitting in the fused software at the time of manufacture or if it has been planted subsequently. Suspicion of the latter happening increase because at this stage too the BEL / ECIL deputed engineers have access to the machines. Why they are there is again a mystery. Technical personnel drawn from departments of the government could have performed any role that is expected from engineers deputed by these two companies.
23. Storage with sealing with	Adequate so far as it goes.	

Contd. . .

Activity	*Examination of present position / safeguards*	*Are these adequate?*
signatures of candidates.		
24. Polling in presence of candidates and observers; Mock poll.	Mock poll is merely an eye wash to convince the candidates about the non-tamperability of the machines if trojan is already sitting in the fused chip. It is said that in the new machines a new date-time function has been added that will record if any key, including keys that are pressed to activate the Trojan. Since these are stand-alone machines, even if there is a trojan it would need to be activated in all the 12 lakh odd booths in the country. Large number of people will therefore have to be part of a conspiracy, not very likely in a 'loud' democracy like ours.	Remember, Trojans can be activated at any stage by one who has the code. It could be done by a voter as he comes to vote or, if the chip has been appropriately dressed, even by a wireless device. The position in the new machines is even worse because for the activation of the date-time function either a new chip has been fitted to the ballot unit or the control unit has been appropriately programmed. In the former, a trojan in the ballot unit chip can foil the plans; and in the latter the trojan program just has to be modified to ensure that the 'riggers' key presses are not recorded. That the new machines were only given to States ruled by the opposition (apart from a few very small States) adds a new dimension. It needs to be noted that we don't need to rig all the 12 lakh booths; a study has shown that 7,000

Contd. . .

Activity	*Examination of present position / safeguards*	*Are these adequate?*
		booths all over the country selectively chosen could make all the difference between victory and defeat for a party.
25. Sealing, moving to counting centres and stored.	Safe as far as it goes.	
26. Counting centres in front of candidates and political parties.	The totalling key is pressed and the result can be seen by all and recorded. Here too BEL / ECIL deputed engineers are there to help if anything goes wrong.	The presence of BEL / ECIL deputed engineers here is highly unnecessary and raises reasonable suspicions of doubtful intent. This is the stage when it is easiest to activate trojans. One or two people can activate trojans in most if not all the machines. The RP Act does not permit anyone but poll personnel and government servants on duty to enter the counting centres. How these non-government employees enter these centres is a matter which needs serious investigation and by itself raises a serious question mark on the entire voting process.
27. After counting, the machines are again stored in sealed rooms.	It is not clear if any post-election check is made. It is not clear if any check is made of the	Before any claim is made of the trustfulness of these machines, a proper

Contd. . .

Activity	*Examination of present position / safeguards*	*Are these adequate?*
	soldering device, serial number and so on to check if they are the same as per factory records. It is also not clear with what security the factory records are being kept and why these have not been handed over to the ECI.	post-election audit of these machines, especially of the PCB, must be made by an independent authority directly under the control of the ECI.
At the very least, what ECI should do to at restore some trustfulness to EVMs?	The most potent leaks are the ones above from items 14-18 and items 20-26. In the former, the maximum danger is because the chip is sent to a foreign company in the latter because ECIL / BEL engineers handle these machines at the time of the polls. This is a clear breach of security and leads to questions on the trustworthiness of EVMs.	Short term: 1. Change the chip in the existing machines and replace them with another processing chip fused in India under direct control of ECIL / BEL engineers. This should be an embedded one-time programmable (OTP) non-volatile memory on the processing chip. Thereafter, ECI should get a third company (maybe NIC) to write a 'sentry' program and fuse that into the chip as well before soldering them onto PCBs. Parties and candidates be enabled to check sentry software through an open standard specification. This will fulfill essential conditions of 'public scrutiny of elections'.

Contd. . .

Activity	*Examination of present position / safeguards*	*Are these adequate?*
		2. In the stages from 20-26, ECIL / BEL engineers should not be allowed and ECI should deploy experts and engineers from other departments of the government, like NIC. They should directly report to ECI. Long term: the time for simplistic solutions is over. A more comprehensive study is needed to incorporate the data bank on National ID, Voters ID, and security and safety measures before the EVM of the future can be devised.

Appendix 1

Untamperability of EVMs — A Reality Check

N. Ramesh*

Varied international experience shows that it is possible to hack even the most secure of electronic systems. Some examples:

- Hacking of GSM and 3G networks.
- Hacking of EVMs in US and other countries.
- Hacking of US Defence Department Drones.
- Widespread hacking of defence networks.
- Hacking of Google in China.

So what does this mean?

It means that non-hackability is unachievable.

In the case of India's EVMs, hacking is possible due to the various factors discussed below.

Multiple INSERT / Failure Points

No clear evidence of the 3 tenets of Secure Software coding practices:

- Test.
- Verify.
- Validate.

---

* Software engineer, USA.

Let's look at the design of EVMs in India and possible vulnerability scenarios:

- At the outset, no one, other than EC, knows what was "burnt" on to the chips.
- No one knows who burnt it and what validations were done to verify that it was burnt correctly.
- Lack of evidence with test data under different conditions.

Standards Adherance

- Who certified the code and release of these machines?
- Lack of adequate information about any testing standards — an IT Act requirement.
- Was STQC (Standardization Testing and Quality Certification) involved? Who performed the tests and what are the validation results, i.e. error rates / failure rates, etc.

Global Experiences of EVMs

- Multiple cases of no-confidence in EVMs across the globe including, USA, Europe, etc.
- Hacking of EVMs means hijacking of democracy.
- Tamperability of EVMs has been proven time and again.
- One of the best validation methods is to provide a receipt as this is the practice in any electronic transaction (ATMs, taxes, etc.)
- Non-existent global standards (ISO, etc.) for EVMs.

Appendix 2

Public Nature of Election Process

Parakesarivarma Chola's Thousand-Year Old Intellectual Property Right of Secret Ballot

EVM or secret balloting while ensuring the public nature of the elections is as old as Parakesarivarma Chola, who, about 1000 years ago wrote the procedure in an inscription on stone. This is also known as Kudavolai stone inscription. (kudam means "pot" as ballot box; olai means "palm-leaf" as ballot).

This was the basis for the Constitution of India which has the basic feature of democratic republic. The inscription was also discussed in the Constituent Assembly. [http://164.100.47.132 /lssnew/constituent/vol4p8.pdf] T. Prakasam, Member of the Constituent Assembly, 23rd July 1947 stated: Adult suffrage is not a new thing. as imagined by some of our friends, handed down to us by Great Britain. Adult suffrage you will find inscribed on the stone walls of a temple in the village of Uttaramerur twenty miles from Conjeeveram, the whole structure of democracy of those days just a thousand years ago, many of us imagine that it is Great Britain that has given us the democratic process of election; that is not so. You will find on the stone walls of that temple written in the Tamil language an inscription to the effect that there was democratic election carried on then on the basis of adult suffrage a thousand years ago. There was adult suffrage as stated there. There were no wooden boxes which could be used as ballot boxes, but cadjan leaves were used as ballot papers and pots as ballot boxes. That is the way in which they carried on the administration of the country, even in the villages; and it is the misfortune of this country that we have fallen on evil days and came under the rule of different kings.

Cholas had an advanced system democratic republic for local-self governance of villages.

I am attaching photographs of the rule books of the 1,000-year old stone inscription; I request Government of India through Chief Election Commissioner of India to seek an international patent for the stunning and stable election process for a democratic republic. (Actual date of the inscription is: mudalam parantakanin padi-nankavatu aandu padinaram naal, that is, the 16th day of the four-teenth year of Parantaka Chola king).

The kudam "pot" used is the electronic machine part of EVM. I challenge anyone to tamper with an ancient pot from Chola days. The terracotta and palm-leaves are non-tamperable and are, respectively, authentic ballot boxes and authentic ballots which can be preserved for thousands of years in the vaults of the Election Commission.

Uttaramerur Inscription: Recording the Mode of Election to Village Assemblies in the Tenth Century A. D.

The text of the inscription is in V. Venkayya, Annual Report on Epigraphy, 1904

Details at: http:// www.scribd.com/doc/26863214/EVM-parakesarivarmachola

King Parakesarivarman, who conquered Madurai.

Date: On the sixteenth day of the fourteenth year.

Royal Order

Whereas a royal letter of His Majesty, our lord, the glorious Viranarayana, the illustrious Parantakadeva, the prosperous Parkesarivarman, was received and was shown to us,

The Village

We, the members of the assembly of Uttaramerur-Caturvedi-Mangalam in its own subdivision of Kaliyurkottam,

Officer Present

Karanjai Kondaya-Kramavitta bhattan alias Somasiperuman of Srivanganagar in Purangarambainadu, a district of the Chola country,

Settlement

Sitting with us and convening the committee in accordance with the royal command, made a settlement as follows according to the terms of the royal letter for choosing once every year from this year forward members for the "Annual Committee", "Garden Committee", and "Tank Committee":

Wards

There shall be thirty wards;

Qualifications

In these thirty wards, those that live in each ward shall assemble and shall choose for "pottickets" (Kudav Olai) anyone possessing the following qualifications:

- He must own more than a quarter veli of tax-paying land;
- He must live in a house built on his own site;
- His age must be below 70 and above 35;
- He must know the Mantrabrahmana, i.e., he must know it by teaching others;
- Even if one owns only one-eighth veli of land, he should have his name written on the pot-ticket to be put into the pot, in case he

has learnt one Veda and one of the four bhasyas by explaining it to others. Among those possessing the foregoing qualifications;

- Only such as are well conversant with business and are virtuous shall be taken and;
- One who possesses honest earnings, whose mind is pure and who has not been on any of the committees for the last three years shall also be chosen.

Disqualifications

- One who has been on any of the committees but has not submitted his accounts, and all his relations, specified below, shall not have their names written on the pot-tickets and put into the pot;
- The sons of the younger and elder sisters of his mother,
- The sons of his paternal aunt and maternal uncle,
- The uterine brother of his mother,
- The uterine brother of his father,
- His uterine brother,
- His father-in-law,
- The uterine brother of his wife,
- The husband of his uterine sister,
- The sons of his uterine sister,
- The son-in-law who has married his daughter,
- His father,
- His son;
- One against whom incest (agamyagamana) or the first four of the five great sins are recorded,
- All his relations above specified shall not have their names written on the pot-tickets and put into the pot;
- One who is foolhardy;
- One who has stolen the property of another;
- One who has taken forbidden dishes (?) of any kind and who has become pure by performing expiation;
- One who has committed sins and has become pure by performing expiatory ceremonies;
- One who is guilty of incest and has become pure by performing expiatory ceremonies.

- All these thus specified shall not to the end of their lives have their names written on the pot-ticket to be put into the pot for any of the committees.

Mode of Election

Excluding all these, thus specified, names shall be written for pot-tickets in the thirty wards and each of the wards in these twelve streets of Uttaramerur shall prepare a separate covering ticket for each of the thirty wards bundled separately. These packets shall be put into a pot. When the pot-tickets have to be drawn, a full meeting of the Great Assembly, including the young and old members, shall be convened. All the temple priests (Numbimar) who happen to be in the village on that day, shall, without any exception whatever, be caused to be seated in the inner hall, where the great assembly meets.

In the midst of the temple priests one of them, who happens to be the eldest, shall stand up and lift that pot looking upwards so as to be seen by all people. One ward, i.e., the packet representing it, shall be taken out by any young boy standing close, who does not know what is inside, and shall be transferred to another empty pot and shaken. From this pot one ticket shall be drawn by the young boy and made over to the arbitrator (madhyastha). While taking charge of the ticket thus given to him, the arbitrator shall receive it on the palm of his hand with the five fingers open. He shall read out the name in the ticket thus received. The ticket read by him shall also be read out by all the priests present in the inner hall. The name thus read out shall be put down (and accepted). Similarly one man shall be chosen for each of the thirty wards.

Constitution of the Committee

Of the thirty men thus chosen, those who had previously been on the Garden committee and on the Tank committee, those who are advanced in learning, and those who are advanced in age shall be chosen for the Annual Committee. Of the rest, twelve shall be taken for the Garden committee and the remaining six shall form the Tank committee. These last two committees shall be chosen by showing the Karai.

Duration of the Committees

The great men of these three committees thus chosen for them shall hold office for full three hundred and sixty days and then retire.

Removal of Persons Found Guilty

When one who is on the committee is found guilty of any offence, he shall be removed at once: for appointing the committees after these have retired, the members of the committee "for Supervision of Justice" in the twelve streets of Uttaramerur shall convene an assembly kuri with the help of the Arbitrator. The committees shall be appointed by drawing pot-tickets according to this order of settlement.

Pancavara and Gold Committees

For the Pancavara committee and the Gold committee, names shall be written for pot-tickets in the thirty wards. Thirty packets with covering tickets shall be deposited in a pot and thirty pot-tickets shall be drawn as previously described. From these thirty tickets chosen, twenty-four shall be for the Gold committee and the remaining six for the Pancavara committee. When drawing pot-tickets for these two committees next year, the wards which have been already represented during the year in question on these committees shall be excluded and the reduction made from the remaining wards by drawing the Karai. One who has ridden on an ass and one who has committed forgery shall not have his name written on the pot-ticket to be put into the pot.

Qualification of the Accountant

Any Arbitrator who possesses honest earnings shall write the accounts of the village. No accountant shall be appointed to that office again before he submits his accounts for the period during which he was in office to the great men of the big committee and is declared to have been honest. The accounts which one has been writing, he shall submit himself and no other accountant shall he chosen to close his accounts.

King's Order

Thus, from this year onwards, as long as the moon and the sun endure, committees shall always be appointed by pot-tickets alone. To this effect was the royal letter received and shown to us graciously issued by Lord of Gods, the emperor, one who is fond of learned men, the wrestler with elephants, the crest jewel of heroes, whose acts, i.e. gifts, resemble those of the celestial tree, the glorious Parakesarivarman.

Officer Present

At the royal command, Karanjai Kondaya Kramavitta bhattan alias Somasiperuman of Srivanganagar in Purangarambai-nadu, a district of the Chola country, sat with us and thus caused this settlement to be made.

Villager's Decision

We, the members of the assembly of Uttaramerur Caturvedimangalam, made this settlement for the prosperity of our village in order that wicked men may perish and the rest may prosper.

The Scribe

At the order of the great men, sitting in the assembly, I, the Arbitrator Kadadippottan Sivakkuri Rajamallamangalapriyan, thus wrote this settlement.

DR. SUBRAMANIAN SWAMY born in Chennai, Tamil Nadu, is a widely known public figure in India having been elected Member of Parliament five times and has twice held Cabinet positions in the Union Government.

Dr. Swamy has a long and continuing academic association (since 1962) with the world famous Harvard University. He was awarded a doctorate in Economics in 1964 by Harvard after his research with two Nobel Laureates, Simon Kuznets and Paul A. Samuelson.

From 1969 to 1991, Dr. Swamy was Professor of Economics at the Indian Institute of Technology (IIT), Delhi from which post he resigned upon becoming Union Commerce, Law and Justice Minister. He also served on the Board of Governors of the IIT, Delhi (1977-80), and on the Ministry of Education's Governing Council of all IITs (1980-82). He has also been a member of the Court of Benares Hindu University and of Santineketan. Dr. Swamy is a prolific writer. Besides numerous articles in journals, periodicals and newspapers, he is the author of seventeen books. He is proficient in many languages, including Mandarin Chinese.

Subramanian Swamy is President and a founding member of the Janata Party since 1990 which was founded by Jayaprakash Narayan in 1977 in the aftermath of the Emergency.

DR. S. KALYANARAMAN is a former senior executive of Asian Development Bank. A graduate in Economics and Statistics, he has a Ph.D. in Public Administration from the University of the Philippines. He is an author of several books including one on Development Administration — a comparative study of six Asian countries — and Director, Sarasvati Research Centre, promoting studies in Indian civilization, creation of a National Water Grid and formation of Indian Ocean Community. His work experience of 40 years spans financial administration and information technology in Indian Railway and Asian Development Bank, managing a disbursement portfolio of US$ 60 billion for over 600 development projects in more than 29 countries in the Asia-Pacific region and setting up IT systems in these organizations.